Scotland 42 England 1

Scotland 42 England 1

An Englishman's Mazy Dribble Through Scottish Football

Mark Winter

First published by Pitch Publishing, 2023

Pitch Publishing
9 Donnington Park,
85 Birdham Road,
Chichester,
West Sussex, PO20 7AJ
www.pitchpublishing.co.uk
info@pitchpublishing.co.uk

A CIP catalogue record is available for this book
from the British Library.

ISBN 978 1 80150 421 8

Typesetting and origination by Pitch Publishing
Printed and bound in Great Britain by TJ Books Limited, Padstow, Cornwall

CONTENTS

This book is dedicated to the small band of close friends, relatives and mental dogs who formed my outdoor sanity squad during the global pandemic. Covid-19 delayed the book's completion by two years, but thanks to all of you for helping me to get there in the end.

INTRODUCTION

I DIDN'T really start to travel until I hit 50. I decided, wisely as it turned out, that I'd bring forward all the things I planned to do in retirement, get over my fear of flying and just crack on with it. If pretty much all previous mileage had been clocked up following Dover Athletic and Leicester City, travel remained very much football-related. If I spent a week in any city, I'd make it a matter of pressing importance to decide which club I would follow in the unlikely event that I lived there.

In Lisbon I became a *Benfiquista*. In Madrid, I adopted Atlético. In Barcelona I'm reserving judgement until I've visited Espanyol. In Buenos Aires, the mayhem of a regular game at Argentinos Juniors would be difficult to resist. Just across the English Channel from my home, Lens and KVO Oostende might expect my patronage, as could Dinamo Zagreb, Vojvodina, and NK Domžale if I ever take up a nomadic existence in the Balkans. Whenever I've found myself in Italy, I've usually gone to Florence to watch Fiorentina.

Bizarrely, it was a *La Viola* game that triggered my mild obsession with Scottish football. Knowing that the 2008 UEFA Cup Final would be staged at the City of Manchester Stadium, I booked match and train tickets and a hotel well in advance for what I'd fully expected to be a Bayern Munich v Fiorentina clash. Both made a hash of their semi-finals, however, so I went to watch Zenit Saint Petersburg beat Rangers 2-0 to lift the trophy anyway.

It was four years later that I went to see Celtic playing at home. Having seen Rangers play twice – I had visited Ibrox with Leicester as long ago as 1982 – this was always going to happen sooner or later. Given that I'd be getting home via a Sunday evening flight from Edinburgh, I took the opportunity to watch Hearts play at Tynecastle. This in turn led to a return trip to see if I liked Hibernian and when the opportunity cropped up to watch both Dundee clubs playing at home on consecutive days, I couldn't get to Tayside quickly enough. And so it went on.

As I started to spend more and more time in Scotland, I was frequently reminded that football, like life, would often provide a sideshow that was so much more enjoyable than the main event. One by one, I introduced myself to clubs that I'd only formerly known as irritants that ruined my granddad's pools coupon and had the very best of times.

Scotland 42 England 1, if not exactly a love story, is one of affection and admiration for Scotland, its football clubs, and people whose friendliness and hospitality are without equal in my experience. If this book fails to sell a single copy, the experiences I've encountered along the way will have made its compilation worthwhile. If you've yet to venture north of the wall, I really can't recommend it highly enough.

RANGERS v
ZENIT SAINT PETERSBURG

UEFA Cup Final
City of Manchester Stadium
Wednesday, 14 May 2008

I'D BEEN looking forward to seeing Fiorentina play for weeks and booked my tickets in March. I'd been a fan since the early 1990s when Channel Four secured the rights to show live Italian games on a Sunday afternoon. Serie A was the best league in the world at the time and *La Viola* were invariably a treat to watch on their day, with Gabriel Batistuta and Rui Costa being the star turns. With their unshakable sense of swagger and their natty purple shirts, they soon became my favourites. Within a year or two I started making an annual pilgrimage to Florence to watch them play. Even though they could still count themselves among the greats of European football, their likely final opponents weren't the Bayern Munich of old and I fancied Fiorentina to edge a tight game and lift the trophy. As is so often the case when I plan stuff I have no control over, a huge fly was seen wading through my ointment a couple of weeks before the final.

All Fiorentina needed to do to reach the final was overcome a dour and uninspiring Rangers side, who'd nonetheless been turned into a side to be reckoned with under the guidance of the late Walter Smith. Despite failing to have a noteworthy shot on goal in three and a half hours of football, they drew both legs of the semi-final 0-0 prior to beating Fiorentina on penalties in front of the Italian club's own fans at the Stadio Artemio Franchi. I responded to the setback in a very grown-up fashion by kicking some furniture about, having already booked two return train tickets to Manchester at ruinous expense. Citizens of Bavaria were equally miffed, I'd imagine, after Zenit battered Bayern 5-1 on aggregate.

Initially I thought I might scratch the fixture, but after an hour of stressful deliberation I opted to go anyway. It was a special occasion, after all, and one I thought I'd be unlikely to get tickets for again. What I hadn't banked on was the lengths some hoteliers would go to in order to make a buck. Before Rangers had even stepped on to their flight home, the prices of Manchester hotels had gone through the roof on the night of the final.

After searching for a B&B for two that wouldn't cost a week's salary, I put in a call to the Manchester tourist board. Fourteen years on, I still struggle to believe that the following conversation really did take place. I assure you that it did.

'Hello, I'd like to book a hotel in Manchester on the night of 14 May, please.'

'Certainly, sir. Is this just for you?'

'No, it's for my 17-year-old daughter as well so a twin room, please.'

'That's fine, sir. Just stay with me for a moment.'

'Righto!'

After 15 music of listening to music I'd wager was nobody's favourite, my telephone sales professional did indeed return.

'I'm sorry for the wait, sir, but I think I've found you just the place. It's a cosy, family run B&B in Altrincham which is a short distance from the centre of Manchester.'

Like many fans of the English non-league game, I'd been to Altrincham as a visiting supporter. Thus I knew it was a

good 15 miles from the centre of Manchester, but figured I
might as well hear him out, now that we'd got this far.

'That would be £365 for the night, sir. Does that fall
within sir's budget?'

I can't recall my exact response other than shock, but I
think I held back from being too rude to a lad doing his best
in a job he probably despised. Later that same night and on
the point of taking my own cardboard box in which to kip
overnight at Manchester Piccadilly, I had a stroke of luck
searching a website that specialised in rooms over pubs and
came up with just the place for £40 a night for the two of us.
The Ox, situated opposite Granada TV Studios, proved ideal
and I've stayed there every time I've visited Manchester since.

I won't dwell on a journey on a train that was on time but
packed, hot, and uncomfortable and crammed with Rangers
fans, many of whom were 'travelling on the off-chance'. If I
were a particular type of weasel I've no doubt I could have
sold my ticket for £1,000. Rosie would have swapped hers
for a decent pair of shoes, being the type of ungrateful mare
for whom her parents should unquestionably take the blame.

Leaving the train, we merged into a slightly staggering
mass of royal blue humanity that stretched as far as the eye
could see and made a racket I'd only previously experienced
in the front row of an Iron Maiden concert. After that we
hopped into the first available taxi that could take us on the
short trip to The Ox in Castleton, we dumped our bags,
refreshed ourselves with a damp face flannel and enjoyed a
surreal experience in the pub garden.

Though having a chat with the locals is all part and
parcel of the experience, Rosie seemed a bit star-struck as
she enjoyed the company of a bloke she knew only as Kevin
Webster, the mechanic in *Coronation Street* who doesn't
seemed to have aged much in the last 30 years. For my part
I chatted to the same bloke, Michael, a United fan who was

waiting to see if he'd be working on the night of his team's Champions League Final in Moscow given that he'd already been promised a ticket.

Refreshed by a couple of snifters, Rosie and I joined the vast blue human crocodile weaving its way to the stadium without the aid of public transport – which seemed to have been cancelled for the day – or a local police force that seemed to have been given the day off. The two of us seemed to be the only ones not decked out in royal blue; a fact that might have cost me my job under different circumstances.

A couple of days after the game, I learned that ITV's cameras had focused on my lass and I for several seconds during the pre-match build-up. As the only ones not wearing colours – and though I say so myself, Rosie is a photogenic girl – we must have stood out like the proverbial sore thumb and while a few folk at home saw us on the box, I was grateful that one didn't. Withholding a name in order to protect the guilty, I shall simply add that a friend of mine was watching the game at the home of his mother-in-law, my boss. Knowing I'd taken a couple of days' sick leave, my friend, an intelligent lad but not always quick on the uptake, made a lame excuse to stand in front of the TV until the adverts came on. Since this day I've stuck up for him on the frequent occasions he shuns husbandly DIY duties to sneak off and play cricket.

It transpired that most of the constabulary of north-west England had gathered at the City of Manchester Stadium, seemingly doing nothing more constructive than standing in the way of a small army of stewards and security staff, trying to get everyone into the ground as quickly as possible around an hour and a half before kick-off. They succeeded admirably, as minor hold ups were accepted with good grace by those who'd experienced much worse in their time.

Inside the state-of-the-art stadium accommodating the full house it deserved, a fabulous atmosphere, with every spare inch of space covered in Rangers flags from all around the planet, greeted the players as they lined up for kick-off. Under the circumstances, it was a shame that Zenit immediately set about sucking the atmosphere out of the place. In truth the game wasn't much of a contest.

It doesn't happen often in the life of a neutral football fan to bear witness to an individual display of a player that will live long in the memory. Today was one of those days as Ukrainian international Anatoliy Tymoshchuk seemed to operate at walking pace and unchallenged inside his own postal district. Tymoshchuk – five years later to become a Champions League winner with a Bayern Munich side that Zenit had battered to get to the final – played five yards in front of a flat back four. With metronomic distribution, Tymoshchuk was instrumental in everything Zenit did well and ensured that those behind him were under-employed courtesy of his superb reading of the game.

If Rangers' players had hearts the size of buckets, it was clear throughout that they'd met their match, even though the game remained goalless with 20 minutes remaining. Zenit then took the lead with a peach of a goal as Andrey Arshavin, days away from becoming Arsenal's star summer signing, provided a sublime pass to send Igor Denisov clear to stroke the ball past Rangers' keeper Neil Alexander. Though substitute Nacho Novo wasted a great chance to take the game into extra time, the difference in pure talent between the sides was emphasised by Zenit's second goal in added-on time. As Arshavin and Fatih Tekke swapped passes to set up a chance that Zyrianov tapped in from barely a yard out, a final score of 2-0 was the very least that the Russian club's almost total domination of proceedings deserved.

It was mid-morning on the following day when I heard there'd been trouble in the city both during and after the game. We were on the train and halfway back to London when Rosie's mother rang to check if she was OK, and only then did we have some idea of what had occurred. When a giant screen showing the game in Piccadilly Gardens had failed, the good-natured atmosphere that had characterised the build-up went with it. As police charged fans throwing cans and bottles, 30 arrests were made. For my part I didn't so much as hear a swear word during the 18 hours my daughter and I were in Manchester. The Rangers fans we met – and Rosie seemed to warm to being called 'hen' – could not have been friendlier.

A few weeks later Rangers went down to another defeat in Europe, losing 2-1 to the fourth best team in Lithuania in the first week in August. Under the circumstances, it was hard to view defeat in a UEFA Cup Final as failure.

CELTIC v HIBERNIAN

Scottish Premiership
Saturday, 1 September 2012

THE B&B I'd booked was a 20-minute stroll away from Celtic Park. If I decide to go there again I'll find the place easily enough. I'll simply get the bus into town from the airport, get off at the last stop, then take a short stroll to Queen Street railway station where I'll spend a few pence buying a single ticket to Bellgrove and arrive in a trice. Alternatively, I might stay in the city centre and take a leisurely walk to the stadium now I know where it is. Having learned a fair bit about travelling in Scotland during the last ten years, I won't repeat getting there the really stupid way.

My first visit to Celtic Park was arranged on a whim. Working in a school as I do, I get a six-week summer holiday, which is all fine and dandy if you've got plenty of cash to scoot off somewhere. The problem is, of course, that the price of holidays go through the roof at this time of year and flights to just about anywhere tend to be full of the kids I'm keen to get away from for a while. In a few days, in answer to the question, 'Did you have a nice break?' I'd have to answer, 'Oh, quiet you know,' prior to listening to endless yarns about how everyone on a decent pay grade had a wonderful time in places like Thailand or the Dominican Republic.

However, with a week or so to go until the drudgery of the normal working week kicked in again, I felt I had to go somewhere, anywhere, just as a means of getting away for a few days. Having spotted that Celtic were playing at home on Saturday and Hearts likewise on Sunday, I picked out what travel agents might call a mini-break if it came with horse-drawn carriages, tourist tat and chocolate.

Having safely negotiated the drive to Gatwick, the flight to Glasgow and the shuttle bus into the city, I'd developed something of a bizarre plan to find my B&B. Of course, it seems reasonable, even for a pedestrian, to type a couple of postcodes into the AA Route Finder website as a means of travelling a short distance from A to B. However, if I'd died of carbon monoxide poisoning walking by the side of a busy motorway, not a court in the land could have found the AA even remotely responsible. While the terrain was hard going for a while, I got there OK, was warmly welcomed at my digs for the night, dropped off my bag and set out to discover what the East End of Glasgow had to offer.

If I'd visited cleaner and more salubrious parts of the world, such considerations didn't concern me once I'd spotted the stadium at the end of the main drag. Why it had taken me so long to visit I really couldn't imagine. An odd sense of wellbeing was all I felt on what was my second visit to Glasgow, but my first without the help of a designated grown-up. Under normal circumstances a football stadium built on the edge of a vast retail estate wouldn't have been within several grid references of my comfort zone. In this case, Celtic Park provides the unique – in my experience at least – sensation of having an industrial park built next door to a football stadium and not the other way around.

In a mood of extreme *joie de vivre*, I was ready for the pub and a pre-match session that would be as least as memorable as the one I'd enjoyed on the other side of city some 30 years ago almost to the day. Wiser counsels prevailed on realising that it was merely ten o'clock in the morning. Given that the club shop (I think big clubs insist on calling them megastores, but I digress) was open, I killed a little time and added to the collection of memorabilia that adorns the bay window of my living room and screams 'oddball within' at passersby. Ravenous following breakfast at 2am, I thought I'd be spoilt for choice for tuck in the adjacent retail park, but the best I could manage was manky burger and chips in a Tesco 'restaurant' that might have dulled my spirits on another occasion. With appetite sated, I was ready for the pub.

I should state that I've now visited any number of excellent pubs all over Scotland. I say this mainly for the benefit of my countrymen who've yet to venture north of the wall and think that all Scottish pubs resemble Rab C. Nesbitt's local. Though Rab is fictitious, from Govan and therefore unlikely to visit these parts, I felt that was a shame, given that he'd have felt right at home in the boozer I found near the ground. Had I remembered the pub's name, I'd have put together a positive online review of the type you're unlikely to find on Tripadvisor.

On entering, I was immediately endeared to the burst furniture in which cotton wool stuffing protruded from the old-English vinyl upholstery. Quaintly, the shelves behind the bar boasted no half-pint glasses, presumably because there was no call for them. The only other customers were five young ladies of not inconsiderable poundage, earnestly and loudly discussing their exploits of the night before and taking great pleasure from the fact that they were making me blush. It would be fair to say that I wouldn't have taken on any one of them in a fair fight. Having selected my tipple of choice from one of the two available pumps, I got comfortable and started to have fun.

As the pub filled up rapidly, I found myself in conversation with a father and daughter pairing from Stranraer and enjoying their company very much. They, more than anyone, did much to persuade me that a visit to Celtic Park was every bit as much a pilgrimage as a visit to a football match. As season ticket holders, it was a pilgrimage they undertook at least once a fortnight. Though they'd both visited their local club in Stranraer, neither could remember how long ago. This became a recurring theme as I met people who'd come from miles around, particularly those making a regular visit from across the Irish Sea. I could happily have stayed until five to three but entered the stadium an hour before kick-off before I got too drunk to fully appreciate the occasion.

There was one thing I particularly loved about the concourse of the stadium which I took a couple of leisurely strolls around. Earlier in the year I'd visited the new Wembley Stadium and, while impressed in the main, I hated how other stuff had been allowed to give the uninitiated the idea that this was anything other than one of the world's most iconic football arenas. While I'm sure she's performed there in her time, I couldn't quite see why Madonna might warrant being included in a mural along with Bobby Moore and Ferenc Puskás. Celtic hadn't made the same mistake, as the club's illustrious history was charmingly portrayed in old newspaper cuttings in green frames. Old-fashioned perhaps, but I found it all quite moving as I went off in search of my seat in the Lisbon Lions Stand.

One thing I would recommend to visitors to Celtic Park is to make great pains to ensure they are in the right seat, as failure to do so contravenes all manner of Glaswegian etiquette. My error – right seat number, wrong block – almost landed me in trouble before the lad whose seat I'd taken realised I was just a harmless old duffer who'd partaken of too much local refreshment and hospitality.

As the game got under way, I have to admit to being disappointed by the atmosphere around the place. Though vocal support was vociferous in a corner of the Lisbon Lions Stand away to my right, it didn't radiate around the stadium.

Complacency might have been a factor, or so I deduced, given that Celtic didn't really need their supporters to become an extra man, given their current dominance of Scottish football. Today, the attendance was in the region of 45,000 in a division in which crowds of three or four thousand had become the norm at other grounds. However, in a ground with a 60,000 capacity, it was the 15,000 empty seats that attracted my attention and somehow detracted from an occasion I was enjoying. Meanwhile, Celtic were giving an object lesson in how to totally dominate a football match without actually winning it.

They made an encouraging start when Mikael Lustig got on the end of a corner from the right and despatched a half volley into the net from 12 yards out. Quite how they failed to add to a lead during a first half they completely and utterly dominated really had to be seen to be believed. They missed great chances, hit the woodwork on a couple of occasions, forced Hibs' keeper Ben Williams into saves he knew precious little about and were rather unsporting in not letting their opponents have the occasional kick. Had Hibs gone 6-0 down in the first half, they'd have been flattered by the modest scoreline. In the event they equalised shortly after the interval with a goal that may have been low on quality, but was an absolute gem in terms of comedy gold.

Either Lustig or keeper Fraser Forster might reasonably have tidied up what was merely a clearance aimed at relieving pressure on the Hibs goal. What actually happened was the pair put on a very passable impression of the Chuckle Brothers' 'to me, to you' sketch that left Tim Clancy to nip between them and score. I'd have chuckled myself, but the reaction of those around me suggested a more sympathetic tut might allow me to see another dawn.

Lustig did atone for his error, restoring Celtic's lead with a scrambled effort that might just as easily been credited as an own goal, but Hibs' second equaliser did much to emphasise the good fortune they enjoyed on the day. If you're happy to accept the BBC's version of events, their website stated, 'Cairney showed superb skill to get past two challenges and then slot the ball past Forster.' Mine is that Paul Cairney evaded a couple of feeble attempts to tackle him and mishit a shot into the bottom-right corner. Hibs fans didn't appear to give a stuff either way, went completely berserk, and reminded their hosts that they were 'the first to wear the green'. It finished 2-2.

I'd made plans to visit Sauchiehall Street in the evening but should have known this wasn't going to happen given that I'd been up since 2am. Knackered well beyond the point of getting my second wind, I simply got myself a bag of chips and watched the world go by as the stadium emptied. I was back at the B&B by seven o'clock and fast asleep by eight.

I should warn that this is how many men over 50 know they've had a cracking day.

HEART OF MIDLOTHIAN
v DUNDEE

Scottish Premiership
Sunday, 2 September 2012

IMAGINE YOU'RE at a party and get chatting to an intelligent girl you find attractive. Things are going pretty swimmingly; you've discovered you have one or two things in common and don't find one another's means of earning a living too repugnant. All good so far and then you get on to the topic of hobbies. As soon as the words 'I'm a football fan' have been uttered it is almost certain that what had been a free-flowing and enjoyable conversation starts to stall before petering out altogether. Having reached the point of no return, the lady will then say something trite like, 'Oh well, I'd better circulate, I suppose,' at which point you'll probably rejoin your mates in the kitchen and get completely plastered.

If you weren't aware of how you're perceived by a significant percentage of the population, I hate to break the news that you, as a football fan, are perceived to be very, very thick and spend most of your weekends thumping heads. People who think like this have made their minds up on this one, so there's very little point in arguing the toss.

For my part I like to counter that, without football, I would know very few people worth knowing or have been anywhere worth visiting. Without football, my general knowledge would be on a par with the average orangutan or someone whose TV set is stuck on ITV2. So I'm pleased to mention that today's visit to Tynecastle later formed the basis of an hour long history lesson, covering the formation of the Pals Battalions of the First World War, a topic I shall return to later.

As I stepped out of Edinburgh Waverley station for what was to be the first of many times, I reflected on the fact that I hadn't researched my trip to Scotland's capital city very well. I knew it had a castle and a couple of football clubs and that Hibs play in Leith and Hearts don't. That apart, a few recollections from a couple of Irvine Welsh novels is all my novices guide to Edina Fair would have mentioned. Luckily I spotted a corporation bus that was heading in the direction of Gorgie as I left the station. Somewhere in the back of my pointy little head, I had stored the information that Hearts fans once published – and possibly still do – a fanzine called *The Gorgie Wave*. So in a rare moment of clarity, I thought I might just toddle off in the direction the bus was heading. Surprisingly, this was all I needed to do.

The walk was quite picturesque to start with, as I ambled through Princes Gardens in the shadow of the castle. Unfortunately, diversion signs and extensive road works connected with extending the city's tram system out to the airport made the walk a lot less aesthetically pleasing than it might otherwise have been. I just seemed to know the way somehow and by instinctively taking the left-hand fork at Ryrie's pub, I pitched up at Tynecastle in no time. With match ticket and lapel badge purchased, I was comfortably settled in the Tynecastle Arms more than two hours before kick-off.

I hadn't planned to be in the pub that early, but I expected to visit the Heart of Midlothian Pals Battalion monument I'd found out about by watching a documentary on BBC4. In 1914, when war was declared, much debate centred upon whether or not it was acceptable for professional football to continue in Scotland. Hearts, who were leading the First Division table by four points at the outbreak of war, decided that it wasn't. A total of 16 of Hearts' playing staff signed up. Seven died in action, while eight others suffered serious injuries and were discharged. Though some returned to play for the club they were, understandably, never the same players again.

Though I'd somehow got it into my head that the memorial would be outside Tynecastle, I discovered that it could usually be found in the city's Haymarket district. It was in storage at the time of my visit due to the tramway construction but would soon be back in its usual location. In the meantime, the warmth and general sense of bonhomie pervading Hearts' foremost hostelry made a middling guzzling session almost compulsory. I got settled in the company of a local lad, now an Arsenal regular and resident in London, who'd come home for a long weekend and was clearly enjoying himself.

Having found himself a good job with even better prospects, he'd bought a good-sized house in Islington and was enjoying the football Arsenal played most weeks, but he'd become disenchanted with the English matchday experience and being treated as a customer. He told me, 'I've usually been called "sir" 15 times before I've even got a pie in my fist.'

Inside Tynecastle there was an air of buoyancy and expectation about the place. Hearts, after clubbing bitter rivals Hibernian 5-1 in last season's Scottish Cup Final, had made a good start to the new campaign and, after Celtic had thrown away a couple of points the day before, they would go top with a win over Dundee. The Dundee fans, including two in full giant panda outfits, were in good voice and number and in equally fine fettle and keen to make the most of their unexpected promotion. Despite finishing in second place in the Scottish Championship at the end of the 2011/12 season, Rangers' financial problems and subsequent demotion to the

SPFL's bottom tier left a gap that Dundee stepped up to fill as the Premiership's 12th club. Though the ground was some 5,000 short of its 17,000 capacity the atmosphere, full of ale-induced good humour, seemed better than at Celtic Park yesterday.

It didn't stay that way for long, however.

I'd barely taken my seat when I had a perfect view of the incident that was to decide the game. I was barely ten yards away when Dundee's Colin Nish took a tumble in the penalty area under challenge from Hearts' skipper Marius Žaliūkas, with the ball seemingly drifting out of play. With vision aided by spectacles and four pints, I took the view that Nish had tripped over fresh air. Referee Craig Thomson, who almost certainly wasn't a bit squiffy, pointed to the penalty spot, however. Žaliūkas merely looked a tad sheepish and couldn't muster much by way of protest before Ryan Conroy drilled a perfect penalty into the bottom corner to give Dundee the lead.

In the 87 minutes that followed, Hearts had one of those afternoons when nothing came off for them. As the oldest player on the pitch by a distance, Dundee keeper Rab Douglas didn't have too many challengers for the man-of-the-match award. Though Hearts were awarded a penalty of their own towards the end of the first half, John Sutton's woeful effort from the spot gave Douglas less concern than when he'd had to field a couple of over-hit back-passes from his own defenders. As Hearts fans trudged out wordlessly at the end, the Dundee Supporters at the far end of the stadium celebrated what was to prove a rare victory in a relegation season.

Six hours later, the day's theme of ineptitude was enhanced as I went looking for my car in the wrong car park at Gatwick.

A few days on, back in regular life, I was doing my best to liven up a Year 10 class – most with an element of dim bulb about them – in a Friday afternoon history lesson. Those who weren't gazing gormlessly out of the window seemed to think that the British Expeditionary Force was some sort of PlayStation game. As the overwhelmed Miss Hooper introduced the subject of the First World War Pals Battalions it was time for her elderly assistant to come to the fore.

'Lads, you enjoy your football, don't you! You've heard of Heart of Midlothian, right? Well, in 1914 ...'

Thus, the attentions of the daft but savourable were held for a while and one or two might have learned something. Mention it quietly, but I think the talented and highly qualified young lady at the front of the class might have enjoyed a little football natter as well.

RANGERS v LEICESTER CITY

Challenge Match
Wednesday, 8 August 1984

RANGERS v HIBERNIAN

Scottish Championship
Friday, 13 February 2015

IN RECALLING my first ever trip to Scotland, I thought I'd work from memory. In 1984 that's all we had apart from libraries. Hazy though my recollections might be, my trip to Glasgow as a 29-year-old still seems like a major life event, made at a time when I'd barely set foot out of England. Save for a day trip to Calais when I was 21, my only other outing outside the country involved watching Leicester City play Cardiff City. In 1984, I was still three years away from stepping on to a plane for the first time.

Now living in an era when young friends think nothing of spending a weekend in Tallinn, Gdańsk, or Dubrovnik, I appreciate how I must sound like a dreadful little Englander. Though many of my mates did travel overseas, I missed out on the debauchery they seemed to be constantly embroiled in at Europe's less salubrious resorts (until the love of a good woman brought them to heel) while I spent all my spare cash on football.

What do I remember about the day? Well, drink was most definitely taken and for the most of it. I left Dover on the four-carriage boneshaker to Charing Cross around 9am and returned some 24 hours later in a dishevelled and disoriented state. The landscape mostly definitely changed once we'd passed Carlisle and I'm sure I saw a forest of pine trees through a fug of Newcastle Brown Ale. On arrival at Glasgow Central we were whisked through a cultural extravaganza of what the city had to offer for five minutes before somebody said, 'Beer then?' and we went on a pub crawl. Our guide was a Glaswegian lad called Gordon, an erstwhile Rangers fan and current regular at Filbert Street after his work had taken him south. Those who can remember Top Cat's mate Benny the Ball and can imagine him in human form have Gordon to a T. Meeting him again 32 years later prior to a Champions League fixture v Copenhagen he hadn't changed a bit, silver hair notwithstanding.

If my recollections of what was Gordon's local have been confused with various Glasgow-based BBC comedies I've watched down the years, I can only apologise. What is certain is that our coming all the way to Glasgow for a pre-season kick-about went down very well with punters who'd done their share of travelling around Europe for a noble cause. Suffice to say we didn't buy a drink all night and it wasn't for the want of trying.

The fact that the game was billed as a 'challenge match' rather than a pre-season friendly came as no surprise given that it was set up by Jock Wallace, a manager who'd served both clubs with great distinction. Jock was only 60 when he died of Parkinson's Disease in 1996 but is still spoken of in reverential terms by Leicester and Rangers fans alike.

As a man who'd seen military service on the streets of Belfast and in the jungles of Malaysia, Wallace was always keen to impress on his staff that the lavish lifestyle they enjoyed was something they'd be expected to work bloody hard for. So while everyone else on the island was watching a half-hearted warm-up game, blood and feathers were flying around ours in traditional England-Scotland fashion. Leicester's Aberdonian midfielder Ian Wilson was sent off in a game that finished 2-2. I can't recall a great deal else, other than that the soon-to-be-former Mrs Winter, picking me up the following morning, seemed reluctant to engage in any conversation, let alone one about football.

Thirty-one years later, John, Gez and I arrived in the centre of Glasgow early one Thursday evening, having made plans to watch a game from each of the SPFL's four divisions. We'd booked to stay in the Euro Hostel on the banks of the Clyde, so Gez and I set off in time-honoured fashion to find a place in a city we weren't familiar with. Invariably this would involved wandering off aimlessly in the wrong direction, going at least five miles off course, before paying a cab driver £20 to take us to a destination that was 50 yards from our starting point. John, the junior of our party by a good few years, simply tapped something into his phone, walked 20 yards towards the river and said, 'Here it is, lads!'

The following morning, we caught the metro to Ibrox to buy tickets and soon got the impression that something was very wrong. Given the fire sale that was going on in the club superstore, you could have been excused for thinking that this was Rangers' last day of existence before the bulldozers moved in. Us vultures bought up a few £4.99 polo shirts that used to cost £35 and legged it back to town and into a packed Wetherspoons. Though Andy Murray's game in a ranking tennis tournament was being shown on several screens around the pub, nobody seemed to be taking a blind bit of notice.

Later, in front of a magnificent façade that might lead one to think of bricklaying as an art form, it was clear that we hadn't picked a good time to visit Ibrox. Following widely documented circumstances that had seen Rangers demoted to Scottish football's bottom tier, they'd made light work of sailing through a couple of divisions in as many seasons. The Championship, in which Hibernian and Hearts were also punching well below their weight, was proving a tougher nut to crack. Worse still, the much-maligned Newcastle United owner Mike Ashley's offer to top up Rangers' empty coffers to the tune of £20m had gone down like a brick in a swimming pool. As thousands gathered outside the main entrance to advise that he'd be made as welcome as broken wind in a Volkswagen, matters seemed on the verge of turning ugly when we neutrals opted to find our seats as soon as possible rather than hang about.

Once inside, a glance at the history of fixtures between the sides in the matchday programme gave a good indication of how far disillusion had taken hold in this part of Glasgow. While reviews of matches over the last 20 years of Rangers v Hibs encounters suggested that a 49,000 attendance was the norm, tonight's gate was a good 20,000 shy of that figure.

Watching from behind the goal, it soon became very clear to us that Rangers fans fell into two very distinct camps. Those of the wrinklier vintage mostly took the view that, while the Rangers team in front of them was the poorest they'd seen in a while, they were doing their best. Effort, while unlikely to achieve much, was applauded in a spirit of defiance, while criticism was confined to muttering into a cup of Bovril.

For those raised in an era of instant gratification, matters were clearer cut. The team in front of them simply 'weren't fit to wear the shirt' and were loudly reminded of this viewpoint regularly. Though harsh words between the two camps were exchanged regularly, nobody came to blows though it was a close run thing at times.

In a game that Hibs dominated from start to finish, their second goal lives long in the memory and gets the occasional re-run on YouTube. Though it was long overdue, Hibs' second in a 2-0 win, volleyed in just a few minutes from time by Lewis Stevenson, was simply the type of goal the current Rangers side were incapable of scoring. Most of the Hibs team were involved in a delicious pass-and-move breakaway that was given the finish it deserved. Showboating, piss-taking, call it what you will, but a few thousand fair-minded Rangers fans applauded generously before disappearing into the night.

Away to our left, Hibs fans were keen to rub the noses of an ancient foe well and truly in it as they celebrated a third league win over Rangers of the season. 'Can we play you every week?' they sang, probably all the way back to Queen Street, prior to Karma biting them firmly on the bum three months later when Rangers beat them 2-1 on aggregate in the play-offs. Rangers were soundly beaten 6-1 by Motherwell in the final, however.

ALBION ROVERS v CLYDE

Scottish League Two
Saturday, 14 February 2015

'HOW COULD you possibly know that?' asked Rosie as I basked in the glory of another *Pointless* answer.

Although I thought I detected a note of admiration in my daughter's voice, sadness and something approaching contempt would have been nearer the mark. She added, 'I swear your head gets fuller of crap as you get older! If he'd asked you where you put the anti-freeze into a car, you'd have been buggered wouldn't you?!'

In reply, I muttered something about having a broad general knowledge being a good thing. This cut no ice with a woman now on a roll.

'Well I suppose that's true, Dad, if your idea of a wild night out is going to quiz nights with people in cardigans.'

Wounded, I rather foolishly mentioned that I'd just added £250 to today's jackpot.

'Except that didn't really happen outside of your own head, father, did it! Besides, this isn't really general knowledge, just some weird and wonderful fact that's going to lead into a conversation about football any minute now.'

I know when I'm beaten, so I just smiled resignedly and finished my tea. On TV, Richard Osman had just given *Pointless* contestants the names of 14 railway stations in order that they might name the towns in which they could be found. Ignoring our very own Dover Priory (one point) I opted for

35

Sunnyside. That's in Coatbridge where Albion Rovers FC live. Not a lot of people know this, apparently.

I've long held the view that it's the unexpected little gems that so often make football travel memorable. We'd more or less settled on a trip to Paisley to watch St Mirren today and it was only a chance conversation on a Facebook page called European Football Weekends that alerted us to the fact that we could go to two games on Saturday at stadiums that were a five quid cab ride apart. It transpired that BBC ALBA – the Gaelic language channel – would be screening Airdrie v Forfar at 5.15pm, barely 25 minutes after the game between Albion Rovers had finished. Left to our own devices, we wouldn't have found this out by ourselves if we'd studied the fixture lists until the dusk of time. How a chap called Dieter from Wuppertal knew – or would want to know – this is still a mystery, but we remain in his debt.

Arriving in Coatbridge on a grey yet unseasonably warm morning at an inadvisably early hour, we made the decision to find Rovers' Cliftonhill immediately, rather than go looking for it at five to three following a gallon of ale each. Courtesy of John's phone that seemed more intelligent than the three of us put together, we found the ground in no time, and it would be fair to say it came as a bit of a culture shock.

Finding the ground open just before 11am, we entered via a gate behind one goal adjacent to a rust-encrusted turnstile that clearly hadn't been used in years. A cavernous, terraced stand that ran along the middle section of one touchline was taped off, clearly derelict, but with a varied array of plants growing through the cracks in the concrete. Behind the other goal was nothing other than more weeds and cracked concrete, while the pitch was probably best viewed from a block of flats behind the stadium. After last night's visit to Ibrox, this was certainly a rude introduction to how Scottish football's lesser lights lived. Though we'd all toured England's non-league circuit extensively, none of us had seen a ground in greater need of a little TLC.

So absorbed were we in our observations that we'd failed to notice an old lad carefully marking the touchline behind us. 'Can I help you young gentlemen with anything?' he asked in an accent so much broader than we'd heard down the road in the centre of Glasgow. Though I fear we held him up in his work, Rovers' groundsman proved to be enlightening company. Knowledgeable, cynical, with a great sense of humour and history and an overwhelming love of his club and the game, we chatted with our impromptu host for what seemed like five minutes. It transpired that we chatted for the better part of an hour and left Cliftonhill well into opening time.

Coatbridge high street didn't appear to have a lot to recommend it at first glance, but after a quick pint in one pub – where we booked a taxi to take us to Airdrie later – we found just what we were looking for in a boozer a few minutes' walk from Cliftonhill and next door to a bookies. The three of us immediately got settled and, patronising though this may sound, it was good to be in another time zone some four decades earlier than where we woke up this morning.

I'm not quite sure when it happened, but there was a point in time when pubs in England opted to refrain from being a social hub for a pint and a natter and become all things to all men; where TVs, jukeboxes and fruit machines all battle for attention simultaneously, while a slab of bread and a slither of cheese and an apple under cellophane can upgrade an establishment into a 'gastro' pub. There were no such problems in this place where old-fashioned customs were cherished and maintained.

Many of the clientele were retired colliers who'd put on a collar and tie to have a lunchtime drink with their sons, prior to putting their bets on for the day. The three of us shared a table with one such pairing called John and Malcolm. Given that both Gez and I are third-generation Yorkshire mining stock, we found plenty of common experience to talk about. Airdrie and Coatbridge once hosted 21 working pits at a time when work was easier to come by. Now, according to John at least, 'There's nothing here for kids to hang around too long for.' He added, 'We're still a community of sorts, but most of it's in here or at the Wee Rovers.' Just one punter, decked out in Rovers' glaring red and yellow, was going to the game, and expressed incredulity that we were too.

Six pints and a short walk later, we presented our bedraggled selves at the Cliftonhill where an extraordinarily pretty face smiled at me from behind a mesh grill.

'Good afternoon!' I offered, in my state of ale-induced bonhomie. 'One pensioner ticket please,' I added, proffering a crisp note of the realm.

At this point the Rovers staffer adopted a brusque persona and a facial expression that might remind one of Nicola Sturgeon's fizzog had it just been firmly slapped.

'I'm sorry, sir. I'm afraid I don't believe you!' she snarled.

Taken aback at the thought that someone might think I was anything other than an elderly curmudgeon with few of his own teeth, I struggled to respond and a heartfelt 'really?' was the best I could manage. My confused blustering immediately brought a beaming smile to a face that could have charmed a duck off the water.

'Only joking, sir!' she said, and she practically sang 'Happy Valentine's Day, Granddad' as she gave me my two quid change.

If we weren't the only Englishmen at the game – a group of Scarborough fans had made the trip as well – the game itself was a strictly Scottish affair as every participant, referee and linesman included, hailed from north of the border. As all 741 of us huddled together in the only stand that was open we watched a decent game develop, with most of us munching on a pie throughout.

Clyde, managed by former Scottish international Barry Ferguson, were the better side against a Rovers team that wasn't quite at the races. Clyde might have known it was going to be their day as their recent signing and substitute, Steve McDougall, put the Bully Wee ahead inside the first 15 minutes with his first touch of the ball. If the game was even and keenly contested, Clyde always looked the more accomplished of the two sides and they wrapped up the game with a late goal from Scott Ferguson. Ten minutes later we made a swift exit to rendezvous with the cab driver who would whisk us across town in time for kick-off at Airdrie.

Later that year, I was en route to somewhere or other and chatting to an opposition fan and swapping stories about the grounds we'd visited in 2015. It was only when he hopped off the train at Doncaster that I realised I'd waxed lyrical about Albion Rovers for ten minutes but forgot to mention I'd seen Boca Juniors play at La Bomboners.

It was unfortunate that we caught Rovers on a bad day, during a run of form that threatened to ruin their season. The loss to Clyde was the second of three home defeats in a week. In the event, these results did no harm as the Wee Rovers won the League Two title by ten clear points. It couldn't have happened to a nicer club.

AIRDRIEONIANS v
FORFAR ATHLETIC

Scottish League One
Saturday, 14 February 2015

I'M GOING to have to visit Airdrieonians again I think, in order to give the club a fair crack of the whip. I didn't exactly have a great time but I think that was more due to my frame of mind than anything that this perfectly friendly and welcoming club did wrong. Barely 20 minutes after our visit to Albion Rovers, Airdrie at least offered a stark contrast.

We got to the ground with a few minutes to spare for an early evening kick-off but by this time the beer had worn off, which is never a good thing around tea time. We didn't have time to get a feel of the place and saw nothing of the town and what it had to offer. What we did see was an Excelsior Stadium that was opened in 1998 but looked unnervingly brand spanking new. Half an hour earlier we'd stepped out of a stadium that had just one stand open because the rest of it was quite literally falling apart. At the all-seater Excelsior there wasn't a square inch of the place that I wouldn't have risked eating my dinner off. The place was in such pristine condition that even the contents of the pies were recognisable as meat. I found it all a bit unsettling, frankly.

At Airdrie, everyone also watched the game from a single stand, as just the main stand was open to accommodate a crowd of 839, which was ten per cent of capacity. We'd heard that Forfar had 'a large Gaelic-speaking following', but if they did it seemed they'd all opted to stay home and watch the game on the box. As we settled down adjacent to the halfway line and the dugouts, three sides of the eerily deserted ground seemed like they'd been constructed on the off chance that Rangers, Celtic (or more likely, Rod Stewart or Elton John) might turn up and make all the expense and effort worthwhile. Naturally, the stadium had a plastic pitch.

Though the traditionalist in me briefly wanted to pack up and go home, I perked up as it looked as though an entertaining game might be in the offing. Forfar, defying all reasonable expectations, were looking to secure an unlikely promotion to the Championship, while Airdrie's season already seemed destined to end in neither promotion or relegation, no matter how good or grim their form over the last two months of the season. However, if Forfar's need for the points was greater, you'd never have known it as Airdrie looked to have the game sewn up inside the opening half an hour.

Marc Fitzpatrick put Airdrie in front with a smartly taken goal after just five minutes. Airdrie's second was controversial, however, and effectively killed the game as a contest with a good few people scratching their heads in confusion. Nobody on either side of the touchline raised so much as a half-hearted appeal when Gavin Malin seemed to fairly curtail Bryan Prunty's run into the penalty box. While nobody seemed to agree with him or see what he saw, referee Gavin Aitken awarded a penalty and showed Malin a red card for denying an apparently clear scoring opportunity.

Prunty duly stepped up to confidently net his 100th career goal before celebrating with his imaginary friends behind the goal (it later transpired that he was celebrating with his son who we assumed was a young lad who wasn't quite tall enough to peer over the fence).

Game over, but at least Forfar manager Dick Campbell did his best to keep us entertained during a game that petered out instantly as soon as the second goal went in.

Campbell, built like a bison in a knee-length padded coat, wasn't happy and didn't seem to care who knew it. If the lads and I didn't know Campbell from Adam at the time, we were the only ones in the stadium who didn't. Clearly upset at the decision that seemed certain to cost Forfar the game, Campbell loudly and constantly bemoaned his side's luck. If he didn't receive much in the way of sympathy, at least Campbell and his tormentors among the Airdrie faithful set up a little cabaret that lasted longer in the memory than the game itself. If the exchanges weren't exactly up to Kenneth Williams' standard in terms of quick wit and ready repartee, neither were they too angry or poisonous. Suffice to say that Campbell felt a glance at the League One table might offer Airdrie fans a more realistic view of their own adequacy, while they in turn felt he was just a mouthy fat bugger who shouldn't eat quite so many pies. We neutrals from south of the wall gave Campbell a unanimous points decision.

In the second half, Scott Fraser scored the Diamonds' third before Michael Travis replied for Forfar with a goal that not even the scorer deemed worthy of celebration.

Though we called it a day and returned to Glasgow on the final whistle, I didn't know at the time that I'd see Forfar, Airdrieonians and Dick Campbell in a live situation again and make a second visit to Airdrie on a grey Sunday afternoon in January.

HAMILTON ACADEMICAL
v ABERDEEN

Scottish Premiership
Sunday, 15 February 2015

IN 2014 I'd popped into my local, The Bull Inn in Dover, on Christmas Eve. Not being the most festive of coves I tend not to get many presents, but on the bar was a brightly wrapped package with red and white bows attached, bearing a tag with my name on it. Given the interest it had aroused around the pub, I made quite a show opening it. It contained a red-and-white-hooped Hamilton Accies shirt, XL size, not new, but in pristine condition. On the front a large strip had been left blank for an advertising logo, leading me to surmise that no sponsorship was forthcoming for this season's shirt.

The top was a gift from Frazer McCarville, an old Sunday football pal. As one of several Scotsmen who'd represented the mighty Bull Fossils in the Dover Sunday League, Frazer, knowing of my fondness for Scottish football, would often share reminiscences about childhood days with his brother Frank. He'd often nag me to give every other club a miss when I next went north of the wall and visit his beloved Accies. Today provided a perfect opportunity for that to happen, given that an early kick-off gave us plenty of time to see the game and catch our flight home.

After a hearty breakfast and leaving our bags in storage, John, Gez and I initially found ourselves in Motherwell. I mention this to illustrate that even the smartest of phones can become useless in the hands of badly hungover English halfwits, lost in Lanarkshire's industrial heartland, such as it is.

Luckily, Hamilton was just a few minutes away via a train that left within five minutes. Although a 25st bouncer refused us admission to a pub near the ground, he offered us a good alternative in The Tap Room where a hair of the dog became the order of the afternoon, supped in the affable company of Aberdeen's travelling fans. Though a televised game – Leicester losing an FA Cup tie at Aston Villa – put a slight crimp in my day, the three of us were in our element.

I actually remember where I was when I learned the Accies had earned an unexpected promotion to Scotland's top flight. On holiday in Pathos, I'd tagged along with a couple of Hearts fans to watch a televised Carl Froch fight in a local bar. As the topic of football cropped up I commiserated with my new-found friends over Hearts' awful season and subsequent relegation to the Championship. When one replied, 'At least Hibs coming down with us softened the blow,' I was confused. On the day before I flew out to Cyprus, Hibs had won the first leg of their play-off final, and I'd expected them to make light work of the second. In the event Hamilton's 2-0 win at Easter Road took the game to extra time and penalties, success in which earned them promotion.

After picking up a few odds and ends in a minuscule club shop, we took our seats in a New Douglas Park stadium that could best be described as quirky. In what is essentially a two-sided ground with a 6,000 all-seated capacity we opted for the main stand and the company of the home fans, while a good turnout of Aberdeen fans were housed in a stand behind one goal.

On the other side of the pitch, a temporary stand that could accommodate 700 fans – known locally as 'The Gazebo'

– was occupied by two ball boys. Given that both stands were raised above pitch level, we had an excellent view.

We'd expected an entertaining and closely contested game today. Accies, despite a poor run of results following the departure of manager Alex Neil to Norwich City, were well placed in the table, not too far from European qualification. Aberdeen had a string of good results behind them which suggested they might have the wherewithal to mount a genuine title challenge to current leaders Celtic. Not for the first time, our expectations counted for nought as Aberdeen battered their hosts from first whistle to last and were 2-0 up inside the first eight minutes.

In an Aberdeen team that was all about pace and power, Northern Irish wideman Niall McGinn was the game's outstanding player and Accies had no answer to his marauding down either flank. The Dons had already missed a great chance before they went ahead after six minutes. McGinn tore down the right and delivered a cross that picked out Adam Rooney, whose header deflected off Accies defender Ziggy Gordon. Though keeper Michael McGovern produced a wonderful save to prevent an own goal, full-back Andrew Considine followed up to score from close range.

A couple of minutes later, Aberdeen doubled their lead following a move that started in their own penalty area. After two Accies players had got in one another's way trying to get a shot in, McGinn ran the full length of the left hand touchline prior to delivering a perfect cross that Ryan Jack flicked in at the near post.

There was no further addition to the score for another 80 minutes – but God alone knows how that state of affairs came about. McGovern produced a string of fine saves, a couple of goals looked somewhat harshly chalked off and some good chances were missed. During the first half we were perfectly positioned to see that a Rooney shot had struck the underside of the crossbar and come down a good two feet behind the goal line. We had a certain amount of sympathy for the linesman who failed to spot this, given that the speed in which Aberdeen got from one end of the pitch to the other had worn him out inside the game's first quarter.

Aberdeen added a third goal near the end when McGinn raced through a gaping hole in Accies' back line – left by the earlier dismissal of Jesús García Tena – and thumped the ball past McGovern. It finished 3-0 but the Dons' winning margin could so easily have been in double figures.

On the flight home we reflected that we might have just watched this season's Scottish champions. Yet, while they cut Celtic's lead at the top to three points with the win, Aberdeen had to settle for a second-placed finish. As for my Accies shirt, I still have it and plan to wear it one day. Slimming down to an XL size remains a plan I'm constantly talking about putting into practice.

GREENOCK MORTON v FALKIRK

Scottish Championship
Saturday, 20 February 2016

IF YOU travel to Glasgow in February, it's a fair bet that you're not doing so for the weather. If it's sport you're hoping to see, I guess you should be realistic about the possibility that postponements might become an occupational hazard if Scottish football played in Spartan conditions is what butters your muffin. This wasn't a consideration that entered our heads after being just a wee bit spoilt on our last visit just over a year ago. We'd seen four games – one in each division – while having a thoroughly good time and vowing to come back as soon as possible.

This weekend got off to the worst possible start, however, as we went a man down 24 hours before we were due at Gatwick. Essentially, I think John had somewhat carelessly double-booked himself and cancelling a football trip was the option that would cause him the least grief.

Landing in Glasgow late on a Thursday afternoon, we'd made tentative plans to go to Falkirk and watch an under-20s game v Rangers that kicked off at 6pm. Though rush hour traffic scuppered that option, we weren't overly concerned. We checked into the hostel on the Clyde, found a decent bar, chatted and drank with the locals and kept half an eye on the televised football in the Europa League.

It would be fair to say that the following day really didn't go very well, as we endured a grim, drizzly day killing time ahead of a Partick Thistle v Aberdeen game we were really looking forward to. We walked for miles, visiting both Celtic and Hampden Park before getting an early dinner ahead of a trip to Firhil via the metro and another walk. Had John and his smartphone been with us, we'd have been saved the bother. We arrived an hour before kick-off only to be told by an apologetic steward that the game had been postponed a couple of hours earlier, thus ensuring that Aberdeen and their fans didn't have a wasted journey.

It would be fair to say that we took the news like spoilt four-year-olds and sulked all the way back to the hostel. After moaning incessantly for three hours we drew a veil over the day and, while the rest of Glasgow partied with its usual gusto, we sent one another off to bed with a good book.

After a night of heavy and constant rain we took the view that if a game in the Scottish Premiership had been postponed – and one due to be televised at that – it seemed prudent to check if any others had been called off before we set off anywhere. The Celtic club shop adjacent to the hostel confirmed that Celtic v Inverness would definitely go ahead. Gez, looking to pay his first visit, was happy with that, while I at least had a backup option. Shortly after midday we popped into a bookies as a means to my not wasting another journey and the following conversation unfolded.

'Hello. My mate and I are here watching football and we're working out where we'd like to go. Would you mind looking online to see if any games have been postponed please?'

'Of course not, darlin', I'll just have a look for you now,' was the usual helpful and affable Glaswegian response from behind the counter we were learning was the norm. The young lady paused while her screen updated and added, 'Just one game called off so far, boys. Macclesfield v Dover in the Vanarama National.'

After thanking her for her trouble, Gez and I reflected on the fact that rather than set off for a postponed game involving our own club, we'd gone for the more exotic option of travelling to another country to do exactly the same thing. How we laughed until we stopped!

As Gez set off for the east of the city, I hatched a cunning plan that should ensure I'd visit a new ground and see a game. I opted for Greenock Morton v Falkirk, reasoning that I should be able to get to the ground by rail for around 1.30pm. If perchance that game was called off, I could at least double back a few stops and hope that another Championship match, St Mirren v Dumbarton, would go ahead.

In the event, my plan was so cunning you could have shoved it into a pin-stripe suit and called it a tax lawyer. As my train slowly trundled out of Glasgow and out past the airport, it was clear I'd get a game in one way or the other.

As we stopped at Paisley St James, activity outside St Mirren's ground barely 200 yards away was extensive and awash with the dayglow oranges and yellows of policemen and stewards trying to look busy, a fact I took comfort from. Starting to relax a little, I sat back and took in the views of the Clyde Estuary that were still spectacular, irrespective of the restricted visibility that the still grim weather ensured.

Quite what I'd expected to see wasn't something to which I'd given a great deal of thought. That said, ships – and plenty of them – must have been at the back of my mind somewhere. All those grainy black and white newsreels had taught me years ago that this is where a large proportion of the world's shipping had once been built. Now, just three shipyards have survived on the Clyde after we English decided that jobs and industry weren't for us, and we could all make a living selling coffee and opening doors for one another. I didn't see so much as a canoe throughout the entire journey.

Former shipyards in Greenock have rather predictably been replaced by leisure facilities and commercial premises but at least a couple of dry docks remain open for ship repairs, which would explain the huge crane that towered above the town, right next door to Cartsdyke station where I jumped off.

I'd already decided where I'd be watching the game from the train window. I've never been one for soulless identikit stadiums, stuck in the arse-end of nowhere adjacent to a retail park and a junction off a motorway. If you can't walk to a game via a pub or two, I'm really not that interested. So it would be fair to say that if my heart wasn't exactly all a flutter as Cappielow appeared through the mist as the train slowed down, my weekend had improved dramatically. Spotting a cavernous, terraced stand that ran along most of the far touchline – the type of which we all love yet have somehow been allowed to drift out of fashion – I'd already picked out the spot where I'd stand. Cappielow was, quite simply, the business; an old-school stadium, complete with a spot of rust, crumbling concrete and peeling paint, smack in the middle of town and five minutes' walk from the train station. If I'd possessed a hat, it would have certainly been tipped at a jaunty angle.

Ten minutes later I'd ascertained that the game was definitely on, purchased a ticket in the 'Cowshed' and, having found that I couldn't get a beer inside the ground, went off in search of a bar. In common with the turn for the better that the weekend was taking, I found one inside two minutes: a proper local, right on the corner of the ground.

Settling down with pint in hand, I pondered for a while over the identity of Morton's celebrity fan. It took a while to recall that it was McLaren, butt of Norman Stanley Fletcher's casual racist jibes, who'd first mentioned the club in an episode of *Porridge*. Aficionados of classic 1970s comedy will doubtless recall that 'Jock' revealed his allegiance prior to an eagerly awaited clash between A Wing and B Wing. Remembering that McLaren was a sitcom character who might not have been a Morton fan at all, I thought I might introduce myself to one or two real people who were. Nice folk they were, too, albeit bewildered at the fact I'd passed up the chance to watch Celtic to watch Morton instead.

When the game kicked off, I could see their point as Morton were having one of those seasons that had mid-table mediocrity written all over it. The game had barely got going when the moaning around me started in earnest. Even the youngsters seemed bitter and careworn, expressing incredulity that this was what they were doing for pleasure on a Saturday afternoon. This was the grumpiest crowd I'd been a part of for a very long time – and that made me feel right at home.

Morton weren't a bad side, working hard for one another but without really creating much. Any half-decent move invariably ended with a poor or overhit final ball and the harder they tried, the worse it seemed to get. Falkirk, by contrast, had been growing into the season and an excellent run of recent results had made them look certainties for a play-off berth in common with more fashionable rivals Rangers and Hibernian. It came as no surprise when they took a lead they never looked like relinquishing.

Morton should have cleared a Falkirk attack that hadn't looked too threatening. However, as an attempted clearance spooned up into the air, John Baird first outmuscled central defender Conor Pepper, brought the ball down with a sublime first touch, then stroked it effortlessly past keeper Derek Gaston.

Falkirk fans, who'd turned up in good numbers – briefly forgetting the soaking they'd endured behind the goal in a modern stand that boasted seating but no roof – celebrated accordingly.

In the second half, Morton might have fluked an equaliser. A corner from the right almost sneaked in unaided and while a long-range effort went behind via the top of the crossbar, a Falkirk win looked more likely the longer the game went on. So it proved, but it came at great cost as midfielder Conor McGrandles, back at his first club on loan from Norwich, came off worse in a 50/50 challenge with Morton's Joe McKee. Though I was too far away to comment on the nature of the challenge, it was instantly evident that McGrandles had suffered a serious injury. After he'd spent the night in Inverclyde hospital it was confirmed that he'd broken his leg in two places.

The following morning, the Sunday papers confirmed that only Albion Rovers' home game had fallen victim to the weather on Saturday. Now on our way to Edinburgh, Gez and I concluded this wouldn't have been the fault of the dedicated groundsman we met last year.

HIBERNIAN v ALLOA ATHLETIC

Scottish Championship
Sunday, 21 February 2016

IF YOU take the left-hand exit from Edinburgh Waverley and pass through a small shopping centre, you'll come to a rather aesthetically pleasing spot called Princes Gardens. If you ignore a bloody great Ferris wheel that's there now and turn your back on it, I can think of no better place to quaff a sandwich and a hot drink and consider the possibility that the world's not a bad old place after all.

Until very recently I hadn't known that Princes Gardens was once a loch that did a rather nifty job of keeping invaders away from the adjacent castle. However, after the north end of the loch was drained in 1763 as a means to aid the construction of a bridge, the western end was also drained to create the park. Although the old loch was a favourite spot for suicides, it seems it was also ideal for proving the innocence of witches. It didn't do them much good, mind, as the skeletons of several were found, with hands and feet bound, once all the water was removed. If nothing else it made the locals think twice about keeping cats.

I've gone off on this particular tangent for a couple of very good reasons. Firstly, to point out that if anyone of mature vintage directs you anywhere via the 'Nor Loch', it's Princes Gardens they're talking about. Secondly, I thought I might waste a bit of space and bung in an interesting fact given that this section will be about football and precious little else. At the risk of jotting down a spoiler alert, I prattle on endlessly about Edinburgh later once I get up a head of steam. The place becomes one of my favourite cities and I visit several times before I get to the acknowledgements at the end. For now I'll just ask you to accept that I treated Hibs in the same way I did Hearts in that I came, I saw, then just buggered off again.

As our train gently trundled from west coast to east, it dawned that I was becoming something of a regular on this line having jumped on and off at a few stations along the way. Stopping at Bellgrove, I reflected on what a pointless exercise it had been to walk miles there from Glasgow Central, given that the B&B I'd booked was a £1.20 train fare and a five-minute stroll away. I wondered if a smashing bloke who'd introduced me to the square sausage, a Celtic fan called Thomas, was still running the place. Further up the line, stops at Coatbridge Sunnyside and Airdrie brought back fond memories for both of us of our two games in an afternoon at Albion Rovers and Airdrieonians respectively. Closer to Waverley, the thought occurred that I'd doubtless be getting off at Livingston if I was to see this project through to fruition. Great railway journeys that Michael Portillo is unlikely to book apart, we pulled into the capital bang on time and about an hour and a half before kick-off.

If you haven't had the pleasure, Easter Road is a particularly easy ground to find. Simply find London Road – and from Waverley it's difficult to miss – and walk down it for a mile. Hang a left on to Easter Road and you can't miss the stadium if you don't walk past it too quickly. Thus, we just about had time to buy tickets and grab a swift half before settling down to watch the ground fill up.

'Fill up' might have been stretching it a bit, given that the 'Leith San Siro' was considerably less than half full of its 20,421 capacity. Those who had turned up were in buoyant mood, however, and still crowing over a win over Hearts in a Scottish Cup replay, but I'd guess that three home games in a week – Morton were due to visit on Wednesday – proved beyond the pockets of some. Left to perm two from three, this was arguably the one that most would choose to miss, even though it was hard think that today's match would end in anything other than comprehensive win for the Hibs. Alloa, who'd yet to win at home in the league, were enduring a rotten season and went into this fixture with just 13 points to their name. Hibs, by contrast, were on a great run of form, currently in second place in the Championship, and still involved in both cup competitions. Though Rangers looked odds-on to return to the top flight, Hibs would cut their lead at the top to five points if they could win their next two home games.

Under the circumstances, I could only admire the 30 or 40 Alloa fans who'd congregated behind the goal at the far end, where Arthur's Seat provided one of football's most magnificent backdrops. Having followed my own team around England in similar circumstances, I feared their short trip home might be a tad muted. For the time being a quick and hearty chorus of 'When the Wasps go Marching In' raised the spirits for a few minutes.

Given the midweek cup win over Hearts, it came as no great surprise that Hibs came out to a welcome that the generous would describe as rapturous. That said, I was disappointed not to have the chance of a bit of a sing-song. I'd been under the impression that Hibs took the field to the Proclaimers' 'Sunshine on Leith', so being a bit of a fan of the specky Hibee tunesmiths myself I'd learned the first verse and the chorus as a means to joining in with the locals. It transpired that I just shouted 'THUNDER' a few times, given that the teams came out of the tunnel with AC/DC's 'Thunderstruck' ringing in their ears.

With the niceties dispensed with and the game under way, I hadn't much of a clue as to the careers of the players I was watching. I didn't take long, however, to work out who was the best player on the pitch by some distance. Having previously seen Hibs pick up four points from two games against the Old Firm in Glasgow I'd warmed to the side and their stylish passing game. Watching them on their own patch was to prove equally pleasing.

Had I boned up beforehand, I would have known that Hibs' Liam Henderson was a teenager from just down the road in Livingston. He'd played at all youth levels as a Scottish international and had already picked up league and cup winners' medals in Norway with Rosenborg, and was here on loan from Celtic for the season. It took him just five minutes to put his hallmark of quality on the game.

The goal that gave Hibs the lead was a replica of one I'd seen in Madrid, when Lionel Messi and David Villa had combined to give Barcelona the lead in a game against Rayo Vallecano courtesy of passing, movement, and precision I'm convinced the pair could still have contrived with their eyes shut. In this instance, Henderson played a 60-yard diagonal ball from the left-hand touchline that only the gifted or foolhardy would attempt. The pass dropped perfectly at the feet of Martin Boyle who slipped unnoticed between two Alloa defenders, took it round keeper Scott Gallagher, and rolled the ball into net. That was effectively that as a contest.

Hibs boss Alan Stubbs had made seven changes to the team that had beaten Hearts in midweek but this never looked like a gamble on his part. Alloa, described later in a BBC report as 'gutsy but impotent', had their moments but seldom looked like salvaging anything out of the game, particularly after Danny Carmichael had give Hibs a 2-0 lead to take into the break.

As the second half slowly petered out it dawned on Gez and I that we'd seen Hibs striker Chris Dagnell play before, as a lad with an enviable scoring record in England's lower divisions. Trying his luck north of the border wasn't working out, according to those around us, and he was substituted towards the end of a game he'd made little impression on. I was to see him again later in the year, turning out for Crewe Alexandra having found his shooting boots again in his spiritual home of England's north-west.

Boyle, making his first start since December, scored his second and Hibs' third before we headed off to Waverley and on to a flight home from Glasgow.

Hibernian's form fell away remarkably. After they lost 2-1 to Ross County in the final of the Scottish League Cup, they also missed out on promotion after a 5-4 aggregate defeat against Falkirk in the play-offs.

It all came good in the end, though, as an-injury time goal secured a 3-2 win over Rangers and Hibs won the Scottish Cup for the first time for 114 years.

I'm reliably informed that the fans' rendition of 'Sunshine of Leith' that day was emotional.

DUNFERMLINE ATHLETIC v INVERNESS CALEDONIAN THISTLE

Scottish League Cup Group Stage
Tuesday, 26 July 2016

THERE'S NOTHING like a midweek trip to Dunfermline to give a chap a sense of his own mortality. I don't mean this in any maudlin sense but I speak from a pragmatist's perspective. There was something about the place to make me think that this is a town I'd like to spend some time in beyond a flying visit. The question is, given that I've just turned 61, how much time have I actually got?

Looking at the matter from a glass-half-full perspective, let's say that I won't slip off the dish until I'm 84. Remaining optimistic, let us further assume that I'll have another ten years of full mobility that will enable me to shin up large hills with all the enthusiasm of a puppy with an extra willy. Realistically, I could just as easily get knocked down by a bus – I'm useless around traffic – so maybe I shouldn't plan too far ahead. So much to see and so little time is a phrase that covers all bases, I think.

Today's visit was always going to be a flying one if I made it at all. My flight arrived on time, though, enabling me to check in at my Edinburgh hostel then double back to Waverley Station in good time to get to East End Park for a 7.45pm kick-off. After a much-anticipated crossing of the Forth Bridge – which was to leave me spellbound, and not for the last time – I set foot in the Kingdom of Fife for the first time and sought directions from the type of friendly and helpful ticket man that Scotrail seem to employ plenty of. Despite the early evening drizzle I enjoyed a stroll through a lush green park, saw a couple of lads wearing black and white scarves walking towards some distant lights and followed them. Although a signpost helpfully advised I was heading towards Trondheim, I thought it best to ignore it for the time being.

Arriving at the ground about an hour before kick-off, it struck home just how much I'd looked forward to this visit. As a season ticket holder at Dover Athletic I've looked out for the results of our island's other DAFC for as long as I can remember. Whether any Dunfermline fans thought of us as the other DAFC – or are even aware of our existence – is something I forgot to ask. Further, in a town of some 50,000 souls, I'd long since been impressed by the number of talented people the town had produced or had strong links with. Two of them, who both played a significant role in my life, are no longer with us.

Though I was already a grumpy old sod when The Skids were in their pomp, I was always a fan of Big Country. Though never the most regular gig-goer, I'd travelled to see them several times and could never understand why they weren't globally popular in the manner that so many less talented bands are. I caught them twice on their Buffalo Skinners tour of 1993 and marvelled at how so much new material instantly seemed like old favourites.

To me, Big Country singer and guitarist Stuart Adamson, who moved to Dunfermline as a kid, had the whole world at his feet with talent to burn in a band whose sound was unique. From what I've read he had his head screwed on as well; living in the town he grew up in, married to a lovely lass, father to a couple of kids and popping down to see his local team whenever work commitments allowed. He seemed like my kind of bloke.

To this day it still saddens me greatly to think of his death in 2001 when, facing a second divorce and a drink-driving charge, he hung himself with an electrical cord in a Honolulu hotel; an empty wine bottle by his side. It is recorded that, at his funeral in Dunfermline's Carnegie Hall, U2's The Edge delivered the eulogy and told mourners that Big Country wrote the songs he wished U2 could write.

Quite how I came to read it in the first place I can't recall but suffice to say that Iain Banks's *The Crow Road* is one of my favourite novels of all time. After watching the book subjected to one of the BBC's better TV adaptations, I've gobbled up everything that Banks, another son of Dunfermline, has ever written. If I admired his work I admired him more for the quiet, stoical, and dignified manner he told the world, via a *Newsnight* interview with Kirsty Wark, how a terminal cancer of the gallbladder meant he was unlikely to live for another year. He spoke with the calm disdain of a man facing the trifling inconvenience of having a tooth extracted. He died, aged 59, in 2013 but remains my favourite British author.

If you've read this far without slashing your wrists, I was actually having a rather nice time after purchasing my ticket for a bargain £6. Ravenous, having eaten nothing since breakfast, I popped into the main stand's cafe, bought a pie and a coffee, then slurped and munched ruminatively as I watched the ground start to fill up. Unsure if I'd ever had a steak bridie or not, I thought I'd better try and see if I liked them. I did. Very much.

The crowd was later announced as 2,580 in a smart all-seater stadium that could comfortably accommodate more than four times that number. Chatting with an octogenarian Dunfermline fan, tonight's theme of local talent passing away before their time continued after I'd asked why a chap called Norrie McCathie had a stand named after him in which a large banner of the man himself was displayed. McCathie, a popular defender who played over 500 games in 15-year career for the Pars, died in tragic circumstances, along with his girlfriend, of carbon monoxide poisoning in his flat in Fife, a couple of days after playing at St Mirren. Three months later, at the end of the 1995/96 season, his team won promotion back to the Premier Division. In 1998 the stand was named after him.

When the game started, I reflected on the fact that I'd started to enjoy watching as a neutral far too late in life. Essentially, when it's not your team you're watching, it really is just a game. So while I've found that there's little in life to compare with my team bagging an injury-time winner, there's much to be said for watching a match in a calm and rational frame of mind. Tonight, many Dunfermline fans would have told you that their team had played pretty well in the main and it simply wasn't their night. An Inverness fan, specifically the lad I met on the train back to Edinburgh, may have felt that extra class told in the end. I concurred with both points of view and sat back and enjoyed the spectacle.

Following three seasons in Scottish football's third tier, Dunfermline had started to give their fans something to cheer about. After financial difficulties had seen the club placed into administration they were now back in the Championship after being taken over by the fans group Pars United and having won the League One title at the end of the 2015/16 season. Still basking in the bonhomie that such victories engender, the locals were very much behind their young team and were universally tolerant of their mistakes. This was just as well as they made several.

The game started badly for the home side when keeper David Hutton miscued a back-pass, succeeding only in clearing the ball to Caley's Iain Vigurs who chipped into an unguarded net from 40 yards out. Dunfermline were arguably the better side for most of the first half and deservedly equalised courtesy of Andrew Geggan's thumping header. Caley regained the lead just before the break, however, when Vigurs' free kick found the net via the underside of the crossbar.

As the rain cascaded down on an increasingly grim and grey summer evening, the tannoy man attempted to rally the troops with a full-volume blast of The Skids' anthemic 'Into the Valley'. It worked a treat, but only for Inverness.

Dunfermline might have equalised a couple of times and had a decent shout for a penalty waved away before Billy King cut in from the left-hand touchline and let fly with a shot that dipped and swerved under the bar to make it 3-1. Within a few minutes Vigurs completed his hat-trick to make it 4-1, heading home Carl Tremarco's pinpoint cross from the left. In the final minute Caley had an effort that didn't go in as Greg Tansey's free kick came back off a post. Typical of the Pars' luck on the night, the ball rebounded to Tremarco to nod in from barely a yard out.

'Vigurs hits hat-trick in Inverness rout' proclaimed *The Herald* the following day with a headline didn't tell the whole story.

Back at Dunfermline Town station, I'd just missed one train and had to wait for an hour for another. Happy enough to wander around in the drizzle for a while, I came across a poster proclaiming that grizzled old rockers Nazareth would be appearing locally within the month.

I had the very good fortune to watch Nazareth in Vancouver in 1987 while in Canada for the wedding of two very dear friends. A great gig it was too, even though the band were old then, almost 30 years ago. Subsequent research revealed that Nazareth's lead singer is from Dunfermline. Though he retired from touring in 2013, I'm delighted to record that, at the time of writing at least, he is alive and well.

EDINBURGH CITY v HAMILTON ACADEMICAL

Scottish League Cup Group Stage
Wednesday, 27 July 2016

AS I was sitting nursing a coffee in the food hall adjacent to Edinburgh Waverley station, Luther Vandross and Janet Jackson reminded me, not for the first time, that 'the best things in life are free'. Though I might be scandalously misjudging the pair of them, I'm guessing they didn't back up this rather barmy statement by handing back their royalties. My healthy sense of cynicism apart, today was one of those days when I saw their point.

Although I'd booked to stay in Edinburgh for five of the six nights I'd be in Scotland, today was the only day I'd get to spend time exploring the city. Ideally I thought I might do so with a lot more cash, given that my flights, hotels, and train tickets had long since been booked and paid for. Yet while I was flush last week, urgent repairs to the car and, more importantly, the dog had taken up much of the money I'd put by for all manner of holiday fripperies. If I boxed clever I reckoned I could get by on around £25 a day despite the fact that Edina Fair, like all capital cities, could be a bit pricey. Economies would have to be made and the first thing to go was a visit to the castle, given that the place seemed to be constantly rammed with the type of tourists I'm invariably keen to avoid.

I take the point, of course, that given I spend much of my time as one of their number, I should spend more time in the company of tourists. I will, of course, visit Edinburgh Castle at some point and take a few notes with which to regale a few chuckleheads in a GCSE History class. What I won't be doing is joining the United Colours of Idiocy in seeking myriad selfie opportunities, checking my phone every four seconds, and looking behind war memorials for irritating little Japanese monsters that don't actually exist.

Even coming from a town dominated – and I'll take no argument here – by the world's finest castle, I was impressed at the manner in which Edinburgh markets its rich historical heritage to prosper from tourist income and employment opportunities. In Dover, customers leaving the castle are effectively told there's nothing else to see and to move on to Canterbury or London and spend all their spare cash there. Leaving Edinburgh Castle, you come straight out on to the Royal Mile and could spend all day souvenir shopping if you have more money than sense. Though I'd imagine business rates are a bit steep, the EU seems to provide plenty of minimum-wage labour in a street that's a goldmine for the creative. If you've got some scarves that are worth £1 a pop, for example, one might reasonably knock them out for £4.99 by calling them Scottish scarves. Those of the cheekier entrepreneurial persuasion could target the truly gullible and ask for £7.99 for a traditional clan tartan scarf, particularly popular with those keen to establish non-existent Scottish roots. Quelling the urge to try my hand at shoplifting, I bought five postcards for £1 and scarpered as quickly as my size 11s would carry me.

As an alternative I spent a couple of hours mooching around in the welcoming calm of the Scottish National Museum and Scottish National Gallery, and had a thoroughly nice time without spending a copper coin save for a £1 voluntary donation on leaving both. With my equilibrium duly restored, I got on with main agenda of the day of visiting Meadowbank Stadium followed by a spot of gentle mountaineering by reaching the peak of Arthur's Seat. The former was easily found on leaving Waverley and taking a right-hand turn into London Road.

Having passed Easter Road, it wasn't long before I was drawn like a moth to a flame to old-fashioned floodlights in the distance and found Meadowbank soon after. After taking a stroll around the perimeter, I thought I'd save the rest for later prior to tackling Arthur's Seat. First, I needed more caffeine and made a rare visit to a McDonald's for a coffee. Thinking I might add some vitamins to the stodge of my holiday diet, I ordered some porridge that claimed to have some apple and blackberry in it.

If you've seen the film *One Day* – a very decent adaptation of David Nicholls' best-selling novel – you'll have spotted Arthur's Seat, at the point when lead characters Dexter and Emma decide to climb to the peak of the hill that dominates Edinburgh. After celebrating their graduation into the wee small hours, they have sex and about an hour's kip before deciding to go hill walking in inappropriate clothing. After striding to the top, with Dexter seemingly accomplishing the feat in slip-on shoes, they run back down again with the intention of having more sex. It would be fair to say that my progress was a tad more ponderous.

Wikipedia will tell you that Arthur's Seat is the main peak of a group of mountains in Edinburgh. Robert Louis Stevenson describes it as 'a hill for magnitude, a mountain in virtue of its bold design'. I simply stood by a loch at its base (or possibly a pond) and said, 'Crikey!' It looked a daunting task to reach the peak, but I was only too aware that this was a task I wouldn't be able to tackle in a year or two. My dodgy knee, with its torn ligaments and a touch of arthritis, was only going to get worse. So off I toddled.

Arthur's Seat, incidentally, owes its name to Arthurian legend. I know nothing of Arthurian legend other than to impart one very valuable piece of advice. If you find yourself on a date with a lady who tells you she's seen *Excalibur* 198 times, you should be suddenly remember an urgent appointment and run to the nearest exit.

I like to think I've travelled a bit in the autumn of my life and have seen a few views that might be considered cinematic. I've travelled down the Andes into Santiago through a series of hairpin bends known as the 33 Curvas. I've seen nature's greatest show on earth, Aurora Borealis, from the window of a Vancouver-bound jet. I've watched the stunning golds, pinks, and purples of a midnight sunset over the Gulf of Finland from the bow of the Helsinki-to-Tallinn ferry. As a resident of Dover the view of the famous White Cliffs from the middle of the English Channel is one I will never tire of, and I can now say from experience that the view from the peak of Arthur's Seat is right up there, affording clear and unspoilt views of the Firth of Forth, the city of Edinburgh and the mountain range that towers over it.

Although hundreds were undertaking the same walk as me, it was still possible to enjoy an hour or three of splendid isolation. I had to shut my eyes on one or two occasions, mind. I'm not selfie society's greatest fan but I completely understand why anyone would take one in this location. Standing or sitting on the edge of a sheer drop to certain death to take one is a bit foolhardy in my humble opinion, so in order to avoid coming over all queasy I stepped up the pace and travelled downhill a lot faster than I came up.

While I was in the area, I thought I might have a stroll around Leith and see some of the parts of Edinburgh I'd read about in the novels of Irvine Welsh. Fellow fans will know of his fascination with the darker side of Scottish society. Rather than waxing lyrical about lochs, tartan and roaming in the gloaming, Welsh's Scotland, usually centred around Leith, is often confined to a world of thieving, glassings, Stanley knives and heroine and not the stuff that tends to feature in the tourist literature. Somehow, I just fancied a pint in a manky pub and have a little walk on the wild side.

If I was looking for Edinburgh's dark heart on Leith Walk, I was to be disappointed as I found myself in a high street that looked much like the one in my home town, albeit it with a lot less litter. There were more takeaways than were good for the health of the district and while a few businesses looked like they were holding on like grim death, no premises were actually boarded up. With its second hand shops, charity shops and lack of household names from the retail trade, there was nothing here I hadn't seen before. That said, Leith Walk might have been on another planet from a Royal Mile that was barely a mile or so up the road.

It was at 'The Fit Ay the Walk' – you'll notice how quickly I've picked up the language – that I noticed what I guess I'd subconsciously been looking for. Directly below the statue of a stern-looking Queen Victoria I chanced upon half a dozen locals, all with a tell-tale purple tin seemingly spot-welded to their fist, engaged in violent argument. Although slurred speech and impenetrable accents made understanding impossible, the shellsuits and ruddy complexions spoke volumes. The only female in the group – 25 going on 60 and the possessor of few teeth – seemed to have had an unfortunate accident, judging from the brown stain on the seat of her otherwise green and purple attire.

Satisfied that I was the only tourist in Edinburgh who'd come across Welsh's 'Jakeys', I figured I'd seen enough and should return to the hostel for a little lie down.

Three hours later I was reliving that crushing sense of disappointment that I'm convinced most British football fans experience as soon as they enter an athletics stadium.

Somehow I feel that the pitch in a football stadium is its centrepiece, whereas it seems like an afterthought when placed inside a running track. As a spectator you're that much further from the action and somehow more disconnected from it.

Meadowbank Stadium had certainly seen better days. Typically, paying punters could only watch from a main stand in which all the orange seats had been faded by the sun; impressive, though, that Scotland could produce enough sunshine for that to happen. Dispirited, I thought I might sit in the stadium concourse, munch on a pie that was becoming a staple of my Scottish diet and wait for the game to kick off in half an hour's time.

Edinburgh hadn't had three teams playing in the Scottish league for over 20 years. In 1995 this stadium's previous residents, Meadowbank Thistle, had changed their name to Livingston and moved to the town of that name. However, by winning the 2015/16 Lowland League Championship and a play-off final against East Stirling, Edinburgh City would welcome Forfar Athletic next week in the Scottish League Two season's opener. For tonight's League Cup group game, Hamilton Accies would offer a different challenge. Although they'd struggled in recent times they were a Premiership club nonetheless and were expected to win comfortably.

I'd looked forward to seeing goalkeeper Michael McGovern play for Accies again but had somehow missed that he'd followed his former manager Alex Neil to Norwich City, ending a 15-year career north of the wall. The outstanding form I'd seen him produce in defeat against Aberdeen clearly wasn't a one-off. A Northern Ireland international from Enniskillen, McGovern had had an outstanding tournament at the 2016 Euros in France. At times, it seemed like he was taking on Poland and Germany on his own in 1-0 defeats to both countries.

McGovern's replacement, Remi Matthews, looked likely to enjoy a quiet evening during the game's early stages, but after he'd picked the ball out of his net twice in the space of a couple of minutes it seemed a shock result might be on the cards. However, although Ross Allum's smart finishing had given City a 2-0 lead within the first 20 minutes, it soon became clear that they'd peaked too early.

Accies, seemingly insulted by this threat to their superiority, pulled a goal back within three minutes courtesy of Alister Crawford's beautifully flighted free kick. It was the visitors' game from this point, and, with less than a third gone, Brazilian Alexandre D'Acol made it 2-2.

If the match became more one-sided as it went on, it was no less entertaining and deserved a bigger audience that the 459 fans who'd paid to get in. One or two watched for free though, as a group had gathered behind one goal in the bar of an adjacent sports centre to watch events unfold. One lad combined spectating and participation to great effect, watching the game while knocking off a few calories on a running machine. Inspired by his fine example, I sprinted down the steps to the concourse to get myself another pie.

Although Edinburgh did enough to suggest they'd be fine playing at League Two level, they lost this one as Accies scored twice midway through the second half through Jordan McGregor's close-range tap-in and Dougie Imrie's penalty.

Having put in as least as much mileage as the players, I was knackered by the time I got back to my hostel in the Cowgate district. I'd enjoyed seeing so much of Edinburgh after previously spending just single afternoons in the city to watch Hibs and Hearts. Though tomorrow's trip to Aberdeen would only be for a few hours as well, I'd been looking forward to it for weeks.

Despite the high-volume excesses of Edinburgh nightlife, I slept like a rock.

ABERDEEN v NK MARIBOR

Europa League Third Qualifying Round
Thursday, 28 July 2016

THE TRAIN to Aberdeen was packed, so it was just as well I'd booked in advance. Unfortunately I'd forgotten to read the small print on the Scotrail website and seemed to have reserved a seat on a service that might have been solely for the use of irritating small children and their equally galling parents.

In the double seat to my left, a young Japanese mother and primary-aged devil child joined me in not uttering a word throughout the journey. Sadly their devotion to handheld games made them the noisiest buggers on the train. Headphones were dispensed with as the whole range of onomatopoeic noises came from their state-of-the-art tablets whenever they shot something. They shot something approximately every four seconds. If the child had been busting caps into the bottoms of virtual prostitutes in *Grand Theft Auto*, his mother wouldn't have had the first clue, so engrossed was she in her own game.

Just behind me, a Geordie woman who could have been a walking advertisement for *Viz* magazine was threatening her ten-year-old with a whole series of sanctions she was never going to impose. The lad, who answered to the name of River, had clearly never heard the word 'no' in his puff. He gave credence to a wealth of recent academic research which suggested that while some children might benefit greatly from organic snacks and a course in conflict management, others just needed a good kick in the seat of the pants. Regularly. For now, a third packet of Haribo and a can of Monster unsurprisingly failed to stop River constantly screaming and running up and down the carriage.

Opposite me, a rather charming little girl – the image of Sophie Ellis Bextor – who only let out a blood-curdling shriek every five minutes or so, asked her mother why Edinburgh's main railway station was called Waverley. She replied, 'Oh, it's just a name darling, it doesn't actually mean anything.'

I thought it best to put in my tuppence worth to help, so I said, 'Actually, madam, I believe the station is named after Sir Walter Scott's historical novel *Waverley* which was written in 1814. It was his first venture into prose fiction and is set in the time of the Jacobite uprising of 1745. Then again, if you wish to bring your child up in ignorance, who am I to judge?'

Only joking!

With no spare seats on the train, I opted to stand between two carriages where I chanced upon an American backpacker whose entire family had just been crushed to death in a freak accident, judging by her tearful histrionics. When I discovered her wailing was a result of being unable to pick up the train's Wi-Fi, I lost sympathy and jumped out at Kirkcaldy and would have done even if the train hadn't stopped there. I hoped there'd be service for normal people along shortly and there was.

I'd booked into a hotel called the Sopranos St Magnus Court; not because it sounded a bit classy and highbrow with its opera connotations but because I love *The Sopranos*, the HBO series about the Mafiosi of New Jersey, and the name grabbed my attention. A very nice hotel it is too and, if your eyesight is a bit keener than mine you can see it clearly from the main entrance/exit of Aberdeen station. A charming young lady checked me in and while her best

Hollywood smile screamed 'Welcome to Aberdeen', her broad Lithuanian-Scottish accent ensured I didn't understand a single word she said. Luckily my room number was on the key she gave me, and I'd stayed in a hotel before. I dumped my bag and went out for a wander.

Mooching around at my usual leisurely pace, I couldn't help but think that whoever had been advertising Aberdeen down the years hadn't done it too many favours. What, after all, do we know about the place? The Granite City? Fair play, many of the city's buildings are hewn from the same rock retrieved from quarries dotted around the area. This might make the city look a bit grey, but I didn't see this as a bad thing but as something that proclaimed the area's individuality and made it look rather smart.

The North Sea oil industry? The port area looked a bit grim, but don't they all! With the oil running out and the industry in decline there were sure to be serious consequences for the area. If the city centre was anything to go by, it looked, despite the appearance of one or two less-salubrious retailers, like nobody was chucking in the towel just yet. As for the town's football fans, like the ones I'd enjoyed a few drinks with in Hamilton, they made light of how they were perceived in the Lowlands as men who married their own livestock and were happy enough to take a joke against themselves. If Aberdeen really was a heavy-industry city in which men were men and the sheep were nervous, I hadn't noticed.

I'd decided to find the ground and buy a ticket before I pitched up for the game later, but, as ever, I got confused by the written instructions I made for myself. I duly asked an old boy for directions, and he told me, 'Just walk to the end of King Street. When you see the cemetery and feel the wind coming in off the North Sea, you can't miss it.'

He was spot on and when I arrived at the famous old stadium, I knew I was back in the big time when I had to be entered on to a database before I could get a ticket. The £13 I paid for it was the costliest I shelled out for during my week in Scotland but I felt that paying such an amount for a Europa League game was put into sharp perspective when, a week or so later, I paid £15 to watch an English non-league game finish 0-0 in Wrexham.

Although I wasn't sure I'd fancy visiting in February – even in July the midges were wearing cardigans – or a swim in the North Sea at any time, I still found myself 500 yards away from an old-fashioned seaside promenade and figured it would be rude not to stop for lunch. There was nothing for it but to buy some fish and chips from the grumpiest man in Scotland and watch the world go by for an hour. Feeling seasonally rakish, I had an ice-cream as well.

The urge to spend a summer afternoon in a pub garden was strong at this point, but wiser counsels prevailed given that kick-off was still some six hours away. Instead, having shelled out for a little luxury in the middle of a week of hostel living, I opted to go back to the hotel, have a long soak in the bath and reacquaint myself with television. I'd paid for it, I reasoned, but would happily have forgone the pleasure of watching Rusty Lee and Anne Diamond winning an edition of *Pointless Celebrities* if I'd been charged a bit less.

Smelling a little nicer than I had for a while, I found my way back to a pub I'd spotted earlier and settled down at a table with a group of Aberdeen fans I reckoned to be about 35 years my junior. We spoke at length about cities we'd visited; Budapest, Prague, Bucharest, and many others that might as well have been on a different planet when I was their age. Different times I suppose, but I'd seen Aberdeen beat Real Madrid to win a European Cup Winners' Cup Final and I felt that was the type of experience that they'd miss out on.

An old Caledonian friend of mine called Ali Kennedy has, for more years than either of us would care to remember, been promising to come to Scotland for 'a big night of European football'. Ali is a Celtic fan who makes tentative plans for us to visit in February or March; a good plan apart from one tiny flaw that the dedicated follower of Scottish football may already have spotted. I usually suggest we go before the schools go back in September just to be on the safe side, but I'm sure we'll get there in the end. For now, Aberdeen was to provide everything Ali had promised me.

I instantly took a liking to Pittodrie. Despite the open corners the official capacity was some way north of 20,000, but the stadium looked much bigger given that all four stands were close to the action in the same manner some top English grounds used to be before everyone started banging on about global branding and moving up to the next level. With vocal support geared exclusively towards getting behind the team, the place was jumping as the teams came out. I was expecting a good game as well, given that I'd been impressed with Maribor when I'd seen them win in Domžale while on holiday in Slovenia.

I often think some fans can be a bit sniffy about teams who are a bit direct. Many of my acquaintances would happily dismiss Aberdeen as 'a bunch of hoofers' and bore me senseless in telling me why. Yet while this turned out to be something of a sledgehammer v scalpel type of affair, it was nonetheless a cracking game of football.

If there was nothing too scientific about Aberdeen's approach to the game, their fans loved it as they poured forward and seldom allowed Maribor out of their own half. With big number nine Adam Rooney (who I'd remarkably see score a hat-trick in an English non-league game at Dover soon after) instrumental in everything they did well, they could and should have led handsomely at the break. One save from Maribor keeper Jasmin Handanović, which kept out a close-range header from Jayden Stockley, ranked as one of the finest I've seen in 'live' context. At the other end Maribor missed the clearest-cut chance of the first half and the sides somehow went in level 0-0 at half-time.

At the interval I refrained from further boosting the share price of the Scottish pie industry and enjoyed the spectacle of a huge tanker seemingly trying turn itself around in the North Sea.

If the second half wasn't as frenetic as the first, it was no less enjoyable. Maribor were in no particular hurry as they prodded and poked to look for an opening with the confidence of a side that knew one would soon come their way. As was the case in Domžale, they didn't look like scoring until they actually did, as Ash Taylor mistimed a tackle leaving Milivoje Novaković to go clear through the middle and fire into the corner.

Novaković gleefully ran off to celebrate with Maribor fans, duly disappearing under the 20 or so who had made the trip. Those supporters then disappeared under the Maribor team and staff, who in turn disappeared under stewards who sought to control the pile-up by the rather bonkers criteria of adding to its numbers. By the time a couple of policemen arrived on the scene – by virtue of showing the same turn of speed as the aforementioned tanker – Aberdeen had kicked off again. It all seemed like a lot of fuss to make over a few blokes who'd reduced their mental age for a minute or two and were merely expressing a little glee.

Although 1-0 with just seven minutes remaining was a terribly harsh reflection on the night's events, Aberdeen hit back to earn a draw that was the very least they deserved. As a deep cross was nodded down by Taylor, Rooney held the ball up and laid if off for Jonny Hayes to drill across the keeper and into the far corner.

Chatting with the locals on the way back to the hotel, most seemed to have enjoyed the game as much as I had but felt their team needed a lead to take to Slovenia. So it proved. After having a penalty saved by a goalkeeper who should have been sent off earlier, Aberdeen lost 1-0 to a comedy own goal in injury time and went out of the competition.

STIRLING UNIVERSITY v
THE SPARTANS

Scottish Lowland League
Friday, 29 July 2016

SOONER OR later, when searching for directions to a football ground, you will come across the statement, 'It's a bit of a trek, so just get a taxi.' Invariably, and I'm speaking from extensive experience here, this is utter bilge uttered by fat lads who could do with a spot of exercise or blokes with more money than sense. So just in case you're planning a trip to the Forthbank Stadium in Stirling, let me tell you how you can get there in half an hour from the city's railway station at a pace a 61-year-old with a dodgy knee will have no trouble maintaining.

Turn left out of the station, cross a bridge that takes you back over the railway tracks, then turn right. Pass the Vue cinema on your right and, staying on the left-hand pathway, follow your nose until you pass a small sewage plant. Keep going until you reach the local sports centre, and the ground is just on the other side of the car park. Honestly, how difficult was that?

I'd started my day in Aberdeen and was on my way out of the city by about 9.30am, already making tentative plans to return. In a half-empty carriage containing no annoying people whatsoever, I settled down with a good book (Isabel Allende's *Daughter of Fortune* since you ask). This state of affairs wouldn't last, but at least this morning's distractions were entertaining and attractive as four ladies of some 30-ish summers got on at Montrose. Immediately, they broke out four champagne flutes, a carton of orange juice and a full bottle of Moët, which they opened with much glee and no little ceremony. It was a bit early in the day for me, not that anyone was asking. Having poured themselves a Buck's Fizz, they added a final flourish to each glass by adding a strawberry. Although I can't tell a good champagne from a glass of liver salts myself, I formed the impression that this might be a classy thing to do.

Comfortable and with glass in hand, the girls had a natter. About nails. For 45 minutes. Although they might have discussed the rights of man while I was in the loo, they'd reverted to nails by the time I got back. When alighting at Leuchars, one of the girls said, 'It's so nice to have a proper conversation for once. Aaron's always talking shite about football.'

I tried not to laugh out loud at this point but failed miserably. Happily, the girls saw the funny side and waved to me as I settled back down with the lovely Isabel until we pulled into Waverley.

Though tempted to have a little siesta, I dumped my bag at the hostel and headed off to Stirling. If everything had gone to plan I'd have been on my way to Inverness for three nights prior to flying back to Luton. When this idea was scuppered by late fixture rescheduling, I figured I'd spend a day in Stirling, take in a Friday night Lowland League game and combine a little Anglo-Scottish history with recce ahead of a future trip to a Stirling Albion fixture.

I have to say that I took an instant liking to Stirling and once again I was struck by how a place can maximise its heritage to promote employment and tourism in a manner that my hometown just doesn't. Stirling, if you weren't paying attention in Year 9 history, played a vital role in Scotland's story, particularly around the time of the First War of Scottish Independence at the end of the 13th century. Therefore, a trip to Stirling Castle serves to announce quite loudly that this is where the English had their backsides handed to them on a plate once or twice. Having worked in a History class for a few years I knew that these parts had suffered at the hands of Edward I who was, by all accounts, a bit of a bastard. That said, Stirling sent us Billy Bremner seven centuries later, so I assumed that slate had been wiped clean and we were friends again.

With the site of the Battle of Bannockburn just down the road and Stirling Bridge a mile or two away, this wasn't a place I was going to do justice to in an afternoon. That said, I still had time to peruse the perimeter of the Church of the Holy Rude (insert your own gag in the space provided) and read a plaque or two. James VI of Scotland – our own James I, the first Stuart monarch and son of Mary, Queen of Scots – was christened here. You'll remember all the trouble he caused by dint of being a bit useless and monumentally unattractive, I expect. A few minutes later, while admiring the view from the ramparts of Stirling Castle, I heard an unmistakeable American accent telling a small tour party a few facts about Scottish history. Unfortunately, all of the 'facts' seemed to have been quoted directly from the script of *Braveheart*, leaving me with the option of either moving on or chipping in.

The tour guide was called Wilbur, or if he wasn't then he should have been – loud, brash, ill-educated and with the full tourist starter kit including a baseball cap and a camera the size of a pygmy hippo. Under normal circumstances I'd have ignored him, but this wasn't an option within a five-mile radius of where he was standing. His mates were good ol' boys visiting 'the old country' in a manner that suggested some spurious ancestral connection would alleviate that they were all tedious, golf-loving bellends. If somebody hadn't already got to them first, I think I could have convinced at least a couple of them that they were lairds or thanes of somewhere or another and sold them a certificate to prove it for a grand. Wilbur was the most irksome of them by some distance, constantly referring to 'Scatlin' and speaking of 'The English' as though someone had just placed a long-deceased mackerel under his nose.

Talking utter bollocks is, of course, an enjoyable pastime. I do it regularly from a position of knowing that 90 per cent of what I'm saying is nonsense and mostly made up for my own amusement. Wilbur, however, was uttering 99 per cent nonsense with the authority of a man who knew what he was talking about. I briefly thought he might be receiving money for delivering such unadulterated twaddle but dismissed the notion instantly.

Maybe I was hazy on a couple of points. That said, if Edward I was defeated at Bannockburn in 1314 it might not have been such a notable achievement given that the Hammer of the Scots popped his clogs in 1307 and wouldn't have put up much of a scrap.

Likewise, I could have sworn that kilts weren't a hot fashion item until some 300 years after Stirling Bridge and that the poem *To a Mouse* was written by Robbie Burns, not Robert the Bruce. William Wallace, unless I'm very much mistaken, was from Scotland's lesser nobility rather than being a 'simple commoner' whatever that might be (either way, I'm pretty sure he didn't get to shag Queen Isabela of France in a tent).

When Wilbur loudly proclaimed that Bannockburn was the last battle to have been fought on British soil, I thought it best to abandon my wee, sleekit, cow'rin, tim'rous beastie persona and just put my colonial cousin straight.

'That'd be the Battle of Culloden, mate!'

'Excuse me, buddy!' Wilbur replied.

'The Battle of Culloden. 1745. The final battle of the Jacobite uprising. That was the last battle to be fought on British soil, not Bannockburn. The English won that one, incidentally. I thought you might like to know.'

Wilburn scowled in a manner that suggested he really didn't want to know and seemed miffed that he'd been caught out as a fraud.

'Thanks, fella,' he replied. 'If there's anything else you need to know, I'll be sure to come and find you!'

Fuck off, in other words, but I thought I might help myself to the final word on this one.

'Oh, OK. Fair enough. I just thought you needed some help. Sorry!' I turned to walk away, then turned sharply and said, 'One final thing just in case you're planning to talk about William Wallace. I'm speaking from memory here, but I think he was from Renfrewshire, not Sydney or New York.'

As I left with a spring in my step feeling rather pleased with myself, a genuine tour guide smiled broadly and wordlessly shook my hand before I made my way to Forthbank. It was my plan to double-check the kick-off time, find a decent pub for an hour or two, then go to the game. Thus, I went into the club's smartly appointed offices and asked, 'Can you tell me what time tonight's game kicks off, please?

'What game's that?' said a lass behind the desk.

'Stirling University v The Spartans in the Lowland League.' 'Oh, I'm afraid they don't play here now!' said the lass, a little more apologetically than she needed to.

At this point another lady joined us from a glass-fronted back office, having heard the conversation so far.

'Haven't they updated their website yet? Hang on a minute, I'll find out where they're playing nowadays as I'm keen to know myself.'

Within a minute, she was back.

'It's a 7.45 kick-off, but they play at Falkirk now. Sorry you've had a wasted journey.'

Given that both ladies were employed by Stirling Albion, I was quite touched by how genuinely concerned they were about my wasted journey. I thanked them for their help and concern, told them that it couldn't be helped and that I'd see them again when I came back for an Albion game. Stirling University has 12,800 students, 1,500 staff but no sod to update the football section's website, apparently.

I had time to get to Falkirk if I put my mind to it, but the truth of the matter was that I simply couldn't be arsed. After four days solid of either walking or travelling around Scotland by train, I was tired. Thus, I got some hot chocolate and some biscuits from the Sainsbury's at Waverley and had an old git's night in back in my cosy single room at the hostel. Not for the first time, the divine Ms Allende got me through the night.

Final score from Falkirk: Stirling University 0 The Spartans 3.

DUNDEE v FORFAR ATHLETIC

Scottish League Cup Group Stage
Saturday, 30 July 2016

LET'S START with a little game of word association, shall we? Name a foodstuff that reminds you of Dundee. You said cake, didn't you?! I thought as much. Not cow pie then? Me neither, so you can imagine my surprise when the first noteworthy landmark I spotted on my first visit to Tayside was a statue of Desperate Dan. Though it's been a while since I picked up a copy of *The Dandy*, I'd rather assumed that Dan was an American chap. I remember that he shaved with a blowtorch and used his superhuman strength in the selfless service of the underdog, but his connection with Scotland was something I'd somehow overlooked. I was confused for a while until some less than painstaking research revealed that DC Thompson, *The Dandy*'s publishers, are based in Dundee. Minnie the Minx and Gnasher are there too, although Dan has been left to doggy sit for Dennis the Menace for reasons that nobody has yet made clear.

It was a shame in some respects that I hadn't timed my visit for a year or two down the line. Although the city will doubtless benefit greatly from a massive development along its expansive waterfront, all I initially got to see on leaving the railway station was scaffolding and large areas that were under construction and boarded up. The city centre, in which all the usual retailers were present, could have been anywhere. Unusually, I hadn't made a pig's ear of following the directions

I'd printed off and, having found the Wellgate Centre, I used the escalators to exit via the top floor as instructed. At this point, I was rather expecting to gloss over an instruction I felt might be widely exaggerated. It read, 'Here you have two choices, via the Hilltown [shorter distance but like climbing the north face of the Eiger] or via Dens Road [much longer but less likely to induce a heart attack].'

The hill in front of me wasn't quite vertical, but it wasn't far off, so allow me a little poetic licence here when I record that Hilltown makes Arthur's Seat look like a billiard table. There was no way I could walk up it as such, but I could just about scale it. Although I doubt that Sir Ranulph Fiennes would have been quite so courageous or downright foolhardy, I decided to have a crack at it simply because it was there. I dare say somebody's erected a plaque at the top in my honour by now.

It was tough going as I struggled through a part of Dundee that looked as though it had known more prosperous times. An assortment of shops, mostly selling foodstuffs from east and central Europe and beyond, were all open for business but looked like they were hanging on like grim death. Behind me, a largely uninterrupted view of the River Tay offered a more pleasing aesthetic, even if it did involve walking backwards for a while. Eventually, after the hill became less steep and I'd turned right at an ornamental clock as I'd been told, Dens Park was right in front of me.

Anyone who has studied Scottish football to even a cursory degree will know that the grounds of Dundee and Dundee United are close together. What I didn't quite appreciate was that they virtually join at the corner flags. Sad act that I am, I paced the distance out and noted that the grounds are 128 paces apart at the nearest point.

With time on my hands before kick-off I visited the shops of both clubs, bought match tickets, a programme, and a club badge in both, and nattered with the amiable staff. In the United shop I chatted at length with a family of Scarborough-based family of Dundee exiles who were home visiting family. Dad seemed thrilled to bits that he'd acquired a pink away shirt for his little lad. The lad, a cherubic little fellow aged five or six wasn't exactly jumping through hoops in receipt of his 'surprise', but I figured this was an obsession he'd grow into, given a hefty shove in the right direction.

Given that my match tickets collectively came to a paltry £11, I had enough left over for a little self-indulgence. Adjacent to Dens Park is a family baker's, established in 1860, called Rough and Fraser. Although my search for the best football pie in Scotland is a work in progress, this fine establishment offered a contender for the title at the splendidly low price of £1.02. One is enough for those seeking a fine dining experience, two is fine for a light lunch and three just about sufficient for a tubby bugger looking to line his stomach ahead of a moderate session in a welcoming alehouse. I should stress that I could not have made an accurate assessment as to what the pies contained, but it could have been Desperate Dan's fossilised testicles for all I cared.

With appetite sated, I found the pub recommended to me just around the corner. Although it appeared to have changed its name from the Centenary Bar to the Ambassador, the recommendation was spot on. Set up to accommodate both home and away supporters – though Forfar's travelling support had opted to sup elsewhere – it had everything I needed from a pub pre-match in reasonably priced decent beer and friendly locals to discuss the game with.

I thought the Dundee fans might be in an optimistic frame of mind ahead of the new season. Back in the top flight and with the visit of most of Scotland's top clubs to look forward to, Dundee could also lord it over their nearest and dearest for at least a few months following United's relegation at the end of the 2015/16 season. In the event, I found most Dee supporters in a sombre and resigned frame of mind.

Three days previously and barely a week before the start of the season proper, Dundee's star man, an English lad called Kane Hemmings, had triggered a clause in his contract enabling him to move back south of the border. Dee manager Paul Hartley wanted to retain the services of a man who'd knocked in 25 goals the previous season but admitted to various branches of the Scottish media that there was nothing he could do to stop the move.

There's nothing new about a player moving from Scotland to England to advance his career. This particular transfer, conducted for an undisclosed fee, was a little different in that Hemmings had moved to Oxford United, only just promoted to England's third tier. My new drinking companions saw the deal as a sad and predictable consequence of high wages, even in the lower reaches of the English pyramid structure, meaning that the standard of Scottish club football was destined to stagnate and decline. A lad of similar vintage and tonnage to myself called Alan summed up the view of pretty much everyone present when he told me, 'I'm always going to turn up every week and I think we'll do OK this season. Mind you, a few others I work with are seriously pissed off that Hemmings went just after they'd shelled out money they don't really have on season tickets. It won't stop there either. Watch Greg Stewart today, as he'll be the next one out of the door, mark my words.'

Alan was spot on. Stewart scored twice against Forfar, and it was to be his last game for the club. Two weeks later he signed for Birmingham City for an initial fee reported to be in the region of £500,000.

Inside Dens Park, modernised but still quaint and quirky, just 2,219 fans had turned up for the visit of Forfar. Although they were well supported they'd not fared well since I saw them at Airdrieonians just 18 months previously, when they missed promotion to the Championship by a whisker. The following season they finished rock bottom of League One and would start again next week in Scottish football's bottom tier. It wasn't difficult to see why today as they barely had a sniff of the ball and were fortunate to only lose 7-0.

If Forfar weren't the toughest of opponents, Dundee played some good stuff with a lad called James Vincent orchestrating from the middle third of pitch. Starting to fit snugly into the balding stalwart category – a term I guarantee you will never hear outside of football – Vincent was just one of those players I'm drawn to watching over the course of 90 minutes, with his extraordinary talent for finding an acre of space that only he seemed allowed into. As he prodded and poked and waiting patiently for an option to present itself, Vincent was simply a treat to watch. Although I thought long and hard as to whether I'd paid £6 to watch a better player, I couldn't think of one.

As the goals rattled in at regular intervals, attention around me seemed to be drawn to events elsewhere. I'd assumed that Dundee, as the strongest club in the group by a distance, were going to win it at a canter. The truth was that they needed a favour from Dumbarton to have a hope of making the last 16, didn't get one, and duly went out of the competition. East Fife finished top.

As is so often the case when I'm really enjoying myself, the final whistle told me it was time to go 'home'. As I tumbled down the north face of Hilltown, I reflected on the fact that I was about to embark on a 130-mile round trip that would take me to my next game approximately 150 yards away.

I must start thinking these things through in future.

DUNDEE UNITED v DUNFERMLINE ATHLETIC

Scottish League Cup Group Stage
Sunday, 31 July 2016

ALTHOUGH IT took me at least 50 years to get any serious travelling under my belt, there's a little game I always play with myself when I visit a new location. I think I may have mentioned before that if I visit a town or city with more than one football club, I need to know which one I would follow in the unlikely event that I moved there. While this has proven to be a pretty straightforward process, particularly in mainland Europe, in Scotland, matters aren't quite so simple.

Rangers or Celtic? I've no particular preference as yet, having had a good time at both. Hibs or Hearts? I thought I'd be a Hibs man before a memorable session with good company in the Tynecastle Arms took me into the ranks of the undecided. Dundee or Dundee United? Later today, I opted to either flip a coin or come back and form a second opinion.

With the benefit of hindsight I should have stayed overnight between the two games. What I hadn't realised was that Scotrail staff were holding the latest of a series of one-day strikes, aimed at combating the company's plans to introduce driver-only-operated trains throughout the region. As a younger man I'd have welcomed this move and would have bunked just about every train I set foot on to save myself a fortune. Nowadays, with friends in a similar situation whose jobs are threatened, I thought the whole thing had the usual stench of redundancy for some and a bigger dividend for shareholders who already had more money than they knew what to do with. I said as much to pickets outside Waverley who were genuinely apologetic about the plight I found myself in and couldn't have done more to help me out. Although the train I'd booked had long since been cancelled, a skeleton service was still operating and I'd have no trouble in getting to Dundee with time to spare. My train back hadn't been cancelled and, after being given firm assurances that it wouldn't be, I decided to chance it.

Arriving at around 1.30pm, my stroll along the waterfront took me past the ill-fated Robert Falcon Scott's vessel, the RRS *Discovery*. It looked tiny and I wondered how on earth it could have survived the 'Roaring Forties' and mile after mile of Antarctic pack ice. The attraction was closed, unfortunately, but with the spirit of Scott very much in mind and with the aid of a local Sherpa, some crampons, and a slab of Kendall Mint Cake, I reached the summit of Hilltown in good spirits. Given that Rough and Fraser was understandably closed and with no time in which to enjoy what The Ambassador had to offer, I opted to go straight to Tannadice and watch the ground fill up.

Today's crowd of just shy of 5,000 represented around a third of the capacity, and it was hard to imagine that 28,000 had filled the stadium in 1966 when the Tangerines entertained and beat Barcelona. I was reflecting on the last time I could recall watching them play (when they lost on aggregate against IFK Gothenburg in the 1987 UEFA Cup Final) when the phone rang. I didn't recognise the number, but the call came from a Dover-based Scottish pal, Hughie. With an absence of niceties or preamble that has become something of a trademark, Hughie got straight down to the point of his call.

'What on earth are you doing up there, Winter? Have you taken up sheep farming?'

I initially considered the possibility that he thought I might still be in Aberdeen before I answered his question with a question.

'How on earth do you know where I am, you old sod?'

'You're a bit difficult to miss, pal. A big ugly bugger in a green shirt tends to stand out when everyone else is wearing orange. Just don't pick your nose as you look a bit conspicuous.'

I'd quite forgotten that the game was being shown live on BT Sport. While I imagined its audience at home might be minuscule, it included Hughie, at least for the time being. Reflecting on the fact that I'd previously been spotted at a televised match on three separate occasions and been on sick leave for all of them, I cut our conversation short as kick-off was imminent.

If the group stages of the Scottish League Cup weren't considered to be big potatoes by the fans, they seemed like a competitive way of starting the new season. This game was certainly nicely poised. United had won all three of their ties thus far and Dunfermline, despite their heavy home defeat to Inverness, could still qualify for the knockout stages with a win. What followed was lively to say the least.

I thought Dunfermline had played some decent stuff in midweek but being a bit brittle had cost them dearly. They'd added a little steel to their game today, however, and provided the perfect pantomime villain in the form of Kallum Higginbotham.

Higginbotham, a Salford lad, had played for a few clubs either side of the border, and is a forward who can play a bit. A recent signing at Dunfermline, he was keen to impress and earned his money today as arguably his side's best player. In the first half, however, his game plan was largely a tale of how many fearsome tackles he could launch himself into without getting booked. I made it nine before the referee pulled a yellow card out of his pocket.

He'd raised a few pulses by then, however, most notably when one older fan, made a little purple around the gills through Higginbotham's rumbustiousness, finally snapped and offered a piece of advice, but rather touchingly made allowance for the young children around him who were taking advantage of United's admirably cheap concession tickets.

'Get off the park, you dirty fffff ... you dirty ... uhmmm ... pie,' he bellowed before wandering off in search of appropriate adjectives.

The kids lapped this up, naturally, and from behind their hands constantly muttered something akin to, 'chortle, chortle, snigger, snigger, you're a dirty pie, number 20' before Higginbotham switched flanks at the start of the second half.

If there was nothing between the sides in the first half, Dundee United always looked to have that little extra creative edge, with Irishman Willo Flood – keeping up the balding stalwart tradition that seemed prevalent in these parts – their best player in central midfield. They took the lead shortly after the break with a straightforward goal; Jamie Robson knocked over a good cross from the left, Temitope Obadeyi flicked the ball on, and Simon Murray headed in from close range. Murray, incidentally, was the only red-headed Scotsman I noticed during my six-day stay, duly destroying a myth I'd brought up with me. With a few minutes remaining, Scott Fraser made it 2-0 from a free kick that was a replica of the one I'd seen Dunfermline concede on Tuesday, thus ending their interest in the competition.

Having checked that my train was still running, I just had time for a pint on the waterfront while perusing the Scottish papers. I noted that if I had gone up to the Highlands, I'd have had an eventful trip given that Inverness and Ross County both won 7-0 against Arbroath and Cove Rangers respectively. One lucky punter, a 54-year-old father of three called Steve Sales, had placed £1.40 on Inverness, Ross County and Dundee all winning 7-0. He won just shy of £60,000.

Had I done likewise, I'd have stayed for a couple of months and finished this book in no time at all. In the real world I was back in Dover inside 24 hours, working through the school summer holidays as a means to financing my next trip.

FALKIRK v FORFAR ATHLETIC

Scottish League Cup Group Stage
Tuesday, 25 July 2017

A COUPLE of years ago I went to watch Fiorentina play in a pre-season friendly at Chelsea. Ignoring a 24-hour tube strike, I figured it was barely a brisk stroll from Victoria Station to Stamford Bridge. So it proved, but decent boozers seem to be a thing of the past in west London these days, hence we found ourselves in a series of ghastly gastro pubs. Although I took the beer prices on the chin, I couldn't afford to eat without selling one of the children. However I was drawn to an item on the menu that stated, 'Haddock, chips and all the trimmings – £12.50.' Well, I had to ask.

Attracting the attention of a charming young Polish girl called Roza, I asked what was meant by 'all the trimmings'?

In flawless English and without a hint of irony, she replied, 'It could be peas, it could be carrots, it could be broccoli. It just depends how creative the chef is feeling at the time.'

Ordering fish and chips in Falkirk is a very different experience, I can tell you.

Initially I'd committed my usual error of finding the ground before heading back to town and seeing what the place had to offer in terms of ale and tuck. As usual, by the time I found the ground, I had maybe an hour and a half to kill but no time to get into town and back. Famished, I was directed to Balfour's, a chippie within sight and a two-minute walk of the stadium. Inside, a lady called Donna was holding court and dishing out her wares.

'What's a white pudding when it's at home, Donna?' I ventured.

'It's mostly fat, suet, bread and oatmeal,' she replied. 'It's the nearest we've got to a vegetarian option, son!'

For a 62-year-old, there's nothing quite like being called 'son' to let you know you're back in Scotland.

I'd arrived in Edinburgh the previous evening and while it was great to be back after a year's absence, I soon found myself feeling somewhat overwhelmed. Although the city was a week or two away from the festival, it was certainly geared up for it as I had four leaflets shoved into my hand before I left Waverley. Outside, the young and the beautiful of far-flung continents took endless selfies of themselves, clogged up the pavements and purchased over-priced tartan-related tat from minimum-wage staff, none of whom appeared to be Scottish. Befuddled, I shuffled off to Princes Gardens for a snooze.

Twenty-four hours later in Falkirk, Donna knew all her customers on first name terms. Sturdy, cherry-cheeked and Pickwickian, she worked alone and took her time, a fact that bothered nobody. They queued patiently and enjoyed her comestible cabaret after a hard day's graft. I liked the lady too, not only for reminding me why I liked visiting Scotland but also for dishing up the best fish and chips I'd had in a while.

After buying the obligatory lapel badge – my collection is now the envy of absolutely no one yet pleasingly manages to embarrass and irritate the children – I went straight into the ground five minutes before kick-off (Donna doesn't do small portions so it took a while to finish my tea outside).

Again, I was given cause to reflect on the fact that a few Scottish football grounds have bits missing. Although Falkirk's is one of the smarter stadiums I've entered in recent times, I was surprised that there was an open area on the far side of the pitch. The guy in the next seat, here as a neutral like me, told me that the ground was effectively a work in progress. The north and south stands behind either goal had opened in 2005 and 2009 respectively. There were no immediate plans to add a fourth and final stand, given that the ground seemed fine as it was. Every seat afforded a good view of the (artificial) pitch and the facilities were excellent. I'm no great fan of new-build stadia, but I rather liked it here.

Some 2,187 punters pitched up for the game, which seemed a reasonable attendance all things considered. Only the main stand was open and comfortably packed enough to provide a decent atmosphere.

I'd enjoyed watching Falkirk play, as one of a few Scottish clubs I was developing a soft spot for. Their fans seemed like a good bunch when I'd shared a carriage with them on the way back from a 1-0 win at Morton and I'd enjoyed watching them on TV in what ultimately proved an unsuccessful play-off campaign at the end of the 2015/16 season. Their 3-2 win over Hibernian was one of the best televised games I saw all season.

By contrast, I've unwittingly made a habit of turning up once a year to watch Forfar take a pasting. Irrespective of how they're doing at the time, my appearance is sure to put the kybosh on their chances of getting a positive result. When I eventually turn up at Station Park, if they don't actually ban me they should probably shoot an albatross for luck.

If being in Falkirk had made me feel at home in Scotland again, it was a young Englishman who caught everyone's attention on the pitch. Myles Hippolyte was a youth player at Brentford who went out on several unspectacular loan spells to non-league clubs in the London area. In Scotland, Hippolyte's fortunes took a distinct turn for the better as he earned cult status with the locals after scoring in a 3-2 win over Rangers. As a result, I'm told that a local chippie now sells a 'Hippolyte Haggis'.

With the confidence a young man gets when he's enjoying the best spell of his career, Hippolyte took just eight minutes to make his mark on the game with a sublime goal; a beautifully struck half volley from the better part of 30 yards out. Nathan Austin – more on him in a year or three – headed a second on the half hour and Hippolyte's second sublime finish gave the Bairns a 3-0 half-time lead that was an accurate reflection of how the game was going.

Five minutes into the second half, Hippolyte completed his hat-trick and immediately left the field to a standing ovation. Falkirk decided that enough was enough for one evening and the withdrawal of all three of their first choice strikers suggested they had bigger fish to fry (sorry) at the weekend. Seemingly grateful for the respite, Forfar were still indebted to keeper Marc McCallum for three superb saves that prevented a repeat of the 7-0 dicking I'd seen them take at Dundee a year ago. Otherwise, I was left to enjoy the panoramic vistas of Scotland's Central Lowlands.

I'd assumed that Falkirk was inland, halfway between Edinburgh and Glasgow, but the fact that it was situated in the Forth Valley at least explained the vast number of seagulls that inhabited the place. Nurtured on Donna's leftovers, many the size of a light aircraft dived in and out of the main stand, clearly capable of a more menacing attack than Forfar had managed all night. As a glorious red and purple sky brought the curtain down on what had been a dismally grey day, the only clouds were poisonous ones that came from the chimneys of nearby Grangemouth.

The Bairns won all of their group games but went down to a surprise 2-1 home defeat to Livingston in the last 16.

Back in London, a Gonzalo Rodríguez goal gave Fiorentina a 1-0 win over a lacklustre Chelsea. Like you care!

COWDENBEATH v DUNDEE

Scottish League Cup Group Stage
Wednesday, 26 July 2017

AT SOME point during the early 1990s, changes to EEC legislation led to around 1,500 clerical workers being made redundant in and around Dover. I was one of them. Times were grim for a while, but I somehow managed to keep the wolf from the door by doing whatever work became available for a couple of years before new career options presented themselves.

For a while, Ray Sutton, an old school mate, and I found temporary clerical work arranging £1 ferry crossings for *Sun* readers. Given that the work was dull in the extreme, we found a few ways of amusing ourselves and getting through the day before being handed our hats and told to never darken the company's doors again having been caught sneaking off for a five-hour lunch break to watch Dover in an FA Cup tie at Welling. Prior to our very welcome dismissal we would entertain ourselves on a Saturday afternoon by having a punt on a fixed odds coupon, which introduced us both to Cowdenbeath FC.

At the time the 'Blue Brazil', as they're affectionately known, had come to international prominence for all the wrong reasons having gone 38 games without a win. Accordingly, they were our losing 'banker' for the day – and won. Perfectly illustrating how our luck was going at the time, Ray and I went on to score zero out of ten on three consecutive coupons. After Ray's wife Debbie christened us 'the Midas brothers in reverse', a bookie friend told us that, had we put a tenner on this eventuality, the odds would have been so long that we could both have paid off our mortgages.

A year or two later, I chanced upon *Black Diamonds and the Blue Brazil* by a priest called Ronald Ferguson. Some 25 years further on the story of Cowdenbeath's trials and tribulations of these times remains one of the most enjoyable football books I've ever read.

Happily, we've all enjoyed more successful times since the turn of the century. Ray and I have been gainfully employed ever since and have enjoyed some great times as football fans. Likewise, Cowdenbeath, while leading an up-and-down existence at times, have enjoyed their share of promotions and spent some time punching above their weight in the Scottish Championship. However, at a time when my journalistic career was hitting the buffers, Cowdenbeath entered a downward spiral that seemed certain to end in relegation to the Lowland League sooner or later. Today, it seemed fitting that I should visit at a time when they're ranked 42nd out of 42 in the overall scheme of things.

Initially, the fixture against Dundee sold itself. It was the only available competitive game in Scotland as all the other Scottish League Cup ties had been played the night before. However, Celtic had to throw a spanner in the works by opting to entertain Rosenborg and give me the opportunity to witness one of those European nights I'd been told so much about. After brief deliberation, I figured that Celtic had enough fans without me and that Cowdenbeath might put my money to better use.

Bang in the middle of town and a five-minute walk from the railway station, Cowdenbeath's Central Park stadium couldn't be more aptly named and it immediately struck me how friendly the locals were on hearing an English accent. Suffice to say that giving Celtic a swerve in favour of a night with the worst team in Scotland went down well.

I went on to wax lyrical about the only man from Cowdenbeath I'd ever known, an old boy to whom anyone who'd ever kicked a ball in Dover owed a great debt of gratitude. Tom Donnelly, who I would guess passed away around ten years ago, arrived in Dover after the Second World War with his Scottish regiment. Having met Elsie, the love of his life, Tom settled in the south-east and became a great servant to the game locally. After founding the Dover & District Sunday Football League in 1966 Tom served as its secretary for decades, ran the competition single-handedly at times, and was always true to his claim of being available 24 hours a day. I don't suppose that Tom's death was solely responsible for the decline of the league he served with great distinction, but it was certainly a factor. Whether or not he ever returned to Cowdenbeath was something I wished I'd asked.

With skies overhead looking a tad dark and ominous, I made myself an honorary Blue Brazilian for the evening under cover in the main stand.

It needs to be said that Central Park is a bit of a tip. As a stadium that also hosts stock car racing, a pitch separated from a perimeter track by giant tyres gives the place a spectacular ugliness that's unparalleled in my experience. That said, my dog Tilly is an ugly bitch, but it doesn't mean I love her any the less.

In the soulless and spotless all-seater world we increasingly live in, I think we can all be a bit sniffy about the state of some football stadiums. Increasingly I find that all I need from a ground is somewhere to stay dry, have a decent view of the pitch and to be in the company of nice people. With entrance for a fiver an added bonus, I'd got pretty much everything I needed for a good night out. I don't suppose that Central Park, playing surface apart, is a great deal different to what it was in the 1950s. More and more I'm asking what on earth is wrong with that? With a few hundred visitors from Tayside adding to a nice atmosphere, a bumper crowd – for Cowdenbeath at least – of 1,321 settled down to watch the game.

The game didn't really give much indication as to how either side might be expected to fare throughout the season ahead. Although Cowdenbeath could be admired for the dogged manner in which they tried to stay in the game, a very obvious gap in class between the sides didn't take long to emerge. As it did, Dundee fans may have thought they'd found a new hero in Sofien Moussa.

Moussa, a Tunisian, is no spring chicken and will turn 30 early in the new year. He hadn't uprooted many trees in a nomadic career that encompassed spells in Norway, Romania, and Bulgaria, but with the looks and playing style of Diego Costa, Moussa looked like the kind of class act who better sides than Cowdenbeath might struggle to contain. In 21 first-half minutes Moussa helped himself to a hat-trick, the second of which came with an overhead kick that would have graced any game. Playing wide on the right, Dundee's Roarie Deacon was a player I'd seen many times on the English non-league circuit. After resurrecting a career that began at Arsenal, Deacon, now 25, had starred in Sutton United's remarkable run to the fifth round of the FA Cup earlier this year. He too looked like he might prosper on Tayside.

With progression to the last 16 all but guaranteed and the visit of Dundee United to look forward to at the weekend, Dundee made several substitutions after the break and got through the remainder of the game in second gear. Under the circumstances I nipped out five minutes before the end to get an earlier train back to Edinburgh, knowing that I'd see both sides play again before I went home on Monday.

STIRLING ALBION v NOTTS COUNTY

Pre-season Friendly
Thursday, 27 July 2017

AFTER A couple of days of practically tripping over kilts and tartan-related tat in Edinburgh, I didn't see any of either in the city of Stirling. I found this particularly surprising given that the combatants of the Battle of Stirling were apparently kitted out in kilts some 300 years before anyone else in Scotland. And this is in a place in which painting your face blue still hadn't gone out of fashion over 1,000 years after the Picts discovered that running around looking like Smurfs was a good way of discouraging invading Romans.

Today, I had other things on my mind than the less-than-painstaking research of Hollywood historians. I was trawling numerous charity shops in the city centre in search of some warm emergency trousers. I'd travelled north without bothering to pack any, thinking that shorts would be ideal for a balmy Scottish summer. I now appreciate that my thinking was flawed and naive and now pack for all four seasons whenever I visit.

Having taken in the history and more scenic part of Stirling during my last visit, I saw the less-salubrious side of the city this time. Just a five-minute walk through the centre told a depressingly familiar story. While one or two high street 'names' had closed their doors for the final time, two pawn shops existed in close proximity and seemed to be doing a roaring trade. There was money in the place somewhere, mind. You can always tell when this is the case if you visit a charity shop. Most of Stirling's were stocked with brand-name, pristine clobber, chucked out by folk who presumably have more money than sense. Half an hour later, I had some 'new' chinos and a couple of good-as-new Ian Rankin novels in my kit bag.

With an hour or two to kill, I thought I might visit Bannockburn and followed a sign that told me that the place was two and a half miles away. I walked the first mile before it dawned that I hadn't got the first clue what I'd find when I got there. Whatever it was, I'd have no time to look at it, given that I'd need to leave almost immediately to get back for a 7.30pm kick-off. After sitting on a bench and watching the bumper-to-bumper rush hour traffic crawling out of the city for five minutes, I headed back.

I was grateful this fixture had cropped up, simply because it was slowly starting to sink in that what I'd set out to do was actually a massive undertaking for me. To finish my book, I'd need to visit 42 Scottish clubs; a tough enough task if I lived, say, in Edinburgh rather than Dover. Essentially, if I spend a week in Scotland I need to visit a new ground every day. The more grounds I visit, the more difficult that will become.

Today I had rather hoped to be in Perth, but St Johnstone had rather inconsiderately scuppered that plan by getting themselves knocked out of Europe at the earliest opportunity, losing twice to the fourth-best team in Lithuania. Thus, when the Stirling v Notts County fixture cropped up on one of the numerous websites I'd been trawling I was chuffed in the extreme; not least because I'd get an extra game in, but because my previous visit a year ago hadn't gone well to say the very least.

After an ordinary fish supper served by a lass whose scowl screamed 'what do you expect for minimum wage', I set off in the direction of the Forthbank Stadium still hungry but feeling only slightly miffed. Knowing the direct route to the ground I was there more than an hour before kick-off, but I was surprised to discover that there was already a game taking place when I arrived. After presenting myself at a couple of closed and locked turnstiles, I wandered into the main office and was greeted by the same lass who'd been my helpful harbinger of doom when we first met last year. Given that our previous meeting revolved around my prattling on about something she hadn't the first clue about, I thought I'd have a bash at making more sense this time.

This didn't go well, frankly.

'So has the game kicked off early then?' I asked hopefully.

'No, it was always due to start at 5.30. The second half's just started.'

'Oh, it said 7.30 on the website. I think we're talking about different games somehow, don't you?'

'I think we might be. I'm talking about the England v Scotland under-16 game. How about you?'

Once she'd ascertained that the lunatic in front of her was harmless, it seemed as though I was providing a little comic relief at the end of dull working day.

'Stirling Albion v Notts County. Pre-season friendly. Kicks off here at 7.30.'

'I'm afraid it doesn't, sir!'

Worrying that we might have reached the stage where she asked if I had a responsible adult who might come and pick me up, I thought I'd try a different tack.

'Can I come in and watch what's left of this game then?'

'I'm afraid not, sir. Now that the second half's started, I'm not allowed to let anyone else in.'

As a clever riposte failed to suggest itself, I opted for a quick 'thanks anyway, goodnight' and slunk off like a badly beaten dog.

I should probably have felt more miffed than I actually did, but started to think this game was the product of a fevered imagination and that I might have gone completely Squirrel Nutkins. Bewilderment wasn't exactly uncommon in lads of my advancing years, after all. Then again, I'd seen my phantom fixture listed on a couple of reputable and reliable websites and I'd definitely seen two blokes wearing Notts County shirts coming out of a Stirling pub less than two hours ago. Purely as a means to establishing my own sanity, I decided to ring my good friend Simon Harris. Simon, if you haven't had the pleasure, could sniff out a fixture on the moon having first booked a cheap hotel and flight deal before he got there. In terms of football, finance or a combination of both, he has a brain the size of Bournemouth.

'Do me a favour could you, Simon? I haven't got internet on my phone, so can you go online and see if you can find the Stirling Albion v Notts County fixture anywhere, as it's starting to do my head in now.'

Simon confirmed he'd be happy to help and, always as good as his word, he returned my call in five minutes.

'Yep, found it! Stirling Albion v Notts County. Forthbank Stadium. Kick-off at 7.30. It's here on the Scottish FA website. The funny thing is it doesn't seem to be mentioned anywhere else.'

I thanked Simon for his time and trouble and confirmed that I would see him next week at Hartlepool for Dover's first league game of the season. Then I gave in and ambled back to Stirling station. Comfortably settled on the train back to Waverley, I buried my head in an Ian Rankin novel, safe in the knowledge that this at least would involve a mystery that would be resolved.

I slept soundly in Edinburgh, safe in the knowledge that if this book is concluded without further mention of the Forthbank Stadium in Stirling, at least you know I tried.

EAST FIFE v ST JOHNSTONE

Pre-season Friendly
Saturday, 29 July 2017

I'M SIGNED up to a Facebook page called Dover for the Delighted. It was set up by a Dover-supporting pal of mine in response to a tawdry national rag referring to our home town as 'a toilet'. Within days, 6,000 people became members.

We've become an easy target down the years, particularly for hacks who spend more time compiling their expenses than researching and writing articles. Going for the soft option and belittling a town that hasn't enjoyed the best of fortunes in recent years has almost become a national sport. It is fair to say that our town centre – which most of us have abandoned lately – is more than a bit grim. Yet what an endless stream of correspondents fail to mention is that some of the world's most breathtaking scenery can be found if you leave our market square and walk for ten minutes in any direction.

The 'toilet' feature was widely view as the worst attack on the town since a couple of well-known 'musicians' – who might reasonably call themselves Two Untalented – came here to twizzle about in front of a tape recorder for 15 minutes, take a few grand off us, then rant about the town's deficiencies on a radio show popular with the hard of thinking.

This is not a mistake I shall be making as I describe my brief visit to Methil.

I mention all this as I was at a beer festival recently, where I was introduced to a Celtic fan who bore more than a passing resemblance to the standard comedy Scotsman of the English imagination, albeit in a Motörhead T-shirt. As we got on with the standard of business of talking shite and football, I told him I was writing a book about the Scottish game from an Englishman's perspective which would involve visiting all 42 of the SPFL clubs in his country.

He replied in the broadest accent I've heard in many a long year, so please make allowance for the following translation. He said, 'Waaaaaaaaaa! Are ye oan drugs, man? Ha' ya been tae East Fife? Tae Methil?'

Made curious by this hearty and emphatic recommendation, I told the fellow I would visit as soon as humanly possible.

If the SFA's website had much to answer for following my second wasted journey to Stirling, a little balance was restored when I found out that I could recover a little lost ground by attending two games in a single Saturday. St Johnstone's early exit from Europe dictated they needed to get a little hastily arranged match practice under their belts, though why they opted for a midday kick-off at East Fife I neither knew nor cared. It simply meant that I could get an extra match in, as the early start ensured I could get to Kirkaldy in time for Raith Rovers' League Cup derby against Cowdenbeath.

Making an early start from Waverley, I bumped into hundreds of fans en route to the game. Not the one I was attending, obviously, but Celtic's friendly at Sunderland had certainly captured the imagination locally and put a few quid into Scotrail's coffers.

On the other side of the Forth in Kirkaldy, several more fans clad in green and white hoops boarded a southbound train, duly ignoring more local attractions. On the number seven bus to Leven, head scarves rather than football scarves were the must-have fashion accessory.

I'd heard that Methil, which doesn't have a train station, is eight miles from Kirkaldy. I dare say that's true, as the crow flies.

What wouldn't I have given to have been a crow during a bus journey that seemed to take an eternity.

There were just two types of passenger who travelled on a bus that seemed to stop every 100 yards or so. The first were cheery octogenarians en route to the cemetery via some shopping mall I wouldn't have the time or inclination to visit. The others, kitted out exclusively in bargain basement tracksuits and trainers, weren't quite as lively, slowed down by the obesity that comes from over-familiarity with the chip pan and an ailment known as cake retention. In a darker moment of thought, I realised I wasn't too far away from being eligible to join either group. For now I seemed to be the only passenger who was travelling more than a couple of stops.

Although I'd half expected Methil and the villages leading into it to resemble some sort of post-apocalyptic hell hole that would make a decent location for a Mad Max film, it seemed tidy enough and relatively litter-free. Although it's a post-industrial town that hasn't quite discovered its new purpose, that hardly makes the place unique, and I was warming to Methil as we pulled into a bus station that was just a judiciously bunged rock away from the football stadium. My imaginary pet crow could have got there in seconds but I had to arrive via a more circular route. I didn't see a single soul heading in the same direction.

For the second time in a few days, I came across a stadium that was well named. Bayview certainly offered a largely uninterrupted view of a bay, albeit one under cover of the grey clouds that had followed me all over Scotland. No matter, as it was only a fiver to get in and everyone seemed pleased and surprised to see me.

Having slipped through the turnstile, I found myself in something of a quandary. Although I counted myself lucky not to have something more pressing to worry about, I couldn't decide whether to buy a pie or not. It just seemed wrong before midday, somehow. After soul-searching for a few minutes, I decided that the staff at East Fife had opened up early for the likes of me when they almost certainly had better things to do. Feeling it would just be plain bad manners to overlook their diligence, I went for the mince option, washed down with a coffee, in the splendid isolation of the main – and indeed only – stand.

On three sides of Bayview's plastic pitch were breeze block walls, every square inch of which were covered in advertising, suggesting that the club's commercial department was on top of its game. For the paying punters, a 2,000-seat covered stand offered a perfect view of the action, safely accommodating as many supporters as East Fife were ever likely to attract. Although the stadium had the space around it for future development, keeping it as it is seemed the most pragmatic option for now.

I'm unsure if the attendance was ever published but, after turning up in dribs and drabs a crowd of sorts, duly boosted by a decent enough turnout from Perth, made the fixture worth the time and effort.

If the game induced the muted enthusiasm you might expect from a pre-season friendly, it was entertaining enough to distract us from a good natter on occasion. The spectators, I decided, were of much the same stamp as any who might attend a pre-season friendly, being essentially the types of punters with much better things to do that they were earnestly and successfully trying to avoid.

St Johnstone were the better side against an East Fife team who were mostly made up of trialists. Although Saints' dominance didn't produce too much in the way of chances, Stefan Scougall's 38th-minute goal did produce an indifferent 'Oh good. About bloody time!' from the visiting fans around me.

The main talking point of the game arrived a few minutes later, after a linesman seemed to have nodded off, presumably because all the action had taken place in the other half of the field. Having got away with a blatant offside, East Fife broke to create an absolute sitter of a chance. Somehow, a lad with number 77 on his back not only missed from three yards out but managed to put the ball out of the stadium.

After David Wotherspoon scored Saints' second around the hour mark, I kept one eye on my watch and another on a game that wasn't doing much to hold everyone's attention as it entered its closing stages. Knowing that the bus back to Kirkaldy was unlikely to be breaking any speed limits, leaving ten minutes early seemed reasonable given that missing it would also involve missing Raith Rovers v Cowdenbeath. In the event, I jumped on the bus just as it was leaving the depot.

Methil? I'm not planning to move there anytime soon but I rather liked the place.

RAITH ROVERS v COWDENBEATH

Scottish League Cup Group Stage
Saturday, 29 July 2017

IF YOU'VE never watched the BBC's *South East Today*, I can't say I'd heartily recommend it. It has its merits, I suppose, but does rather give the impression that we're all rich, except for some in the Medway towns who don't possess luxuries such as teeth, we support Brighton & Hove Albion and spend most of our time moaning about the lack of a decent train service.

Having used Southern Railway a few times as a means of getting to Gatwick, I've discovered first hand that their customers don't need to look too far to find something to whinge about. Constant use of the phrase, 'It's nuffink to do with us, guvnor, it's Network Rail's fault!' must start to rankle after a while, I'd imagine. Luckily, my region is served by South Eastern Trains and the service is mostly fine and dandy, with a high-speed link to London St Pancras that can get me to parts of the country and back in a time I wouldn't have believed possible a while ago.

Although I'm a big fan of high-speed rail services, there's just one instance in which I feel a little haste might reasonably be employed. I've travelled in and out of Fife a few times now and can confirm that although the track runs parallel to Raith Rovers' Stark's Park, the train I'm on invariably gets up a full head of steam and passes it inside a couple of seconds. I may be alone in this, but I can't help thinking this is just downright rude.

If I'd passed any grounds on the number seven bus back from Leven, there'd have been plenty of time to take in the aesthetic pleasures of any ground we rolled past at a leisurely four miles an hour. I had to make do with the scenic delights of a derelict power station that had given employment to thousands during more prosperous times. Although Methil wasn't exactly Val-d'Isère, I couldn't accept the view of one travel writer who'd placed the town fourth in his 'even worse than you thought' list and I wondered if there are twinning associations for towns that aren't posh.

Closer to Kirkaldy, I marvelled at the local accents, as demonstrated by a couple of wifeys of the parish. Such was the difference in dialect, we could have been a million miles from Edinburgh. As is the case with many of a certain vintage, they spent most of the journey talking about ailments, though I only knew this given that 'shingles' was one of the few words they said that I could actually make out. As we pulled into what seemed a charming seaside town, I made yet another mental note to put a post-retirement walk along the Fife Coastal Path nearer to the top of my bucket list.

There was something about Stark's Park that made me wish that Scottish football's halcyon days weren't quite so far in the past and unlikely to ever return. Derogatory though that may sound, I liked the ground that, despite needing a lick of paint, didn't seem to have lost any of its character in the process of modernisation. It didn't require a great leap of imagination to see a full house anticipating a game against one of the country's top clubs. This wasn't quite today's state of affairs, though.

The official attendance was 1,480 for what was essentially a derby game, though I gathered that the two clubs didn't play one another too often these days. Even though the towns of Cowdenbeath and Kirkaldy are just ten miles apart, Stark's Park didn't have much of a derby atmosphere about it. If any

Blue Brazil fans had made the short trip along the A92, I failed to spot them. Indeed, the McDermid Stand (named after world-renowned crime author Val's father, who was a long-serving scout for the club) which normally housed visiting fans was closed.

In fairness to Fife's footballing public, this seemed like a good fixture to miss irrespective of bragging rights and cheap tickets, as the game was first and foremost a dead rubber. Given the Dundee clubs' qualification for the last 16, today would only decide who finished third and fourth in a group in which Buckie Thistle's *nil points* had guaranteed bottom spot.

This is not to say that Raith didn't play some cracking football at times. A cut above their opponents, 'Fife's finest' knocked the ball about confidently and scored a couple of effortlessly created team goals – though Lewis Vaughan and Liam Buchanan – inside the game's opening half an hour. A 2-0 lead was always going to be enough as Raith opted for economy of effort rather than go for the five- or six-goal winning margin they might easily have accomplished out of second gear. Cowdenbeath, every bit as outclassed as they were during their home defeat to Dundee, couldn't muster a single shot on target, never mind find the goal that might have briefly made the fixture marginally more interesting.

A wander around the concourse below the stand made for a more riveting diversion at half-time, where wall-mounted photos and newspaper cuttings proclaimed the more illustrious parts of Raith Rovers' history since 1883. In 1994, after beating Celtic on penalties to win the Scottish League Cup, they became the first club from outside of the top division to qualify for Europe. After knocking out clubs from Iceland and the Faroe Islands, Rovers came up against perennial European champions Bayern Munich in the second round.

This particular occasion is celebrated in glorious black and white in a photo from Munich's Olympiastadion that proudly proclaims, 'Bayern Munich 0 Raith Rovers 1.' If every picture tells a story, this picture doesn't tell the whole one as Bayern narrowly won both legs and went through 4-1 on aggregate.

I spent most of the second half thinking about my hosts rather than watching them. Was former PM Gordon Brown really a Raith Rovers fan, or was this simply the claim of a rugger bugger looking to mop up a few votes? When Sam Leitch – not David Coleman as many believe – said, 'They'll be dancing in the street of Raith tonight,' was he actually being ironic rather than ill-informed?

If Raith Rovers were to meet Bayern again in a competitive European game, just how many millions would need to be thrown at the club to make that a possibility? If it's evaporated milk, why is it still in the tin? It was that sort of afternoon and, a wildly animated young gentleman in a Hibs shirt apart, I think we'd all lost interest long before the end.

En route back to Edinburgh and a penultimate night in a city I was starting to love, it seemed clear that I'd need to give the structure of this book a tweak and a rethink. Though the group stages of the Scottish League Cup offered plenty in the way of variety and number of fixtures, much of what I'd seen in the competition had effectively been warm-ups for the coming season.

Although I'd need to earn a few quid to finance my next trip, I figured I might run the risk of a few postponements and visit for some blood-and-feathers affairs in the middle of February. In the meantime, the Dundee derby should round off my 2017 visits rather nicely.

DUNDEE v DUNDEE UNITED

Scottish League Cup Group Stage
Sunday, 30 July 2017

THERE'S A sequence in *American Beauty* when Annette Benning's character, in a state of post-coital bliss after shagging an estate agent, tells us, 'That's just what I needed!' On tonight's train back to Edinburgh for a final night in the capital I felt very much the same, but wasn't going to say as much in a packed second-class carriage. And while a comparison between sex and Scottish football isn't something that should be explored too deeply, I did at least find myself in a euphoric state that a really good game of football can induce. Although I'd have a great time and some memorable experiences on this most recent trip, the football, mostly due to an absence of any truly competitive edge, had been disappointing. Today's derby game, the best I'd seen in Scotland since Aberdeen hosted Maribor in the Europa League, had all the ingredients necessary to awaken anyone's love of the game, no matter how dormant.

Initially I hadn't planned to visit any Scottish ground more than once, wishing simply to visit all 42 of the country's league clubs as quickly as funds and work commitments would allow. Although I'm sure they do their best, blokes who compile fixture lists don't do much to help me out in this respect. However, BT Sport figured that today's Tayside derby was their best bet for a TV audience, hence the game being moved to a Sunday. Given it was the only fixture played in Scotland that day, I opted for another train ride rather than a stroll to the peak of Arthur's Seat. I can't help but think that BT Sport and I made a damn fine decision.

After crossing the Tay it became clear that Dundee's waterfront development had continued apace since my last visit precisely a year and a day ago and there were shells of buildings behind the hoardings and scaffolding now. Having renewed my nodding acquaintance with Desperate Dan, Gnasher, and Mini the Minx, I fairly skipped through the Wellgate Centre and found that I was becoming a dab hand at urban mountaineering, scaling the face of Hilltown in a personal best time on my third attempt. At the peak, God was in his glory and Rough and Fraser were open to cash in on an unexpected windfall and provide me with the Tayside ambrosia of a couple of pies. I was, as Stephen Fry might have put it, bang up for it.

If the ambassador wasn't exactly bursting at the seams when I last popped in, they were doing a roaring trade today as both sides of Dundee's footballing divide were looking to make a day of it. Not that any rugby folk would believe it, the atmosphere was warm, friendly, and jocular. The nearest I came to a cross word was when a lad in his early 20s, clad from top to toe in bright orange, was told by his Dundee-supporting friend, 'If you're coming in a Dee pub, you'd better get the drinks in, ya daft wee c**t!' He did.

Inside Dens Park, the atmosphere belied the fact that, in terms of reaching the last 16 at least, this fixture was almost as irrelevant as the games I'd seen earlier in the week given that both sides had accrued nine points from three wins apiece. Both sides could still win the group, however, and that was enough to add a little edge to a game that was always going to be lively anyway. If the fans cursed and shook their fists at one another, you'd have been hard pushed to have detected anything in the way of genuine malice.

I'll be brief with regard to the match content, other than to say it was a superb game, as both sides went at one another at a furious pace that never relented. The tackles flew in and although referee Kevin Clancy – constantly berated by both sets of fans while having a cracking game himself – produced his yellow card four times, nothing came close to being x-rated. Paul McMullan gave United the lead seconds before half-time, Mark O'Hara equalised on the hour and both sides hit the woodwork in a frantic search for a winner. After warmly congratulating one another on a job well done, there was a small matter of a penalty shoot-out that would secure an extra point and top spot in the group. The last of the ten penalties saw United keeper Harry Shaw save Roarie Deacon's under-hit effort to give his side a 4-3 win. United fans in the Bob Shankly Stand celebrated like it really mattered, Dundee fans shrugged their shoulders as though it really didn't, then both left the stadium like the close friends I'm sure many of them are.

I'd cheered Dundee throughout the game; a fact I didn't give much thought to until I was back in Dover. I'd become fond of them, certainly, and I thought that maybe I'd found my Scottish team. I had a good number of clubs to visit before I made that call, however, and maybe the pre-match drinks had helped me decide that I didn't want to be the only neutral in the ground. Either way, it was the perfect way to say goodbye to Scotland for another year.

The next game between the sides was a cracker as well. I watched it live on BT Sport just a few days later. After they'd been drawn together on the same ground in the last 16, Dundee reclaimed bragging rights by winning 2-1. They drew Celtic at home in the quarter-final and I dare say you can guess what happened next.

THE SPARTANS v EDINBURGH UNIVERSITY

Scottish Lowland League
Friday, 9 February 2018

IF YOU'VE been paying attention – and I would if I were you, as there'll be a quiz at the end – you'll know that I should have seen The Spartans play in the summer of 2016 but had a wasted journey to Stirling to see a game that actually took place in Falkirk. If I hadn't planned to see them play during my first visit of 2018, I was rather glad I did. If travel has taught me nothing else it's that what you expected to be a sideshow often proves to be the main event.

With several grounds still to get to, it was becoming increasingly difficult to plan ahead and I hoped that the February weather and the Scottish Cup fixture scheduling wouldn't be too unkind. Essentially, I'd booked a train and a hotel well in advance as a means to getting the best deals, then hoped that the draw for the fifth round would provide me with new grounds to visit on Saturday and Sunday, together with a rescheduled league fixture on Friday night. In the event I was happy enough with two out of three, irrespective of the fact I'd be based in Edinburgh, but making two trips to Ayrshire over the weekend.

When the hoped-for Friday night fixture at somewhere like Livingston failed to materialise, a little light research revealed that a Lowland League game would take place in an Edinburgh suburb and Lothian Transport would happily take me there on a bus.

Arriving on Thursday night, I'd had the usual pang of trepidation that comes with comes with booking the cheapest B&B on offer and hoping that I wouldn't be spending the next four nights in a zero-star rat trap. In the event I found what would become my home-from-home for the next five years in the Sakura, just off Nicholson Street, in a room that had all the little essentials that are pretty much the starter kit for making an old git happy. Booking before Christmas for £25 a night proved an excellent plan given that the Ibis 500 yards away was asking £165 to stay on the Saturday night of the Scotland v France Six Nations rugby fixture.

Given a full day in Edinburgh on Friday, I thought I might explore a bit. A street map in an Ian Rankin novel I was reading drew me to the Water of Leith, so I thought I might check it out, thinking it was probably a lake in a public park. It took a while to find as I left the usual hubbub of Princes Street behind me for the day to have a long and blissful stroll along a path beside a river that runs through the city before it flows into the Firth of Forth at Leith.

Completely oblivious to the fact I was smack in the middle of a capital city, I tickled the ears of a few passing dogs, bade their owners a hearty greeting and made nodding acquaintance with half a dozen herons and a decidedly confused looking cormorant. Thoroughly enjoying my first full day off in weeks, I stopped for a coffee at one of Leith's swisher establishments, buttoned my coat and did the whole thing over again in reverse. With not a cloud in an implausibly cornflower blue sky and the feel of the sun on my back for the first time in months, I made the most of my good fortune and the short daylight hours.

When I set off for The Spartans' ground around 6pm, the temperature had dropped alarmingly. Spartan conditions, in fact, in which I generally like to watch my football. I'd worked out that a 27 bus from The Mound would drop me off at the Morrisons store that's a five-minute walk from Spartans' Ainslie Park stadium in Edinburgh's Pilton district.

Those of us who are up on our contemporary Scottish literature will have heard of Pilton. Ian Rankin and Irvine Welsh both tend to be a bit disparaging about the place and if you ask any Scotsman for directions, there's a decent chance of him starting his reply with, 'Oooo, you don't want to go there!' After tapping Pilton into Google, I came up with a Wikipedia entry, only to discover that this usually loquacious search engine could only muster 84 words to describe the district. Here are 12 of them: council housing schemes, deprived, high crime rates, anti-social behaviour, joyrider and stealing. If the Lothian Tourist Board is thinking of setting up a branch in the area, the staff will have to work bloody hard for their money. Thus, I think I might be about to buck a long-standing trend by writing a few positive words about the place.

A first glance at Ainslie Park put me in mind of Bayview at East Fife with an all-seated stand along one touchline and hard, uncovered standing around three sides of a 3G pitch. Arriving ridiculously early as usual, I was one of the first through the turnstile where I stumped up around £7 for admission, a programme, and a half-time draw ticket. At this point a fellow of similar vintage to myself and decked out in The Spartans' red and white offered me a hearty welcome followed by an apology, 'We're ever so sorry, but the bar's shut tonight, as we've booked it out for a function. If you fancy a cup of tea, you'd be welcome in the boardroom before the game starts.'

It was only when I flicked through the match programme that I discovered it was club chairman Craig Graham who'd invited me into the boardroom for a hot drink. The motto here, perhaps, is that where the hospitality of some of Edinburgh's outskirts is concerned, you shouldn't believe everything you read.

Having warmed myself up with a coffee and a sausage roll, it became very clear that this was a club that ran very much for the community's benefit. On an adjoining area behind the main stand, a couple of youth games and a women's fixture were taking place, a group of kids were taking part in a mass kickabout on a court behind one goal, while a local cheerleading group had taken over the clubhouse. All in all, maybe 150 kids had turned up on a bitterly cold Friday night to do something or other. Meanwhile, it was eerily quiet on the housing scheme behind the far touchline, leading me to believe that the Glue Sniffers and Joy Riders Club AGM had been cancelled until further notice.

I rather enjoyed the game. Although local opinion was unanimous that The Spartans were some way below their best, I enjoyed contrasting Scotland's fifth tier with the English version that was my staple back home. Certainly, this was more aesthetically pleasing than what I might usually expect on a Saturday afternoon, with a thoughtful, passing game being a direct contrast to the more agricultural 80 per cent perspiration style that's become the norm in England's National League.

Thus, I enjoyed watching two sides trying to knock the ball around rather than simply lamp it up the park at every opportunity. While Spartans and their 120 or so fans looked set to endure a frustrating evening, David Greenhill scored with virtually the last kick of the game to earn a win that sent everyone home happily. Though they missed out on promotion via the play-offs, The Spartans were crowned Lowland League champions in May.

An hour or so later I found myself at the local infirmary, miles from the city centre, not through any altercation with the locals but simply through being an old codger who couldn't make head nor tail of the bus timetable without his reading glasses. So after catching the number 21 instead of the number 27, the driver of the number eight took pity on and old and bewildered Englishman and told me he was going my way, duly dropping me off within a few yards of my guest house on his journey to the North Bridge. With the weather expected to turn nasty over the next couple of days, I only hoped my trips to Ayrshire would run as smoothly.

KILMARNOCK v BRORA RANGERS

Scottish Cup Fifth Round
Saturday, 10 February 2018

YOU'D BE amazed just how quiet it can be at half past eight on a Saturday morning in the middle of Edinburgh. I know I was. I'd never seen the place as anything other than busy, vibrant, and bustling, but on a grey, drizzly, yet unseasonably mild morning, very few of us were out and about. Either the street cleaners had finished for the day or attitudes to litter were a little more robust in these parts. With time to kill, I enjoyed a first stroll through The Meadows, walked around the back of the castle, through the Grassmarket and down to Waverley via the Royal Mile and left on the 9.30am to Glasgow Queen Street.

Gazing out of the window from time to time, I reflected on how easy it had become for me to find my way around and drift about on autopilot without fear of becoming irredeemably lost. Although I'd managed to make a drama of it on previous occasions, I negotiated the 15-minute walk from Queen Street to Glasgow Central without incident, found the Kilmarnock train and was there barely a couple of hours after leaving Edinburgh.

I found the ground in next to no time, purchased everything I needed courtesy of a couple of bored young girls in the club shop and found myself free to explore for three hours. I'd planned to do a few things before kick-off, having found that Dean Castle looked appealing, as did the Burns

Monument that didn't seem to be too far away. The trouble was that the drizzle, the type that seeps into your clothes before you've had the chance to notice, seemed to have settled in for the day, lessening the appeal of the kind of walk I'd thoroughly enjoyed the day before. Thus, I walked the length of a high street that was pretty indistinguishable from many others on the British mainland, walked back again, then went for the good old default option of spending a couple of hours in the pub. The one I chose was Fanny by Gaslight (try Googling that and you'll come up with some intriguing options) which proved a decent choice, not least because I'd remember the name of it without having to write it down.

Fanny by Gaslight was very much a home from home and so similar to many pubs I frequent south of the border. As Partick Thistle were making a decent if ultimately unsuccessful fist of having a crack at Celtic in the early televised cup tie, I settled down in the affable company of Joe and Barry and got a round in. Smashing old boys though they were, they did much to emphasise why the gulf between clubs like Kilmarnock and Celtic had developed into a chasm. Though both were born and raised in Kilmarnock, neither had visited Rugby Park in decades. Both were Celtic fans who didn't go to their games either. Both enjoyed their football but opted to watch it in a warm and welcoming pub where the happy hour(s) coincided with the latest televised game. A glance outside at the continual drizzle of a dull February afternoon defied anyone to suggest that Joe and Barry had got it wrong.

By contrast, half a dozen Brora Rangers fans were making the most of their Highland League club's few hours in the limelight. They'd travelled in hope rather than expectation, safe in the widely held belief that it's the day out that mattered, even if the 90 minutes in the middle of it might not be much to write home about. Although they weren't hoping for or expecting much more than honour in defeat, optimism increased in direct correlation to every pint supped. In essence, the classic non-league away day that had been my staple for the last half century or so.

Since turning 50 I've learned the valuable lesson that, if I wish to avoid a raging hangover for the next three days, it's time to leave when I really start to enjoy myself. Although I had time for another beer or possibly two at a push, I started to retrace my steps to the ground around two-ish.

In the close season I'd read an article on Kilmarnock in *When Saturday Comes*. In a section that asked fans about their hopes and expectations for the forthcoming season, a Killie fan had expressed the wish that his club would move to a smaller stadium. He reasoned that there was little point in having an 18,000 all-seater stadium, if you only had three or four thousand fans to rattle around in it. The atmosphere at a smaller venue would be considerably enhanced, he argued. At the time, this struck me as a somewhat barmy notion. Inside Rugby Park, I could see his point.

This is not to say that Kilmarnock don't have one of Scotland's better stadiums, but with only 4,278 fans turning up today, only the 400 or so who'd made the 500-mile round trip from Brora seemed to be enjoying themselves and offered much in the way of vocal encouragement. Behind me, a group of 20-odd young lads tried to get a chant or two going, but with a conspicuous lack of success. This wasn't surprising, I figured, given that Killie found themselves in one of those no-win situations that cup draws tend to throw up from time to time. Given the four-division gap between the two sides, anything other than a comfortable home win would have been viewed as a failure of sorts. Under the circumstances, I suppose it's no great surprise that the locals who did show up were expecting more of a procession than a contest. For a while, I thought it might not pan out that way.

In the first half Kilmarnock were considerably more patient than their supporters, as Brora made a very good job of compressing play and making their hosts look a very ordinary side indeed. Although Brora deserved to go in level at half-time, a young Londoner on loan from Aston Villa, Aaron Tshibola, put Kilmarnock in front on his debut for the club.

For Killie fans the day's major talking point and excitement came on the concourse under the main stand. Given that the legend of the Killie Pie had reached as far as my little corner of south-east England, I'd inserted one into my face within a couple of minutes of coming through the turnstile. Very deserving of its place in the annals of top notch football tuck it was too, so I thought I might treat myself to another at the interval.

Unfortunately said pies had sold out within five minutes of the half-time whistle, duly provoking remarks of bitterness, weariness and calls for rebellion among the populace. 'Fourteen thousand short of capacity and I still can't get a f***ing pie. That's just careless!' was how one lad – carrying enough puppy fat to survive an Ayrshire pie shortage should one occur, frankly – put it. Resourceful to the last, I strolled up to the away end where pies were still plentiful and got a Brora fan to sort one out for me and bung it through the fence.

If the Killie fans around me were peckish, cold, and ripe for revolution, the mood didn't last too long as Kris Boyd's elderly legs showed a surprising turn of speed to go clear through the middle and make it 2-0 with a smart finish. For all their grit and admirable endeavour, it was a deficit that Brora simply didn't have the wherewithal to come back from.

Although extra class and fitness told in the last 20 minutes or so, Brora didn't suffer the hiding that the 4-0 final scoreline implied. And while Eamonn Brophy and Stephen O'Donnell both scored peaches of goals from long range, Kilmarnock eased through to the next round without dampening the spirits of the Brora fans who went home in good voice and spirits. Most were rat-arsed in other words, having made the most of their day out.

In an ideal world I'd have stayed in Kilmarnock overnight and made the 17-mile journey to Ayr in the morning. In the real world, things were to prove a little more problematic.

AYR UNITED v RANGERS

Scottish Cup Fifth round
Sunday, 11 February 2018

HERE'S WHAT could have happened in an ideal world. After yesterday's game at Kilmarnock I could have had a few more beers, stayed overnight and enjoyed a leisurely breakfast before undertaking the short trip to Ayr. Had I got out of bed early enough, I probably could have walked it. Given the relatively early kick-off at Somerset Park I could have watched the game, caught a south-bound train as far as Dumfries, then nipped down to Carlisle to catch the Euston train and been home in time for MOTD2. Though things occasionally happen this way in low-budget films, matters never pan out quite so simply for us football fans, given that fixture scheduling and cup draws tend to make life as difficult and expensive as possible for us.

As a reasonable chap, I've always taken the view that essential engineering work has to be done at some time and that Sunday is the best day of the week for it to be undertaken. I'm less reasonable when I happen to be travelling on a Sunday, naturally, given how much can possibly go wrong if my planning – as is so often the case – isn't quite up to muster. In the event I needn't have worried as today's replacement bus service from Paisley to Kilwinning, though tedious at times, kept moving in the right direction and gave me the opportunity to see a part of Scotland I hadn't seen before. Chatting with some Rangers fans, I confessed that I'd watched their club play a few times but had yet to see them win. They were joking, I think, when they discussed the possibility of chucking me off the bus via the rear window. Once reunited with the train service the final part of the journey passed in a flash, giving me the opportunity to say, 'Ah, so that's where it is!' a few times as we passed through Troon, Irvine, and Prestwick Airport.

I took to Ayr instantly but regretted how little time I would actually spend here. I'd made half-baked plans to walk along the beach then run along the Clyde estuary from where I'd heard you could see both the Isle of Arran and the tip of Northern Ireland on a clear day. Yet while Friday had been an unseasonably clear and warm day, this Sunday had much more of a bleak Scottish winter about it. It started to snow as soon as I stepped off the train and got heavier as the afternoon progressed. The game would undoubtedly start – as they tend to when the TV cameras are around – but whether or not it would finish was up for question. With not much time available to do much else, I opted to head straight to the ground given that plenty of fans of both clubs were already headed in that direction.

Given that the game would be a guaranteed sell-out, I'd worried about getting my hands on a ticket but needn't have been concerned. My call to the club was answered on the second ring (without the benefit of a pre-recorded message telling me how important my call was) and my ticket was bought and paid for within a couple of minutes. Living up to their nickname of the Honest Men, Ayr had admirably resisted the temptation to cash in on a plum draw and ticket prices were kept at normal levels, with my old git ticket costing a piddling £12. As I picked mine up and perused the souvenirs in the club shop, the Rangers team bus pulled up outside. Predictably, one or two locals made a derogatory remark about Glaswegians and their perceived tenuous relationship with soap but, on a day when they'd be outnumbered by about nine to one, they did so rather quietly.

I'd looked forward to this game since the draw was made and couldn't help but think I might bear witness to a memorable occasion and that a big upset was on the cards. Ayr went into the game on a great run of form, running head-to-head with Raith Rovers in a bid to win the League One title and promotion to the Championship. At kick-off they'd scored more goals than any club in the SPFL. Likewise, Rangers were on a good run themselves and if they weren't quite challenging Celtic's total domination of Scottish football they were starting to suggest that they might in a year or so. They were prone to the odd slip-up, mind, hence my belief that this would be a really close-run thing.

I'd opted for a terrace ticket in the home end and an old-school stadium of the first order was virtually empty when I went through the turnstile and stood undercover adjacent to the Ally MacLeod hospitality lounge. Like all Englishmen, my overriding memory of MacLeod is of a fellow with a constantly anxious expression, often with his head in his hands, wondering how the 1978 World Cup winners-in-waiting had got things so horribly wrong. If the late Scotland manager had been remembered for comedic reasons south of the border, I wasn't about to say so in the stadium where he made his name and turned Ayr United into a highly respected top-flight club.

Sheltered from the increasingly heavy snowfall and marginally warmed by a hot pie and beverage, I was starting to enjoy myself. As the ground filled up rapidly it was clear that this would be a home game for Ayr in name only, as Rangers fans took up a generous ticket allocation and took over three sides of the ground.

When the game started, it soon became evident that Ayr's players and supporters were keen to make the most of an occasion that doesn't come along every day. On a day when the blizzard conditions might be expected to sort the mice from the men, every player on both sides wore a short-sleeved shirt and shunned the wearing of gloves. Inside the first five minutes Ayr took an early lead to create scenes of utter pandemonium around me.

The goal came as Rangers' Wes Foderingham made an awful hash of attempting to clear the ball upfield. Ayr's Alan Forrest made the most of the keeper's hesitancy, blocked the ball and reacted sharply to scramble it over the line.

I wasn't sure what to make of the 20 minutes that followed as Rangers slowly but surely began to take control of the game. They created numerous chances that were either missed in outlandish fashion or smacked against the frame of the goal. Though one might think that their luck was out, and it simply wasn't going to be Rangers' day, the realist might concur that an equaliser would come sooner rather than later. Though the latter proved to be the case – Colombian striker Alfredo Morelos equalised around the half-hour mark – the sides went in level at the mid-point of a game that was as absorbing as I hoped it might be.

There's usually a turning point in this sort of affair, I find; a moment when fans will look back and mutter, 'Yep, that's where it all went tits up.' From Ayr's perspective, the bosoms started to point in a northerly direction from the moment early in the second half when Foderingham saved with his legs to prevent Declan McDaid from restoring the home side's lead. When Jason Cummings put Rangers ahead soon after with a delicious back-heel, that was the end of that!

If Ayr had scrapped manfully in a vain attempt to cover up a gulf in class that became more apparent the longer the game went on, few around me seemed to doubt that their chance had long gone. Within six minutes of going in front Rangers had extended their lead to 4-1. Rather than drop down a gear and close out a game that was clearly won, Rangers' dominance in the last 20 minutes bordered on cruel. Looking capable of scoring every time they crossed the halfway line, they took two more of the several chances they created to win 6-1.

Had the game kicked off at 4pm rather than 2.30pm, I doubt that it would have gone ahead and played to a conclusion. My concern was how to get back to Edinburgh in a blizzard that didn't look like relenting. As a man from a country in which a millimetre of snow will close the schools for three days, I was forced to consider rearranging plans that would prove prohibitively expensive and time-consuming.

I needn't have worried. Scotrail operated as per programme, so to speak, and had me warmly tucked up in the capital within three hours. The following day, I was at home researching the cost of hotels and train fares ahead of my next trip in May. It should be warmer then but with Scotland there are no guarantees.

PARTICK THISTLE v MOTHERWELL

Scottish Premiership
Tuesday, 8 May 2018

PRONE THOUGH they are to delays and sphincter-clenchingly unfunny pre-recorded announcements that make me want to clog up their toilets with anything that comes to hand, I rather like Virgin Trains. Given that some customers haven't grasped the concept of a quiet carriage, I shelled out an extra tenner and treated myself to a first-class ticket today. All quite marvellous stuff if you stop and think about it. I left Dover on the 10.49am and, even allowing for an hour mooching around St Pancras, the 1pm from King's Cross had pulled into York at around a quarter-to-three. After a spot of lunch I buried my head in a good book. Another couple of chapters dedicated to that scruffy, dour-yet-effective maverick cop Inspector Rebus later, I looked up to see sheep grazing precariously on the cliffs of the Northumberland coast. This is the life, I thought, and I wasn't far wrong.

Arriving at Edinburgh Waverley bang on time, I undertook the short walk to the guest house that was fast becoming my Edinburgh home and unpacked. Popping out to enjoy the pleasure of a pink and purple skyline of a late spring evening in The Meadows and Princes Gardens, I'd have been completely in my pomp if I hadn't suddenly been taken violently ill.

I'll spare you the gory details of my evening in Edinburgh other than to add that moaning and porcelain were to feature frequently. By four o'clock the following afternoon – fortified by nothing other than Lucozade and Imodium – I felt brave enough to venture out into the big wide world and sally forth to Glasgow. Excuse me if I assume you're familiar with my route by now.

I've mentioned earlier that my previous visit to Firhil was a waste of time, as a long-anticipated fixture against Aberdeen was scuppered by heavy February rain and a pitch with an allegedly poor drainage system. Though my mate Gerald and I discovered a weird and wonderful way of getting to the stadium that day – which involved far more twizzling about on the Glasgow metro than was anywhere close to necessary – it was easier this time, leading me to relate a simpler route to the would-be attendee. Simply hop off the metro at St George's Cross, head north on the Maryhill road, hang a right at the undertakers and you're there (I should stress at this point that, if we're not accompanied by a designated thinker with a rudimentary grasp of 21st-century technology, my friend and I often find that it takes an awful lot longer to find a stadium if you follow the slow route).

After popping into the clubhouse a mere few seconds away from an unfortunate and messy biological accident, I emerged exhausted and in no mood for beer or pies which does rather curtail a fair percentage of the joys of Scottish football. No matter, as with barely half an hour to survive until kick-off a stroll around the stadium, a visit to the ticket office and a natter with some friendly and surprisingly upbeat locals got me in the mood for the game.

In search of a souvenir or two, I found a purveyor of such bits and bobs doing a roaring trade with one of my countrymen, clearly from the south-east like myself. Experience taught me that this might be a good time to keep my own counsel and felt fully justified when the fellow started deriding the stars of the English Premier League and started on the patronising 'this is where the real passion's at' drivel, while making a big show of buying a red and yellow Partick scarf. Speaking softly and using as few words as possible, I bought a lapel badge and scarpered.

Inside the ground the company of a steward proved much more to my taste and liking; a knowledgeable cove and football lover who, like myself, had been at Rangers' UEFA Cup Final in Manchester almost ten years ago to the day. In my experience, English stewards aren't afforded the time to chat and when one does speak to me it's usually to point out the dangers of stepping on a yellow line or the carnage that could occur if I fail to hand over the top of a soft drink bottle. Many of them seem to have necks wider than their heads and an NVQ Level 3 diploma in being generally unpleasant. Fortunately, my newfound friend was of a different stamp and seemed in no doubt that nothing was likely to happen tonight that might interfere with his enjoyment of the game.

I really hadn't expected to be impressed by Firhil, but it's a cracking ground on three sides, retaining noise and atmosphere even in these days of antiseptic all-seater stadia and pristine toilets. Somehow, live games on BT Sport seem to draw attention to a grass bank behind one goal, where Chris Sutton and his mates often assemble and encourage me to swear at the telly which is, of course, nice work if you can get it.

As the game got under way, Partick fans in a crowd of just 3,320 came across as an overwhelmingly pleasant bunch with a *que sera, sera* attitude to what was occurring in front of them. This was a vital game for Thistle, the penultimate one of a particularly tough season during which the prospect of relegation was never far away. A win against Motherwell would at least guarantee a two-legged play-off against

Livingston and maybe even an outside chance of leapfrogging Hamilton Accies and handing the relegation concerns to someone else.

With a Scottish Cup Final engagement with Celtic to look forward to, Motherwell weren't exactly expected to bust a gut to nab the three points on offer. In essence those followers of what the tannoy man described as 'the only team in Glasgow' were confident of a win. If only we all had a fiver for every time we talked ourselves into this way of thinking, what!

In truth, Thistle didn't play very well tonight. They were competitive enough and couldn't be faulted for effort, but lack of pace, creativity and movement up front did much to illustrate how they'd got themselves into such a pickle over the course of the last nine months. Though it must have been frustrating to watch, I could only admire the home fans who offered nothing but encouragement and a vocal support that belied their lack of numbers. Chatting at the interval, my steward friend and I agreed that the game had 0-0 written all over it in indelible marker pen.

A single point wouldn't prove to be of much use to a Partick side that realistically needed six points from their last two games to have even the faintest chance of staying up without going into the play-offs. In the event, they were denied that as Motherwell snatched a winner early in the second half. The goal came as referee Bobby Madden adjudged that Baily Cargill had bundled over Chris Cadden adjacent to the left-hand corner of the penalty box. If the award looked soft, David Turnbull's delivery was perfect for Ryan Bowman to glance a header into the far corner.

Motherwell, having been battered 5-1 at home by St Johnstone at the weekend, weren't in such a generous frame of mind tonight, as Thistle hit back without looking remotely likely to turn the game around. With defeat confirmed,

Partick would need a result at Dundee on Saturday just to be involved in the play-off final.

Back at Glasgow Queen Street, I chatted with a few Partick fans who'd already taken defeat on the chin and were looking forward to a day out in Tayside at the weekend. As one 20-something lad put it, 'If you live in Glasgow, it's easy to go and watch a team who wins every week, but where would be the fun in that?'

Where indeed?!

ALLOA ATHLETIC v DUMBARTON

Scottish Championship Play-Off Final First Leg
Wednesday, 9 May 2018

I HAVE a very dear friend called Hilda, a Manchester United fan and extraordinarily good cook who subscribes to Sky TV. If I drop enough hints during the week she's usually happy enough to invite me round for dinner and to watch a Leicester City game at the weekend. At some point during the match she'll invariably place a tray on my lap, holding a delicious, melt-in-the-mouth concoction that has been marinating throughout the day. Usually around the point when the Foxes snatch defeat from the jaws of victory, I'll be tucking into a second helping of dessert. Peach roulade is a signature dish and highly recommended if you're ever in the area.

Unashamed freeloader though I unquestionably am, I do like to return the compliment from time to time. As a Virgin Media subscriber I'm well placed to reciprocate all the while BT Sport cover the Champions League and United manage to qualify for the competition. Although the food – or the football, if we're brutally honest – isn't quite of the same standard, I do my best. Aldi knock out a cracking individual steak and ale pie to accompany a spot of mash and vegetables. For pudding (I live in a less salubrious part of town and don't do dessert) I usually push the boat out with the most expensive ice-cream with a name that sounds both Italian and vaguely poncey.

It was during one of our low-key midweek soirees (Aldi own-brand lasagne, followed by sticky toffee pudding and custard) that Hilda and I watched United win the 2017 Europa League final. Although I did my best to feign an interest, it really wasn't much of a game. United, dominant without ever getting out of second gear, won 2-0 against an Ajax side who simply failed to turn up on the night. With around 15 minutes remaining and United closing down a deadly dull encounter, Hilda startled me out of a five-minute nap when she said, 'This isn't as good as Alloa v Brechin, is it!'

A few days previously, during the early part of Saturday evening, Hilda and I were channel-hopping in the hope of avoiding the relentless dross in which our major channels increasingly seem to specialise. I'm guessing that the major European leagues had wrapped up for the season as we chanced upon the second leg of the Scottish Championship play-off final on BBC Alba, Auntie's Gaelic language channel. Initially we decided to give it ten minutes. What followed was the most enjoyable televised game I'd watched in a very long time. Somehow, the Gaelic commentary – they had to revert to English after the game, as none of the participants seemed to speak anything else – added to the occasion in that, while we suspected that the commentary team were talking utter bollocks, we couldn't be sure. Relieved of my sworn duty to shout half-drunkenly at the telly, I simply got comfortable and watched the game.

Well, it was a cracker. After Brechin had won the first leg 1-0, both sides attacked from the first whistle and really put on a show. A 4-3 win for Alloa saw the tie finish all square on aggregate and Brechin retained their Championship status by winning 5-4 on penalties.

Almost one year on to the day, all this came to mind ahead of my next Alloa game. If tonight's evening meal wasn't a hearty affair – a bowl of Mediterranean tomato soup at the Bobbing John, Alloa's local 'Spoons pub – it was just as welcome, being the only hot food I'd eaten in four days. Having spent most of the day in bed at the B&B and feeling rotten, a bowl of soup proved just the ticket as I set off for the game in a chipper frame of mind.

On reflection, maybe last season's play-off defeat had been a blessing in disguise? Promotion certainly hadn't done Brechin any favours as they picked up just four points all season, becoming the first Scottish side in 126 years to fail to win a game in a league campaign. Following a five-minute walk along Station Road to Recreation Park, it was a bit of a treat to join a queue to get into the ground and pick up a buzz of expectation. After they'd beaten Raith Rovers in the semi-final – Rovers had blown the chance to win automatic promotion on the final day of the regular season – consensus suggested that the Wasps would be giving the Championship's (relatively) big boys a run for their money later in the year.

Inside the stadium – which put me in mind of a smaller version of Ayr United's Somerset Park – the atmosphere was as good as I'd encountered in Scotland, albeit in a crowd of not much over 1,000. With Dumbarton fans turning up in good numbers both sets of fans got behind their teams in a manner I love to see, but seldom do in England, in that they were vocal without resorting to the negative chanting that so often spoils an occasion.

Although the game didn't need an early goal to liven it up – both sides threw the full assortment of kitchen fitments at it from the off – it got one after just six minutes. A fine goal it was too for Dumbarton and one I had a perfect view of from behind the goal, as Stuart Carswell hammered in a 25-yarder that dipped and swerved and was destined for the top-left corner from the moment he hit it. A real collector's item, apparently, being only Carswell's second goal in eight seasons. Moments later, Alloa might have equalised in almost identical fashion but the Sons' keeper Scott Gallagher produced an outstanding save to tip Jordan Kirkpatrick's effort on to the inside of a post.

Although I could possibly come up with an exception to the rule if I tried, I can't recall ever enjoying any of the several play-off games I've seen down the years involving my own club(s), invariably enduring them as a nervous wreck. I was certainly enjoying this one, however.

If Alloa were a treat to watch, they were frustrated by a Dumbarton side who implausibly put me in mind of Atlético Madrid. Defending from the front and looking to counter on the break, they invariably put a tackle in at the right time or had a body in the way to block any number of goalbound shots. Pleasingly, they did so without ever resorting to excessive time-wasting, feigning injury or constant, niggly fouls.

As Dumbarton celebrated their victory at the end, they did so in a reserved manner that suggested that the tie still had plenty of mileage in it. For my part I'd already decided to forgo other pleasures in the capital and make my way over to Dumbarton for the second leg on Sunday.

For now I had the thorny problem of getting back to Edinburgh, travelling as far as Croy via a replacement bus service. It was touch and go for a while but we arrived almost a whole minute before the 11.12pm train to Waverley. If you've never seen a 63-year-old with a gammy leg cross a footbridge in 43 seconds flat, you'd have been impressed. I certainly drew a generous round of applause from the locals.

LIVINGSTON v DUNDEE UNITED

Scottish Premiership Play-Off Semi-Final Second Leg
Friday 11 May 2018

I HAVE to say that the walk from the railway station to the Almondvale Stadium was rather aesthetically pleasing. If you've ever visited a new town in England you'll understand why I was surprised. Though it's adjacent to the main road into town, the Alderstone pathway runs almost all the way downhill to the ground, offering a tranquil start to a pleasant and almost balmy spring evening. Trees and hedgerows not only disguised the fact that I was so close to the main road but also deadened the dull drone of the rush-hour traffic. Relaxed and at peace with the world, I made the acquaintance of several magpies, a rabbit or three and a Scottish wildcat. On reflection it may have been an ordinary domestic cat having a wild night out, but I'm no expert. Though I got lost somewhere near the local hospital, the trip took the 25 to 30 minutes I was told it would.

Still suffering from the effects of a dicky stomach, food and drink weren't a priority, so I arrived about an hour before kick-off as I'd planned. After discovering that the Almondvale was now the Tony Macaroni Stadium – named after a chain of Italian restaurants – I had a good look round. I had a chat with a few Dundee United fans – all of whom had the relaxed, cynical, yet comical approach to the game that I'd come to expect – who agreed that life outside the top flight had been OK for a couple of seasons, but a third might be a bit tiresome. With United having lost the first leg 3-2, resignation and optimism were voiced in just about equal measure.

There are good reasons why Livi's stadium seems a bit of a strange place. The main one would be that if you're starting from scratch in a new town without much clue as to what your hardcore support might be, how ambitious or pragmatic should you be? Having been a part of a 4,000 crowd inside a 30,500 capacity stadium at Milton Keynes, it was hard for me not to conclude that a stadium a quarter of the size would have fitted the bill. Likewise, the Reynolds Arena in Darlington is perhaps the perfect example of getting things as wrong as possible. In my opinion the Tony Macaroni represents a good compromise in a country in which only five clubs regularly attract five-figure crowds. With an all-seated capacity of 8,000-odd and with all four stands accommodating approximately the same number of fans, the ground is neat, compact, and tidy. That said, a visiting Hearts fan called George Hobbs summed the place up quite succinctly when he said, 'The ground is so neat that you half expect the players to be on plastic bases and flicked around the pitch.'

Since moving to Livingston and adopting the name of the town, the club had lived through interesting times. In the first ten years of their incarnation Livi were promoted through the leagues into the Premiership, had qualified for Europe at the end of a maiden top-flight season and won the Scottish Cup in 2004. Just five years later they were back at the bottom level after a deal was struck to prevent the club going into liquidation. After further ups and downs, the club's recent five-year stint in Scottish football's second tier ended in relegation at the end of the 2015/16 season. After making an instant return, they were looking to earn a second successive promotion and a place back in the Premiership via the play-offs.

Exciting times for Livi fans, no doubt, which made me wonder why there weren't more of them. Despite another successful season, finishing second behind runaway leaders St Mirren, Livingston were one of the Championship's most poorly supported clubs with an average attendance of just 1,350. While the club anticipated a crowd of nearer 2,000 tonight they were to be pleasantly surprised when 4,508 turned up, leading to stands behind either goal being opened up to accommodate a few latecomers. All in all, I couldn't help but agree with Mr Hobbs's assertion that the stadium was a bit odd. The bar was tiny and packed, the club shop was tiny without much stock in it, yet corporate facilities were capacious but under-used. The old boy next to me summed the club up rather well when he told me, 'Most of the locals have a soft spot for Livi, but they're a lot of people's second team. When they pitched up here, all the football fans I know had allegiances that were fully formed. If you think that Edinburgh's 15 miles that way and Glasgow's 30 miles that way, I don't think they've picked up much in the way of hardcore support. I come and watch them a fair bit though if they're at home and Hibs are away.'

More encouragingly he added, 'Most of the younger lads I know who go to games come here, mind, so maybe the club will do well once all of us old buggers have died out.'

With so much at stake for both clubs, I suppose it should have come as no surprise that the occasion was more memorable than the game itself.

Though I hadn't really known what to expect of Livingston, they were pretty unique in terms of the styles of play I've seen in Scotland thus far. If crisp passing and movement was the way forward for some, this lot were robust, competitive, well organised but far from being a treat to watch. Following one of English non-league football's more direct sides, it was a style I'd become accustomed to. Just like my own beloved Dover Athletic, I guessed that if Livi received any compliments over the course of the season they would be delivered grudgingly ('We know what to expect from Dover' and 'Dover are good at what they do, I suppose but ...' are the most regularly used quotes of opposition managers whose expensively assembled squads have just been battered). Suffice to say that Livi didn't need 25 passes to cross the halfway line but took the collective view that Dundee United would not like it up 'em! Doing what they do best, Livi extended their aggregate lead to 4-2 with a goal after six minutes. It came as Keaghan Jacobs lamped a free kick into the penalty area from just inside his own half, Declan Gallagher nodded the ball across the face of goal and Alan Lithgow headed in unchallenged from barely a yard out.

If Livingston were a tad agricultural in their approach, the energy they put in was remarkable on a warm night at the end of a long, hard season. Needing three goals to win, United looked petrified under the aerial bombardment that kept coming their way and always looked odds-on for a third consecutive season in the second tier. They did equalise on the night, however, as Scott Fraser, tightly marked and with his back to goal, worked an angle for himself and fired in after being set up by Scott McDonald.

Although the Tangerines had no option other than to give caution a wide berth, the second half was set up for some thrills and spills that never really materialised. The game was no longer much of a contest but Livi still offered plenty to admire as a side largely made up of players let go by other clubs, playing with an energy that contrasted starkly with what I'd seen from Partick Thistle on Tuesday night. In the forthcoming play-off games between the sides – which I'd watch at home on BT Sport – I knew who my money was on. To the surprise of absolutely nobody, tonight's game finished 1-1.

Back at Livingston station, Tangerines fans took defeat well and with resignation. Consensus suggested they'd blown a great opportunity in the first leg and needed a decent lead for the second. With a mixture of optimism and bravado, they suggested I watch them again soon when they were certain to make it third time lucky.

As for Livingston – whose players warmed up tonight wearing T-shirts bearing the logo 'In Hoppy We Trust' – they beat Partick in both legs of the play-off final (2-1 and 1-0) to return to the top division. Though his players' confidence proved well founded, David Hopkin chose to leave the club on a high after guiding them to successive promotions.

ST JOHNSTONE v ROSS COUNTY

Scottish Premiership
Saturday, 12 May 2018

JUST IN case you haven't heard, Perth is lovely. Everyone will tell you so irrespective of whether they've actually been there or not. They'll have a friend who's been, even though they can't be too specific as to who that friend might be. Duly equipped with information gleaned from the bloke-said-must-be-true chain of thought – in my case a Buckie Thistle fan who hasn't set foot in Scotland for years – I set off for a place widely known as 'The Fair City'.

I think I may have mentioned elsewhere that I'm seldom prone to making snap judgements about a place. A few hours anywhere – with the possible exception of Stevenage – simply isn't enough time in which to get anything other than an inkling as to what a place may be like. What I'm long-windedly trying to say here is that I'm going to have to spend more time in places I visit if I want to get as broad a perspective of Scotland as possible. Already beyond the halfway point of what I set out to do, where have I really been? Essentially I've spent a few nights in Edinburgh and Glasgow, had an overnight stay in Aberdeen and popped in and out of places to watch a bit of football. In future, I think my horizons need to be broadened.

The silly thing is that I thought I'd planned this trip rather well. I'd booked trains that would arrive in Perth early and leave late, giving me plenty of time to take in much of what the city has to offer. Beyond this, I suppose I just pitched up and instantly expected to be enveloped in the loveliness for which Perth is famed. That wasn't quite how things worked out.

Arriving around midday, I was standing outside Perth station getting my bearings when I bumped into half a dozen Ross County fans. A canny bunch they were too and seemingly keen to enjoy what looked almost certain to be their last game in the Premiership for a while. Essentially, the Staggies needed a win today coupled with a Partick Thistle defeat at Dundee, which would see them go head-to-head against Livingston in a promotion-relegation play-off final. Though I gathered that they would be well supported today, it seemed that fans would be travelling in hope rather than expectation.

Discovering that these lads had all been to a game in Perth before, I asked for advice as to how I might best spend my time before and after the game. After a brief yet considered consultation a spokesman replied, 'We're off to the local Wetherspoons to get absolutely blootered. You're very welcome to join us if you fancy it.'

My reply ran along the lines that recent health concerns – I was pretty sure by now that I had food poisoning – made drinking heavily inadvisable, I'd love to join when I made it up to Dingwall in the not-too-distant future. Knowing that I had a long walk ahead of me, I opted to head off in the direction of the ground once a kindly soul or two pointed me in the right direction.

I enjoy a long walk, often baulking at the suggestion that I might like to squander my hard-earned income on a taxi. With the weather clement and time on my hands, a stroll was unquestionably the order of the day. Everyone's in agreement that Perth's a lovely city, after all, so I wasn't expecting my perambulations to be anything other than soothing and aesthetically pleasing. Sadly, if I'd done my homework to even a cursory degree of competence, I'd have discovered that the road to McDiarmid Park would take me miles away from both the River Tay and the centre of the city.

In terms of a journey that took me an hour and a half, it would be best not to share an overwhelming sense of tedium and just record the highlights. I passed a BP garage, a branch of Farmfoods and some extensive roadworks near the stadium. It wasn't cinematic. At the stadium, a poster advertised the game and invited visitors to park a car in a series of potholes for £5.

Although I could have sworn it was more recently, McDiarmid Park had opened in 1986 and was starting to show signs of wear and tear. As is the case with most out-of-town stadiums, which are never a good idea in my humble opinion, there wasn't much to do other take a stroll around the perimeter of the ground then go into the bar for an hour.

For the second time this season I found Saints fans to be a friendly, relaxed bunch, though I'd yet to see them involved in a game that provided them with too much to get worked up about. Like their pre-season match I watched at East Fife, their final fixture had nothing riding on it, at least for their 3,000 or so faithful fans. If the place didn't have a frisson of excitement about it, bonhomie wasn't in short supply, albeit it the end-of-term variety. I gave the beer a miss, but the company was good as fans of both clubs mixed happily and renewed old acquaintances in a manner that fans of other sports might tell you doesn't happen at football.

If Ross County had left it late to try and salvage a happy ending to a grim season, they had a damn good go at winning their final league game in the hope of at least postponing their relegation. They got off to the best possible start within three minutes as Jason Naismith's cross was deflected into the path of Craig Curran who squeezed a shot between keeper Alan Mannus and his near post to put the Staggies in front.

Over the course of the 90 minutes County, for my money at least, were the better side. Although they'd enjoyed some great times since the turn of the century – they were in the Highland League as recently as 1995 – it could be argued that they were due a little rough to go with so many seasons of smooth. They and their fabulous support deserved a win today, but as is so often the case with teams at the bottom of the table, they didn't get one.

Having created next to nothing all afternoon, St Johnstone launched one last attack from which David Wotherspoon struck a half-hit effort that was blocked on the 18-yard line. Wotherspoon did much better when the ball rebounded back to him to curl a real peach of a goal beyond and around the keeper to make it 1-1 at the end of an average game. In the event, County's fate had already been sealed by Partick's 1–0 win at Dens Park.

Although McDiarmid Park looked considerably older than her 29 years I rather liked the place, irrespective of the fact that, like Kilmarnock's Rugby Park, so many empty seats would detract from anything approaching a lively atmosphere.

Today, the ends behind both goals were closed and I couldn't imagine they'd be opened again until the next time Glasgow's big boys came a-calling.

Although I'd booked a later train back to Edinburgh in order to have a look round, the trek back to the city centre used up most of the time available to me. Thus, I spent my last half an hour in one of Scotland's nicer cities in an empty waiting room, reading a book about Scotland (Irvine Welsh's latest tome was released in hardback earlier in the week). It was here, I think, that I decided to stay in more towns and cities as a means to make this project worthwhile.

DUMBARTON v ALLOA ATHLETIC

Scottish Championship Play-off Final Second Leg
Sunday, 13 May 2018

IF YOU'LL excuse me for dipping into my book of 100 handy cliches for a moment, it's a funny old world. If I'd stayed in Edinburgh today, I could have taken a 20-minute stroll from my B&B and watched Hibernian draw 5-5 with Rangers. Had I opted not to spend a week in Scotland, I'd have gone to Wembley to watch Leicester City's 5-4 defeat to Spurs and been home in time to watch Barcelona's first and only defeat of the La Liga season, as they lost to Levante by the same score. Despite all these once-a-decade goalfests passing me by within the space of about six hours, I was delighted with my decision to spend the day in Dumbarton. Of course, I never expected to construct a sentence including the words 'delighted to spend the day in Dumbarton', which only goes to show that life in your 60s can still be full of surprises.

Although I'd opted for the slow train to Dumbarton East, that was another choice I was perfectly content with. The journey took the better part of two and a half hours but I had an Ian Rankin novel to read on a virtually empty train that provided me with what proved to be my own personal lavatory. Given that my bowel was every bit as old and irritable as myself, this was to prove no bad thing for everyone concerned.

Arriving some three and a half hours before kick-off, I followed the instructions provided by the excellent footballgroundguide.com website and found the stadium in ten minutes. I took one or two photos outside what I thought was a deserted place when a voice behind me made me jump about three feet in the air.

'Not too many decent pictures where you're standing, son. Follow me and I'll show you one of the finest sights in Scottish football.'

The man I took to be the club groundsman escorted me through the stadium reception, past the empty changing rooms and out on to the pitch.

'Go and stand on the centre spot, turn around and you'll see my point,' I was told.

I did indeed. I'd seen the 334 million-year-old volcanic rock (upon which Dumbarton Castle is built) behind the club's main stand before online. Seeing the sheer size, majesty, and permanence of the thing in real life is a remarkable experience that's destined to stay with me for a very long time. I took a few photos, thanked my guide profusely and wished him luck in what we anticipated would be another tight game.

It was around this point that the afternoon went awry for a while. Having felt rough for the duration of my latest week in Scotland, I'd barely eaten and was starting to feel a bit weak and feeble as a result. With my appetite returning with a vengeance I went off in search of a Sunday roast on a plate the size of a manhole cover, followed by something stodgy drowned in custard. Unfortunately I wandered off in completely the wrong direction for a couple of miles and found myself at a bleak shopping centre where I found the food choices plentiful and disappointing in equal measure. Given the choice of KFC, McDonald's, or Subway, I settled on the former and stuffed my face through necessity but without pleasure or enthusiasm.

I should state at the outset that it was the state of my stomach rather than the Colonel's secret blend of herbs and spices that made me feel this way, but within seconds of finishing my meal I felt as rough as the proverbial badger's arse. After walking there a tad gingerly I spent a wretched half an hour in the Stag's Head pub adjacent to Dumbarton East, mostly in the toilet or trying to take in the last knockings of the Hibs v Rangers game. In the end I had to throw in the towel and hand an almost full pint glass back over the bar, explaining that it was my constitution rather than the beer that wasn't up to muster.

With an hour and a half to kill until kick-off, I toyed with the idea of just finding a seat in the corner of the stadium and having a snooze. In the event I made one of my better decisions and went into Dumbarton's clubhouse, ignoring the 'members only' sign on the door.

Needing a beer like I needed a hole in the head, I tucked myself away in a quiet corner where I might blend in with the wallpaper and not bother anyone. With the clubhouse filling up an hour before kick-off, some pre-match entertainment had been laid on in the form of a four-piece R&B band (I need to go off at a tangent at this point, just in case this book goes to print and is read by someone who only speaks MTV English. When I say R&B, I mean the music performed by the likes of Rory Gallagher, Nine Below Zero and Doctor Feelgood rather than any over-produced caterwauling. Got that? Excellent!).

Although I'm not much of a gig-goer these days, I've swung my pants on occasion and have long since held the view that live music is so much more enjoyable if the band playing look like they're having a good time themselves. These boys – glorying under the name of Harmonica Lewinsky – had clearly been playing with pleasure as an overriding motivation for a very long time. With a lovely sense of self-deprecation ('welcome to our first ever stadium gig') the band went through a set they'd clearly played many times and could have performed blindfolded. I dare say the beer helped but they sent the fans out to their seats in far more buoyant mood than when they'd arrived in a state of anxiety that was easy to pick up on.

I won't wax too lyrical on match content but will simply record that I watched a game that reminded me why I love football, without the angst that play-offs induce for the committed, and watch two sides I'd taken a shine to slugging it out to decide who'd take regular beatings in the Scottish Championship next season.

The thought of either side competing at this level is remarkable if you stop and think about it. Dumbarton, with the traditional industries of the Clyde Estuary now largely a thing of the past, is now effectively a commuter town 13 miles from Glasgow. However the town's football club, in their 2,000-capacity stadium, have spent the last five seasons going toe-to-toe with the likes of Rangers, Hearts and Hibernian. If you put the entire populations of Dumbarton and Alloa into Ibrox, there'd still be 10,000 spare seats. Under such circumstances you can only admire those connected with either club for simply striving to be the best they can.

After Alloa had missed a gilt-edged opportunity to cancel out their 1-0 deficit from the first leg just 15 seconds into the game, the contest became more absorbing the longer it went on. If the first half had been a largely nip and tuck affair, it was Alloa who dominated the second, playing some cracking stuff.

While I held the opinion that it wasn't going to be Alloa's day, the Dumbarton fans around me were adamant that it would. It was they who were to be proven right.

If Dumbarton's defending in the first leg had been controlled, it became increasingly desperate the longer this game went on. Finally Alloa got the break they deserved in the 93rd minute when a cross was deflected into the path of Ross Stewart, who drilled the ball into the bottom-left corner.

If his elation was understandable, Stewart's goal celebration was ill-advised, performed in front of Dumbarton's younger and more boisterous fans. A missile or two was thrown but the final whistle and the prompt and sensible actions of the stewards got things back on an even keel.

Having used the brief interval before extra time to grab myself a can of a local restorative elixir known as Irn Bru, I was startled by a giant of a man in an orange jacket who told me, 'I'm sorry, sir, but I'm afraid I'm going to have to take that off you.'

Full marks to the fellow for being on top of his game and he couldn't have got to me quicker if I'd been carrying an automatic assault rifle. As a flawlessly polite and reasonable chap, he allowed me to take a minute and finish my drink away from the pitch. I returned just in time to see Jordan Kirkpatrick decide the game in Alloa's favour, driving a superb shot across and beyond the keeper and into the top-right corner.

If Alloa had deserved to win promotion on the evidence of these two games, it was hard not to feel for Dumbarton; a town and club that had shown me nothing but hospitality from the moment I stepped off the train. Before today's match the club's board announced that, whatever division they ended up playing in, they would be slashing the cost of 2018/19 season tickets to bring more fans through the turnstiles. It's a brave move and one I hope works for them.

Later that week and back in Dover, I discovered two things. The first was that I'd spent all my time in Scotland suffering from a nasty strain of food poisoning known as Campylobacter by those who can pronounce it. Secondly, while undertaking a little light research, I learned that, following a wedding that hasn't received much in the way of publicity, Prince Harry and Meghan Markle would become the Duke and Duchess of Dumbarton.

The Palace has yet to comment on rumours that the happy couple will be applying for cut-price Dumbarton season tickets just as soon as they return from honeymoon.

BERWICK RANGERS v HAMILTON ACADEMICAL

Scottish League Cup Group Stage
Tuesday, 24 July 2018

THE HIGH-SPEED train to Edinburgh Waverley slows down considerably on its approach to Berwick-on-Tweed, crossing the Grade I-listed viaduct at a gentle pace, affording a spectacular vista of the border town and the River Tweed winding its way towards the North Sea. Like the view from the Forth Bridge, it's one I never tire of and is one that stirs up some pleasing emotions. Heading north, I warm to the idea that I'm less than an hour away from the end of a long day's travel and the start of a holiday. Heading back, I'm looking forward to seeing friends and family again after a few days away. Whichever way I'm heading I'll invariably think that Berwick is a place I should stop and spend some time. Well, today's the day.

Until very recently what little I knew about Berwick was football-related, unless you count the nonsense about the town being at war with Russia for years due to a clerical error on a peace treaty. Just about anyone who's attended a quiz will know that, whether they like football or not, Berwick are an English club who play in the Scottish league system. Many of us codgers who do follow the game recall the day in 1967 when they knocked the mighty Rangers out of the Scottish Cup. As 12-year-olds in a more innocent age of fewer distractions, my school mates and I spoke of little else for a day or two. Apart from watching an episode of *Auf Wiedersehen, Pet* and recalling that Ali Fraser's mum was fond of the place, I'd be hard-pressed to name a town I knew less about unless we include the yarn of the mystery cleric.

On the train home after a particularly ale-sodden away day with Dover Athletic, we'd reached the tired and emotional stage when the anecdotes were flying thick and fast, irrespective of the fact that we'd heard most of them before. Having got on to the topic of odd folk we went to school with, a Geordie lad who is sadly no longer with us shared the tale of a class-mate evidently destined for great things as a professional footballer. In the event, 'the best footballer the north-east has produced since Jackie Milburn' suddenly hung up his boots after finding God, went off to theology college and was last heard of as one of Northumberland's foremost men of the cloth.

Of course, I'm happy to accept without question that my friend went to school in the 1970s with a chap called Eric McDerrick. That he went on to become Eric McDerrick the Cleric from Berwick seems a little more far-fetched somehow and possibly the product of a fevered imagination that comes with drinking too much fizzy pop, while seeking to prove his existence by pointing out a Facebook profile. Though my expectations of a rendezvous aren't high, I won't be the first or last visitor to seek out the man who, for Dovorians at least, has achieved mystical status as some sort of Scarlett Pimpernel of the cloth.

Without too much time on my hands before a 7.30pm kick-off, I dismissed normal custom and practice and spoiled myself with the extravagance of a £3 cab ride, driven by an affable local lad with a fondness for rugby league, and was inside my digs within five of minutes.

Today I was feeling a tad anxious having booked the cheap option of a five-bunk room that I'd be sharing with four complete strangers. Although I'd shared with mates before, this was a new venture for a fellow who enjoys his own company and can live without conversation for days at a time. In the event I needn't have worried. Just before 11 that night, somebody said, 'Shall we have the light off now then?' and within a few minutes the geography teacher, cycling Nazi, escaped murderer, and travelling salesman (well, you can always tell, can't you!) and I were embarking on a spot of the dreamless in our comfortable cots. The only problem was that I'd completely forgotten how badly five grown men cooped up in a confined space for a few hours smell. Guessing that we'd all unwittingly showered using *eau de trench foot*, I was out and about sharpish the following morning.

All this was a few hours away, of course. In the meantime I checked into a spotless and quite charming hostel known as the Granary, dumped my kit bag and ventured out into the warm summer evening. Courtesy of my affable cab driver, I binned my written directions and went with, 'Turn left, left again, cross the stone bridge, turn left again, and walk uphill until you see a sign for the ground. You can't go wrong.' Surprisingly, I didn't and headed straight for the bar.

Having spent my last week in Scotland accompanied by a virulent strain of food poisoning, I'd missed having a beer with the natives and sought about making up for lost time with half a dozen Accies fans in their 20s. Much of our conversation concerned a surprising recent transfer south of the border. Having been impressed with a number nine I viewed as one of the best in Scotland, I'd looked forward to seeing Adam Rooney play again and wouldn't have to wait long or travel far for that to happen. It wouldn't be at Pittodrie though, but at Crabble, the home of my beloved Dover Athletic. Earlier that week Rooney, having just turned

30, rejected the offer of a new contract at Aberdeen in favour of signing for Salford City to play in the National League, England's fifth tier. Although we didn't dwell on what this meant for Scottish football, the Accies lads accepted this as proof positive that 'English football's gone completely f***ing mental'. If this wasn't exactly a winning intellectual gambit, I didn't feel it was a viewpoint I could argue with.

Although I normally have an aversion to multi- or dual-purpose stadiums, I rather liked Shielfield Park. It's effectively a two-sided ground that doubles up as a speedway stadium with a wide cinder track surrounding the pitch. Although one end is completely closed off by the bend of the speedway track you could, technically at least, watch from behind the goal at the other end, albeit a long way from the pitch. Giving up on this option after about four seconds, I watched the first half from a covered terrace called the Ducket that runs along the middle half of the pitch. After the interval, I sat in the all-seater stand on the opposite touchline.

As has often been the case when I've watched a Scottish League Cup game, the 90 minutes was entertaining yet very one-sided. It was largely dominated by an English lad called Mickel Miller. In what might be termed a Rooney in reverse, Miller was trying his luck in Scotland's top tier having impressed in English non-league.

A graduate of Jamie Vardy's V9 Academy, Miller had scored a boatload of goals for Surrey side Carshalton Athletic, leading Hamilton to sign the 22-year-old in January for an undisclosed fee.

Having been broken in gently by Accies boss Martin Canning, tonight's game against lower-level opposition gave Miller the perfect opportunity to show what he could do in front of goal. It took Miller just five minutes to open the scoring with a goal I'd have fancied scoring myself, heading in unchallenged from virtually on the goal line. For the

Borderers it was simply a case of damage limitation from this point, though they might have made more of a game of it if they hadn't allowed Accies full-back Scott McMann his own postal district from which to fire over cross after cross to put them under almost constant pressure. From one of them, Miller dived to score another close-range header and make it 2-0 at the break.

As I took a seat for the second half, which Accies keeper Ryan Fulton might also have viewed as a viable option, Berwick at least scrapped manfully in a game they were going to get nothing from. Having won it himself, Miller tucked away the perfect penalty to complete his hat-trick before another young Londoner, Rakish Bingham, deflected in a shot from Dougie Imrie to round off the scoring. Satisfied with my evening's entertainment, I shuffled off to join my smelly sleeping companions.

The following morning I watched the sun come up over the River Tweed as the local fishermen set their nets for the day. As I unwrapped a sandwich, a seagull settled down on an adjacent wall. By way of appeal he tilted his head to one side in Lady Diana fashion, as if he wanted to be the seagull of peoples' hearts. Essentially, he was making a polite appeal that said, 'If you're not going to eat all that, would you mind terribly ... ?' It made a refreshing change from his cousins at home whose basic message was 'gimme a chip, or I'll have your 'kin eye out'. Given that I'd packed it before and it was a bit manky, I let him have it all. He quaffed the lot in about four seconds, and I swear he winked at me before he flew off.

I carried on along the riverside path and cut back into town, found a cafe that had just opened for the day and took my coffee to an outside table. Each passerby offered me a smile and I wished I had time to hang around for longer. I had a booked train to catch, however, so picked up my bag from the hostel, checked out and walked to the railway station via the same riverside path I'd just ambled along.

As I waited for the Aberdeen train that would drop me off at Arbroath, the train on the opposite platform headed for King's Cross pulled in and a vicar got off some 50 yards from where I was standing.

Although I shouted 'Eric' quite loudly he didn't turn round, leading me to consider that some mysteries are just better left unsolved.

ARBROATH v ROSS COUNTY

Scottish League Cup Group Stage
Wednesday, 25 July 2018

CONSIDER THAT the humble crow – or any other bird who can fly in a straight line for that matter – would be 555 miles from Arbroath if it perched itself on the roof of my house in Dover. Also consider this was a trip I planned at short notice and maybe five people knew I was here if they'd bothered to listen to me. 'Dad's away, possibly in Scotland,' would have been the best my children could have come up with. Under the circumstances what happened next, as they say on tired, outdated game shows, was a bit of a long shot.

Having coughed up a bargain £8, I was one of the first through the turnstiles into Gayfield Park around an hour before kick-off. Staff included, there might have been 30 people inside the stadium. You'll not be surprised, I'll wager, to hear that I was a tad taken aback when the first bloke I ran into said, 'Hello, Mark. What on earth are you doing here?'

This sort of thing happens much more often than it should. If it didn't, nobody would win the National Lottery. This is the second time this has happened to me in Scotland after two teaching colleagues remarked how I bore 'an uncanny resemblance to a chap we work with' when they found me dithering about in Edinburgh's Princes Gardens.

On this occasion it was retired lecturer, serial quizzer, and Dover Athletic fan Mick Palmer I ran into. On reflection maybe I shouldn't have been too surprised, knowing that

162

Mick and his good lady wife holiday in Scotland most years and have been known to catch the odd game.

I took a liking to Arbroath from the moment I stepped off the train and started to make my way to a B&B I knew was barely 500 yards away. Failing to understand directions I'd written myself, I soon got lost and was surprised when a local taxi driver turned down my custom.

'I can't take your money, son,' she ventured. 'It's right there,' pointing at an entrance I could have jumped into if I'd taken both my medication and a decent run up.

I'd expected my overnight digs to be as cheap as charity shop pants somehow, reasoning that not too many people would be heading north for the summer to spend time in a remote town constantly battered by the North Sea. Unfortunately I rather tend to base my reasoning on how many football fans might be heading to a place on any given day, which tends not to be how these things work. It turned out that Arbroath, given its proximity to the Carnoustie golf course, is a popular location at this time of year, particularly given that some major tournament or other had taken place a couple of days previously. Although a few balding old duffers in offensive knitwear and ludicrous trousers were still ambling around the parish, most had returned home enabling me to book into a pricey but welcoming and tasteful B&B.

Before leaving home, I'd marvelled at how England-based Scotsmen could spin a yarn and make up an answer to a question rather than say, 'Sorry, I don't have the first clue,' when asked something about their country of origin. It was in such circumstances that I was offered a couple of explanations as to why Arbroath are known as the Red Lichties.

According to a fan of Forres Mechanics, a Lichtie is a fish with a similar migratory pattern to the mullet and is prized in these parts as a cheaper alternative to the celebrated Arbroath Smokie. Plausible, I thought, as was the assertion that a Red Lichtie is a distinctive helmet once worn in the now-defunct coal mining industry of the Angus region. Sadly the truth is much less entertaining than sitting in a pub for a couple of hours taking utter balderdash in good company. Although the notion still has one or two doubters, it's widely believed that Red Lichties are simply red lights placed on Arbroath's harbour entrance to guide the town's fishing fleet home at night.

Although the fishing and jute industries of this old Jacobite settlement had all but vanished, Arbroath is simply a seaside town that has more than its fair share of charm. Not particularly outstanding in any way, but devoid of the litter and ravages that have made parts of some seaside towns in my part of the world quite horrible. If the town of just 24,000 souls had its rougher parts, I was oblivious to them. After spending much of the last 36 hours on a train, the simple pleasure of a stroll along a seaside promenade was just the ticket. Fish and chips, with the former tasting as though it had been zipping about in salt water in the very recent past, was top notch as was the ice-cream that followed it. Light-headed from my overdose of salt seat air – contrasting rather nicely with the Kent seaside town aroma of vinegar, vomit, and raw sewage – I retired for a pre-match snooze with a rare air of contentment.

Three hours later, after I'd supped a couple of pints of 80 Shilling across the road from the ground in Tutties Neuk – described in some quarters as 'the best pre-match boozer in Scotland' – I was immediately taken with Gayfield Park, as I'm never more at home than in a stadium that caters for just how straightforward a regular fan's needs really are. Although the ground has a capacity of less than 5,000, there's covered terracing on three sides and a seated stand that runs along the touchline adjacent to the main road. Refreshingly short of corporate facilities, anything other than an occasional coat of paint would just ruin the place, with the North Sea so close it almost laps against the terracing.

If my previous night's entertainment had been one-sided and uncompetitive, these two well-matched sides came up with a close and thoroughly entertaining 90 minutes that wasn't reflected in the final score. And while I thought referee Steven Kirkland had a much better game than the locals gave him credit for, having a pantomime villain at the heart of the action never fails to raise the pulses when things aren't going the way you want them to.

Kirkland's first 'crime' was to show an early yellow card to Arbroath's Michael McKenna for simulation when local opinion saw a clear-cut penalty turned down. As a cracking game developed, both sides attacked with abandon, crunching tackles flew in and whatever Kirkland's fee for the night was it certainly wasn't enough. Bad words were bandied about quite liberally on the terraces as Arbroath had two more half-decent penalty shouts waved away, prior to insult being added to injury as County broke to take the lead with a smartly taken goal through Billy McKay.

The visitors might have taken a healthy lead into the interval but for a couple of smart saves from Lichties keeper Darren Jamieson. In the event, Arbroath did eventually get the penalty they'd spent most of the first half appealing for. I couldn't see that Cypriot defender Stelios Demetriou had done a great deal wrong but he was pulled up for a foul on Ryan Wallace, leaving McKenna to tuck away the perfect penalty.

Following the swift demolition of a steak pie, I left the terraces to join my fellow Dover ultras in the main stand for the second half in a seat just behind the home dugout and a rather dapper-looking Arbroath boss Dick Campbell. As a man of similar vintage to myself, I'd taken a liking to Campbell when friends and I had enjoyed his one-man cabaret at Airdrie while he was managing Forfar. If Campbell hadn't been the happiest of campers that evening, he was in a very different frame of mind today. Bald as a badger and kitted out like the winner of a suavest bouncer competition in club jacket and tie, Campbell had the aura of a happy man doing a fine job with lads who had the makings of a very good side indeed. A bit long in the tooth for a crack at it now, I wondered how he'd have fared managing south of the border. Like a good few Fifers before him, I reckon he'd have done rather well.

Either way, Campbell's aura of confidence was to prove justified, though it took a sending off to swing an even game Arbroath's way. Booked earlier for a heavy tackle, County's Tony Dingwall went down a little too easily looking for a free kick and was duly shown a second yellow card and a subsequent red. Arbroath's numerical advantage soon told.

Within a few minutes, Wallace's corner from the left was flicked in at the near post by McKenna. His hat-trick goal came in similar fashion as County failed to deal with another Wallace corner, allowing McKenna a free header that just about crept into the net. Although 4-1 was a flattering winning margin, Arbroath finished with a flourish as substitute Kane Hester burst through the middle and fired into the top right hand corner.

Only Ross County qualified for the last 16 in which they were knocked out by Hibs.

Wandering back to the B&B, another lasting memory of a night out in Arbroath was of Mr and Mrs Palmer heading back to St Andrews via the car park near the harbour. Glowing with a sense of romance that only Scottish football can engender (?!) they strolled hand-in-hand like a couple of newlyweds. They'd be staying for a few more days, while I'd be heading off to the summer job, looking to finance my next trip.

QUEEN OF THE SOUTH v
INVERNESS CALEDONIAN THISTLE

Scottish Championship
Saturday, 10 November 2018

'HAVE YOU done Carlisle yet?' If you haven't been asked the question, it's on its way. If we accept football as a religion as I believe many do, Carlisle is our Jerusalem, our Mecca, our Lourdes. If you answer in the negative, particularly if you hail from the south of England, you're going to be dismissed as a heretic, a non-believer, a part-timer, a chap who simply can't be trusted. In your shoes I'd get it done and out of the way and gain full acceptance into the oddball brotherhood you've somehow aspired to.

When I did finally get around to visiting Brunton Park – to watch Carlisle beat Yeovil 2-1 in a half-decent League Two game in 2016 – the challenge had somehow been negated by the extraordinary improvements in rail travel that have been breathtaking when viewed across the course of my lifetime. I'd originally planned to visit with Leicester in 1983 (coincidentally, a famous footballing son of Inverness, Kevin McDonald, scored City's winner that day) but couldn't justify the time away or the expense, having gained a wife and a hefty mortgage less than a year previously. It would have involved a weekend away, an overnight stay and shelling out the better part of a week's wages. When I did eventually undertake the trip I didn't leave Carlisle until just before

7pm, yet was still tucked up in bed in Dover around six hours later.

Having discovered that a Dover-Carlisle outing was a bit of a doddle, I wondered how much further I could go on a UK day trip. The current answer is Dumfries on an 812-mile round trip, but if I can improve on that you'll be the first to know.

It was finances, or rather lack of them, that made me opt to see if I could make a Queen of the South game on a day trip. Although I'd made tentative plans to stay in whichever town I was visiting until I finished the book, that idea was scuppered when the dog developed a cancerous lump on one of her front paws. Although she's fine now and as perky as an 11-year-old Labrador can be, it cost me north of a grand to restore her to full health. She's worth every penny, but surgery ate up all the cash I'd put aside from my summer job.

While I'd planned a weekend away to watch a couple of games as I had in the summer, the news that fares would be much cheaper over an international football weekend (with fewer fans travelling the length and breadth of the country as a result) couldn't have come at a better time. Thus, four corned beef rolls, three coffees, half a packet of HobNobs and 120 pages of an Isabel Allende novel later, I pitched up in Carlisle.

They call Carlisle the City of the Lakes. It all sounds all very idyllic and Wordsworth-esque, which leads me to warn that the short-term visitor is far more likely to see a gaggle of dayglow orange, semi-naked women of considerable poundage toppling off their six-inch heels than anything remotely aquatic or poetry inspiring.

I'd assumed that my previous visit, when I was about the only visitor not on a stag or hen party and looking for somewhere convenient to throw up, might just have been a one-off.

With half an hour to kill between connections I knew I'd been mistaken as every arrival from the east disgorged its cargo to remind me why I'd declined my daughter's frequent invitations to watch an episode of *Geordie Shore* with her. One lass, who could multitask by walking while applying foundation with what appeared to be a trowel, practically knocked me off my feet by clattering me with a meaty thigh that put me in mind of Malcolm Macdonald. Although I received a 'sorry, pops' and a smile to ease my pain, I sought my train out of town rather than hang about for the next stampede.

It was all very different on the Scotrail two-coach boneshaker heading north through Dumfries and Galloway en route to Glasgow Central. Just about still in England while passing through Gretna, we were very much in Scotland on the train even if the Lowland accents were softer than I'd heard just a few more miles north. Minutes later, rural Scotland stretched out in front of me on quiet country roads where Land Rovers were the transport of choice, in the small part of the country where Tories bumbled about in green wellies and wax jackets.

Leaving a picturesque Dumfries station, it seemed a shame that I'd have precious little time here given my tight schedule. I followed spot-on instructions to 'hang a right at the Burns statue, take a sharp left, cross the bridge over the river [Nith], take the first right and you'll see the floodlights', as indeed I did.

Although it isn't always the case, I'll often find that there'll be something that will endear me to a club and its stadium. In Queen of the South's case I found it instantly when a fellow dishing out the match tickets asked me for proof of age before he'd offer me a concession; presumably because he assumed I was a young whippersnapper trying to pull a fast one by getting in as a coffin-dodger. I flourished my senior rail card, handed over a tenner, then whistled a jolly tune belying the fact that I'd been up since 4am.

I knew instantly where I'd be watching the game from as a fine, cavernous old covered terrace beckoned me in a manner that previous visitors told me it would.

My only real surprise today was that only 1,223 fans had turned up on a glorious afternoon to watch a game that got better the longer it went on. From my spot on the terrace, I was frequently distracted by the singing section; being of a very different stamp to what I'd become used to at home, where late teen boneheads in Stone Island jumpers have become all too prevalent and familiar. This lot were all around 12 or 13 and looked like they were auditioning for a Lionel Bart musical. Although the occasional chorus of 'the referee's a wanker' marginally detracted from their cherubic, Pickwickian personas, I rather liked their innocent enthusiasm for the game, free from the cynicism that would come along with age.

On the pitch, I'd looked forward to seeing Queens' Stephen Dobbie play, given that his goalscoring exploits had made the headlines in recent times, at one point sharing the mantle of Europe's top scorer with Lionel Messi. If the goals had dried up a bit lately, Dobbie had a good game today and was instrumental in setting up the opener.

Not for the first time, Dobbie got behind Caley's left flank to drive a peach of a ball across the face of goal. In attempting to clear, defender Brad McKay succeeded only in whacking the ball against Lyndon Dykes before it rolled apologetically into the net. Caley's back line and keeper collectively claimed handball against Dykes more through embarrassment than conviction, but the goal stood.

If Queens' opening goal had an element of good fortune about it, they scored a couple of beauties in the second half during a period in which even Caley boss John Robertson felt,

'They could easily have gone seven or eight nil in front.' Just after the break, Dykes's perfectly weighted pass sent Dobbie clear to round the keeper and make it 2-0. Within ten minutes it was 3-0 courtesy of the best goal I'd seen in a while as Josh Todd curled a shot into the top-left corner to round off a quite brilliant pass and move sequence that had started in Queens' own penalty area.

Home and dry then! Well, not quite.

What followed gave credence to my view that there's so much fun to be had from observing a game as a neutral; an assertion that so many of my deeply committed mates struggle to accept. Of course, there's nothing quite like the unadulterated glee that comes from watching your team come from behind to win with the last kick of the match. Then again, it's so much easier on your mental health if the team that changes from 'the greatest team the world has ever seen' to a 'feckin' useless bunch of bams' within the space of ten minutes isn't yours.

I hadn't realised at the time that I was watching an Inverness team that hadn't been beaten in 24 Scottish Championship games. While a run like that doesn't come without skill and spirit, they got back into the game as a direct result of the home side failing to heed my warning to 'keep an eye on that big lad' and Jamie McCart rose unchallenged to head in Joe Chalmers' free kick.

If that was a soft goal, Caley's second, which came just three minutes later, was a genuine, 24-carat, Sunday league shocker. Tom Walsh cut in from the left to get in a cross that appeared to evade everyone prior to dribbling into the far corner. Presumably because the ball had brushed gently against his sock en route, substitute Nathan Austin was credited with the goal.

With the crowd noise coming exclusively from Caley's 150 or so travelling fans, the comeback was completed with the third goal of a remarkable ten-minute spell. Again it owed more than a little to the comedic side of the game as Callum Fordyce's attempted clearance missed the ball by about a yard and a half but did connect perfectly with the rectum of Caley's Sean Walsh. Walsh tucked away the penalty with ease and, but for Queens' keeper making a fine save at the end, Caley would have won it with the last kick of the game.

Walking out with the stunned and silent home fans, I picked up the pace in the knowledge that one missed connection would result in my getting stranded overnight, probably for six hours at St Pancras. I made it back to Dumfries station in good time, but not before noticing that a restaurant on my route back is called The Doonhamer. Carelessly, due in part to the locals insisting on calling their team 'Queens', I'd quite forgotten that Queen of the South are known as the Doonhamers.

I never knew the origins of the nickname, so figured it would be fun to ask an exiled Scot when I got home. If you've been paying attention then you won't be too surprised to hear that a Doonhamer was often used to smite an invading Englishman, out to crush a few rebellious Jacobites. Apparently, 'that fat lad who was in *The Full Monty* had one in the first series of *Game of Thrones*'.

The truth, while being much less fun, has its origins in the distinctive Dumfries dialect. Natives of the area working away, particularly those in the railway industry, would refer to Dumfries as 'doon hame' (down home) hence the nickname.

Personally, I was 'doon hame' around 1am, at work by 6am and hoping to earn the cash to come back in January.

QUEEN'S PARK v
BERWICK RANGERS

Scottish League Two
Saturday 26 January 2019

ALTHOUGH THEY say size isn't important, I'm not so sure. Take Hampden Park for example, a stadium with a proud boast about how many fans it has been known to accommodate. In 1970 some 136,505 punters turned up for a European Cup tie between Celtic and Leeds United. Almost 50 years on that attendance remains a record for a game in a UEFA competition and surely won't be beaten. In 1960, while opinions vary on official numbers, 135,000 were believed to have watched Ferenc Puskás's Real Madrid side make it five European Cup wins on the trot by battering Eintracht Frankfurt 7-3.

If the same numbers turned up for two games at Hampden today, over 160,000 would have to wait outside in the car park. Although capacity in these safety-conscious times is 51,866, I couldn't help but think that seemed a bit titchy for a national stadium given my Scottish friends' assertion (though they only seem to watch football on telly these days) that, 'Scotland fans can fill any stadium in the world.' If that statement rang a bit hollow today, the good news was that myself and 443 others like me waited barely any time at all in the queue for the steak pies.

Going into 2019, I had just 14 new grounds to visit and hoped to finish this book by the end of the year. My main problem was that many of those stadiums belonged to clubs who might reasonably be expected to kick off at the same time on a Saturday afternoon, not being a particularly attractive proposition for Sky and BT Sports. Happily, a couple of Sunday lunchtime kick-offs in the Premiership provided the opportunity to see two games over the course of a weekend in both January and February. Coupled with play-off week in May and the group stages of the Scottish League Cup in July, I hoped to be calling 'house', most probably somewhere in the Highlands, at some point during the school summer holidays.

Having booked into the cheap and cheerful Euro Hostel on the banks of the Clyde, a two-minute walk from Glasgow Central, I thought I might need to add a little elasticity to my schedule. Knowing that January in Scotland has been known to throw up the odd postponement and train delay I gave myself three options of a game – at either Queen's Park, Stenhousemuir or Clyde. In the event, my train arrived in Glasgow bang on schedule at midday. Damp, grey, but mild weather ensured the country's entire programme went ahead, so I dumped my bag and set off for Hampden.

I'd waddled around the place before so I knew that Scotland's national stadium was just a short walk from Mount Florida station, itself just ten minutes out of Glasgow Central. Arriving at around 1.15pm and confirming that the game was on, I figured I'd while away an hour or so in the Scottish FA museum upstairs from the stadium's pristine main entrance where you'd normally be expected to bowl up in your best suit. The conversation that followed between a security bloke and myself went exactly like this.

'Is it OK to wander around for a bit?'

'No, not really.'

Duly chastened, I found myself a comfy leather sofa, watched Sky Sports News and waited for the turnstiles to open at two o'clock.

Inside the concourse of the single stand that's open for Queen's Park's home games, I was made curious by the number of fans adorned in black and amber colours not worn by either of today's combatants. A brief chat with one of them alerted me to the fact that today's visitors were Berwick Rangers, not Cowdenbeath as I'd imagined, hence there was no disparity. Far from being offended, the fellow in question accepted my explanation that this is the sort of confusion that often arises when 63-year-olds attempt to study a fixture list without their reading glasses.

I'd mainly picked out this fixture in the knowledge that Queen's Park wouldn't be playing at Hampden for much longer. I'd read about the club's travails in a recent copy of *When Saturday Comes* and thought I might delve into the matter a little further. Naturally, when you need to know anything about a football club, the best person to ask is always, but always, the guy selling the 50/50 draw tickets and I saw no good reason to amend this tried and tested formula today.

Although stoical about the whole affair the chap in question, who failed miserably to flog me a winning ticket, felt that his club didn't have much choice when it came to selling the stadium to the Scottish FA. With the country's governing body constantly making noises about switching international fixtures to Edinburgh and Murrayfield, Queen's Park simply weren't in a position to call anyone's bluff. As the only fully amateur club in the SPFL it was difficult to imagine how they might survive without the income that international fixtures and cup finals provide. While the sale price of £5m seemed a piddling amount, the club hadn't provided the finance that had turned Hampden into a state-of-the-art stadium we were currently nattering in.

As things stood, Queen's Park planned to move into what was essentially a training ground next to Hampden that, with a bit of work and goodwill, seemed more than adequate to meet their needs.

Although their halcyon days coincided with Queen Victoria's first flush of youth, this all seemed like an ignominious step for a club who were once at the top. Having won the Scottish Cup ten times, only Rangers and Celtic have picked up the trophy more often. They're also the only Scottish club to have appeared in an English FA Cup Final, finishing as runners-up in both 1884 and 1885. If times have changed, the club's motto *Ludere Causa Ludendi* (To play for the sake of playing) remains the same. They certainly played a bit today.

Going into today's game, Queen's Park – relegated via the play-offs last season – and Berwick sat third and second from bottom of the League Two table. If similar records in the division suggested this might be a close game, it proved to be anything but.

If the first 15 minutes had proven relatively even, all that changed once Queen's Park got the benefit of what looked a straightforward award of a penalty that was emphatically whacked in by Scott McLean. Berwick's response to going behind involved an innovative and original tactic of walking backwards rather slowly for the remainder of the game.

Having seen their 4-0 Scottish League Cup reversal to Hamilton Accies six months ago I put aside the idea that Berwick might not be very good, making allowance for the fact that they were up against a top-flight side. Today, even their staunchest supporter would tell you that their performance was just rotten.

As Queen's Park, known to their fans as the Spiders, got on with the business of slaughtering what had been put in front of them, I drifted off to thoughts of my own 'career' and memories of a couple of fine goals that would still be viewed regularly on YouTube if they hadn't been scored in the era of the Box Brownie. Let's forget that for the moment that they were scored past a) an elderly postman with dodgy knees and b) a 24st bus driver. I've no doubt that both efforts will flash before me during my last moments on God's clean earth, along with the memory that, had Messi himself struck the shots in question, the end results (assuming Lionel was on his game) would have been exactly the same. While these two golden memories were the highlights of 25 years of grubbing about in the lower reaches of the Dover & District Sunday League, Spiders midfielder Curtis Roberts accomplished the same feat within the space of ten first-half minutes.

Every bum in the house lifted off its seat as Roberts smacked in a half volley and a rising drive of quite awesome velocity to put the home side 3-0 up inside the game's opening half an hour. To my left, 30 to 40 Berwick Rangers fans reflected on the fact that a 200-mile round trip to Glasgow on a damp, grey January afternoon hadn't been their smartest move.

Although I wasn't aware of the fact until I got home, Berwick played the entire second half with ten men. This state of affairs came about when their goalkeeper Kyle Allison, having spent the previous 45 minutes highlighting the shortcomings of the defenders in front of him with steam coming out of his ears, finally lost the plot and was sent off in the tunnel at half-time. His replacement, Sean Brennan, was to have an equally distressing time.

Queen's Park could have scored a lot more, but McLean, Galt (two) and Hawke moved the score on to 7-0 before Rangers, as a result of the home side becoming a bit too cocky, produced a consolation goal that consoled absolutely nobody through Jordan Orru.

I'd had a good afternoon spent in the company of fans relishing every minute of a 7-1 result that doesn't come along too often. Consensus was that, given that this was my first visit to a Queen's Park game, I should come more often. Although the point was raised that, technically, I should have watched the game with all the other Englishmen in the away section, I think the comment was made in jest.

Arriving back at Glasgow Central, it seemed that everyone was celebrating something or other, particularly those Celtic fans who'd come from all over Europe to make one of football's must-do pilgrimages. For my part I couldn't have picked a more inappropriate place to spend a final weekend of dry January. I'd had enough excitement for one day and the effects of getting up at 4am were starting to take their toll. Thus, I was happy enough with an early night, a televised FA Cup tie and a packet of biscuits.

As a young man I'd often wondered why old people go to bed shortly after dark. If you've wondered about this yourself, the simple answer is that we're old and knackered and just doze off easily.

ST MIRREN v HIBERNIAN

Scottish Premiership
Sunday, 27 January 2019

WHEN THE knock at the door came at 4.03am precisely, there was unspoken agreement as to who should answer it. Notwithstanding the fact that nobody should have the misfortune to see me kitted out only in my 1,000-wash grey pants, Gerald had long since called shotgun on claiming the lower bunk. In the upper, there was no way I was getting down in anything other than instalments and this wasn't happening before breakfast, unless the premises were being evacuated. Besides, I was pretending to be asleep. Gerald, stolid, unflappable gentleman that he is, did the decent thing.

Our caller was a sturdy girl of some 40-ish summers whom an athletic lad might attempt to run around, purely for the exercise. Smoke was coming from somewhere, leading me to assume she'd swallowed Geppetto, who'd lit a fire in the hope of being sneezed out again. In truth she had a fag on the go, albeit it in a non-smoking building. Licking her lips, she eyed Gerald up in a manner that concerned both of us before getting down to the reason for her call. In a tone that suggested expectation based on previous experience she said, 'Is our Moira in here with youse?'

Still half asleep, Gerald turned around and gave the room a cursory glance before replying, 'No, love. If she was, I'm sure we'd have noticed. Sorry!'

Our caller, who we later discovered was the matriarch of a hen party from East Kilbride and was named Lorraine, gave a barely discernible nod of understanding and toddled off without another word. 'You're very welcome,' I said, or would have done if I'd been brave enough.

In the morning at breakfast, we were both quite stoical about the whole affair. You get what you pay for covered the aforementioned scenario, we felt. Besides, Lorraine had merely disturbed us for a couple of minutes, caused us to lose about 20 minutes of sleep, and had given us an anecdote to take home which is, of course, the whole point of travelling in the first place. As we set off for Edinburgh and Hibs v Alloa we opened the door to a stunning, raven-haired, and dishevelled young lass with her shoes hanging around her neck. We figured this was almost certainly Moira but thought it best not to ask.

Almost three years later, I'm on the same floor of the same hostel in the same city at roughly the same time. Only my mood, which was becoming fouler by the minute, had changed. I'd paid a decent rate for a single room this time and had made a point of specifying my desire for a bit of peace and quiet. Sadly my room was next to a couple who only functioned on Volume 11. As the male of the pairing went through his repertoire of Irish rebel songs, the female, without saying anything even faintly recognisable as a word, responded with relentless peals of what those in the witching fraternity might refer to as evil cackles. Although a visit to reception brought about a swift cessation of the row, sleep proved elusive and I was first down to breakfast.

The upside of having a disturbed and sleepless night was that I was out and about bright and early and got to see the centre of Glasgow in a whole new light. You might have your own ideas about how Glasgow could look in the aftermath of a Saturday night, but mine proved completely wrong. The place was spotless as I opted for a walk along the banks of the Clyde on a crisp, cold morning as the sun rose just behind Parkhead. As a succession of young women jogged past, each had a smile and a hello for me. While my mood of *joie de vivre* lasted, I popped back into the hostel, made up a breakfast roll, and handed it to a rough sleeper just rising from his bench by the river.

Although no great fan of street art I marvelled at the murals that adorned the city, noting that Frank Zappa needed a touch-up and a fresh coat of paint. Charmed by what looked like a gingerbread house behind Buchanan Street metro which was actually a coffee shop, I parked myself outside with a hot beverage and spent a happy hour watching the city waking up. With a little reluctance, I checked out of the hostel and went in search of the bus that would take me up to Paisley.

There are an increasing number of terms that fill an Englishman with dread and 'replacement bus service' is foremost among them, particularly in my native south-east. However, not for the first time I should record that this is something Scotrail seems to do rather well. The bus left bang on time and chucked me off at Paisley Gilmour Street in short order.

On arrival I was reminded that asking for directions from a fat lad usually elicits a predictable response. Today's affable chubster, while confirming that my printed instructions were spot on, added the usual negative after sucking in air through his teeth, 'It's a bit of a trek, mind. You'll be needing a taxi!'

While the only thing I gallop towards nowadays is my frail dotage, I needed nothing of the sort as the stroll to the stadium took barely 20 minutes. This included the time it took to assist a group of RB Leipzig fans in need of refreshment. My conversation with their spokesman went something like this:

'Excuse me, do you live locally?'

'No, I'm visiting like you boys. What do you need?'

'We're going to the St Mirren game later and thought we'd go to a bar first, but we can't find one.'

'C'mon lads, this is Scotland. You're not trying very hard, are you?'

Right on cue, a sports bar barely five yards away opened its doors to guttural murmurs of teutonic delight and a mad dash for the bar as the towels came off the pumps.

I'd have joined them but had things to plan, needing a swift exit from Paisley after the game. I reckoned on the match finishing around 3.25pm, which should give me plenty of time to get back to Glasgow Central in time for the 4.38pm departure. If I missed that I could also reckon on missing work the following day and shelling out another £200 on various expenses. Thus, a walk from Gilmour Street to the stadium and back should straighten out all the imponderables.

If the route to the (ahem) Simple Digital Arena wasn't exactly scenic, being mostly industrial/retail outlets all the way, Paisley seemed a nice enough place once I'd gone through to the other side of Gilmour Street. In The Last Post, the local Wetherspoons, fans of both clubs were mingling happily. Saints supporters were more optimistic and buoyant than might be expected of supporters looking at a swift return to the Championship and were confidently expecting a win today. By contrast, those who'd made the trip from the capital weren't in a joyous frame of mind having not seen their team win for a while. Adding to their discomfort was the fact that manager Neil Lennon had been suspended by the club and would almost certainly be leaving within the next few days.

As a chap with fond memories of Lennon's playing days at Leicester I took the view that the man could do no wrong, but Hibs fans duly took my views with a pinch of salt given that they were voiced by an Englishman sitting in a Scottish pub drinking tea.

A glance at the Premiership table suggested that what was happening at the bottom of the table was more intriguing than at the top. Celtic's indifferent away form had made the title race a little more interesting than usual, but none of the chasing pack could find any consistency with which to make a genuine challenge. As a betting man I'd still have taken Celtic to win the title by a good ten to 15 points. Matters were much more fluid at the bottom. St Mirren were rock bottom going into today's fixture but would move above both Dundee and Hamilton Accies with a win.

Once inside the stadium, I felt I could have been almost anywhere. It's smart, functional, and comfortably accommodating as many fans as Saints were likely to attract, but somehow lacking that lived-in look a few seasons would provide. While I'd envisaged all sorts of weather problems that might coincide with a January visit, sunshine hadn't been one of them. In the event the setting sun made viewing events at the far end of the stadium difficult, yet with all four corners open to the elements it was getting really bloody cold when the game kicked off at 1.30pm.

In the first half, a decent game looked like breaking out without quite getting there as both sides looked well matched in an affair that was littered with basic errors and niggling fouls. Thus, the fine goal that gave Saints a half-time lead was very much out of keeping with the fare on offer. It came courtesy of a classic piece of wing play as Brad Lyons went haring down the left-hand touchline, leaving a couple of defenders in his slipstream. Reaching the dead-ball line, Lyons cut back a fabulous low cross to the near post. Simeon Jackson – who I'd last seen playing and scoring at Walsall – poked the ball in from two yards out.

If Hibs were disappointing in the first half, they bucked up considerably in the second with Stevie Mallan providing that little extra quality in midfield that was to prove the difference between the sides. If you check out the goal highlights on YouTube you might spot me offering a half-hearted opinion on the legality of Hibs' equaliser early in the second half. If you look very carefully along the 18-yard-line you might spot a scruffy old duffer with a pie in one hand, pointing out with the other that substitute Oli Shaw had strayed marginally offside prior to scoring with his first kick of the match. I wasn't alone in pointing this out, but the record shows that Shaw provided a clinical finish to Mallan's delicious diagonal ball inside the full-back to put Hibs on level terms.

Within a few minutes, Hibs took the lead. Mallan's corner from the right was met by a Florian Kamberi header that was blocked on the line. Typical of Saints' fortunes on the day, the ball dropped perfectly for Darren McGregor to score from close range.

As a sense of deflation settled around three sides of the stadium, few could argue that St Mirren deserved to be trailing at this stage. They might have turned the game around if Hibs' goal hadn't led a charmed life on two or three occasions. In the event, Hibs wrapped up their first win since mid-December by scoring a third goal with the last kick of the game. With Saints committing men forward, Hibs broke quickly, Kamberi held the ball up on the 18-yard line, laid it off and Mallan, with the confidence of a man in form, rolled a delicate shot into the bottom-right corner.

With equal precision yet marginally more speed, I headed for the exit at this point. After leaving the stadium at 3.23pm a lightning turn of pace near the GPO depot ensured my progress was, though I say so myself, providing inspiration to the local elderly, as I duly made the 3.35pm bus back to Glasgow Central and the 4.38pm to Euston with half an hour to spare.

An hour before midnight I was tucked up in bed in Dover.

STRANRAER v DUMBARTON

Scottish League One
Saturday, 16 February 2019

ALTHOUGH WE'RE quite well hidden at times I've concluded that blokes like me are all over the place, sitting there quietly, minding our business, and bothering nobody. Only the tell-tale signs mark us out as football fans – if you don't know what to look for, you'd never know – and we always seem to find one another.

For once, it was a relaxed and pleasant trip up to Glasgow on a Friday afternoon with all the usual irritants missing. No boorish Americans sharing their life story with the whole carriage, none of the constant bleeping of the electronic games that are turning us into a nation of clinical morons, no *Apprentice* wannabes loudly conducting their business, no sharing of happening iPod tunes from Talentless Twat featuring Uncle Knobhead. Even that sphincter-clenchingly awful, pre-recorded message in the toilet – that somebody in the Virgin organisation must consider a real hoot – had broken. All seemingly of a like mind, we passengers sipped tea, read, exchanged the odd few words, and gazed admiringly at our green and pleasant land as we sped through it.

I don't think I'd spoken since leaving Euston, but a chance remark from the table opposite about QPR triggered a happy memory just as we were pulling into Warrington Bank Quays.

'I saw my first ever Leicester game there in 1968. I've still got the programme,' I blurted out, adding that I lived quite near to Loftus Road when I tried my luck in London in the late 1970s and became a regular visitor.

Introductions made, it turned out I was talking to Barry, a QPR fan from Canterbury, and Steve, a Gillingham fan from Deal, both residing within a 15-minute drive of my place. We got along famously as we swapped anecdotes from Barnsley to Buenos Aires and Carlisle, where both were headed for a 92 trip the following day.

Though a commonplace and mundane exchange, I mention it for one reason. When Barry and Steve alighted at Preston, no phone numbers were swapped or addresses exchanged, we simply wished one another well and agreed that we'd see one another around. My guess, though we're just three guys who chatted for 20 minutes on a train, is based on previous experience, and leads me to believe that we probably will.

Back at the Euro Hostel on the Clyde and in the same room I'd vacated three weeks previously, I was in no condition to hurl myself into Glasgow night life, no matter how briefly. Although this vibrant, friendly city had done so much to destroy so many preconceptions I'd held about the place, I was looking forward to seeing more of Scotland. Given that I had an early start in the morning, I bought myself a catering-sized bag of cheesy nibbles, got comfortable and watched the Irn Bru Cup semi-final between Ross County and East Fife on BBC ALBA. Within minutes of the Staggies' 2-1 win, I was out like a light and stayed that way courtesy of neighbours familiar with the word consideration.

A good night's kip proved just the ticket as I was first down to breakfast again prior to boarding the first train that would get me to Stranraer. I didn't necessarily have to leave Glasgow until midday but didn't want to make the same mistake I made last year when my only time in Ayr was spent at the game v Rangers. Today, I'd planned a much more leisurely day in Stranraer that would give me time to explore both before and after the game. In stark contrast to my last trip to this part of Scotland, the weather was glorious.

Boarding the 8.08am four-carriage affair that would divide at Kilmarnock, the thought occurred that I seemed to be spending most of my time in Scotland heading in a different direction to everyone else. Yet while the train was virtually empty for the first hour of the journey, I had some great company in the form of a blind lady who got on at Barrhead. After her husband had put her on the train, I was touched by the trusting manner in which she responded to my offers of help. I was humbled that, as a lady who adopted the I'm-nice-to-people-and-people-are-nice-to-me approach to life, she'd let me steer her into the correct carriage (we were both in the wrong section of the train), help her off at Ayr and entrust me to carry the bag that contained her purse. This is how life should work all the time, of course, but it troubled me to think how this scenario might have played out on the London tube on a bad day.

Travelling on from Ayr was simply a joy. With the Irish Sea constantly appearing on my right and the varied shades of green of rural south-west Scotland on my left, we trundled on at a gentle pace until we basically ran out of land. Stopping briefly just outside Girvan, I watched a ploughing competition which I felt summed up the journey quite succinctly. Having passed Stranraer's Stair Park on the way into town I reasoned I simply had to follow the railway track back to find it. Although that wasn't quite the way of things, I found the ground within about 15 minutes, leaving me with four hours in which to explore before kick-off.

While I appreciate now how ridiculous this sounds, I'd expected to see two things when I arrived in Stranraer: a) ferries and b) the Isle of Man. Ferries I did see, but not in Stranraer. They were just about visible some five miles away on the other side of Loch Ryan, where they now sail from a place called Cairnryan. Even with x-ray specs I'd have been hard pushed to have spotted the Isle of Man, given that it was 60 miles south of where I was standing. I was also in Dumfries and Galloway, not south Ayrshire as I'd first thought, but closer to Larne in Northern Ireland than I was to Dumfries. Although all of this came as a bit of surprise. I guess it shouldn't have given that I only studied Geography to CSE standard, getting a dismal pass mark at that.

Irrespective of my occasional inability to be able to find my own backside with both hands, what I did find was a pleasant town with plenty to recommend it. I guessed that the local ferry industry hadn't moved too far away for it to have a negative impact on employment. Either way, the local high street didn't seem to have endured the usual ravages often suffered by coastal towns, with several small independent traders side-by-side with the household names and the ever-present charity shops.

Having purchased presents for my girls – a trip to Scotland, tradition dictates, involves the gift of a scarf – my attention was drawn to a tiny museum situated next to a pub, so I popped in for half an hour before it closed for lunch.

Every port town has a tragic tale to tell and assumes the world knows all about it. Although the Zeebrugge disaster occurred 32 years ago, claiming the lives of 193 crew and passengers, that terrible night will live forever in the memory of those from Dover old enough to remember it. Thus, I was drawn to the story of Stranraer's own maritime tragedy when, in 1953, 133 lives were lost when the MV *Princess Victoria* sank in the North Channel.

The vessel, built in Dumbarton, was virtually a new ship having been launched as recently 1947. Although a gale warning was in force, Captain James Ferguson took the decision to put to sea on what was viewed to be a short and safe crossing to Larne, just 20 miles away. Given that Loch Ryan is a sheltered inlet, the force of the wind was only apparent on clearing the mouth of the loch. With conditions dictating that it was impossible to turn back, continuing the journey to Larne proved both unavoidable and fatal. Although there were 44 survivors it is notable that none of ship's officers were among them. The bodies of 100 people who died in the disaster were eventually recovered, with some washing up as far away as the Isle of Man. As was to be the case just off the coast of Belgium in 1987, 'Arrangements for clearing water from the car deck were inadequate.'

If my mood was understandably sombre for a while, I soon perked up by taking a lengthy stroll around Agnew Park and the edge of the loch – an area favoured by clearly very responsible dog owners and young families. My interest was soon attracted by the local wildlife which was, to say the very least, abundant. With the dockside area vacated by the ferry companies, a variety of seabirds had set up home and were clearly thriving. Though no slouch myself in the natural history stakes, birds don't fall within my area of expertise and many of those around me were species that, in the natural state at least, I'd never seen before. Having a few keen birders in my circle of friends (they'd all consider 'twitcher' a term of abuse, so tread carefully) I fired off a few texts that went something like this.

'Hello mate. Looking at seabirds in Stranraer. Just seen some little black and white ones with reddish feet and long orange beaks. What are they called?'

'Oystercatchers.'

With kick-off fast approaching, rest and refreshment were required. Reflecting that I'd once stopped to buy warm clothes on a July afternoon in Stirling, I grabbed a coffee from the friendly staff of a cafe called the Driftwood and sat outside to enjoy the warmth of the February sun on my face.

Soon after, I found myself in another park. Stair Park, to be precise, where Stranraer's football ground is situated, sharing the same name. A rather pleasing stadium it is too, having been situated on this site since 1907, with its centrepiece being a newish covered stand that runs roughly half the length of one touchline. A smaller stand stood on the opposite touchline, with hard standing available at a tree-lined end of the ground and an almost flat covered terrace at the other. With a capacity of 5,600 it would comfortably accommodate today's 327 paying punters. Going with the flow of the majority, I settled myself in the main stand and was afforded a perfect view.

Although I'd originally headed north with the option of a trip to either Montrose, Clyde, or Stranraer, I opted for the latter mainly to watch Dumbarton; a club I'd taken a shine to dating back to last season's Championship play-off final. Typically, having my star hitched to their wagon hadn't done them a blind bit of good. Less than nine months ago they were only seconds away from a sixth consecutive season in the Scottish Championship. Last Saturday they'd dropped to the bottom of the League One table and would have their work cut out if they were to avoid back-to-back relegations.

Today Stranraer, due to celebrate their 150th anniversary next year, looked like a side that had yet to win in 2019. By contrast Dumbarton, as their fans around me were keen to confirm, put together their best performance in months. Pacy and purposeful, the Sons had much the better of a first half that somehow finished goalless. As they continued to create and miss good chances in the opening minutes of the second half, it was hard to escape the feeling that this was the kind of performance I'd seen so often at my own club. Any minute now I figured Dumbarton would let in a soft goal at the other end and go on to a lose a game they should have sewn up in the first half an hour.

In the event, Dumbarton took the lead with a fine goal from Ross Forbes, whose first-time effort from the edge of the penalty box was still rising as it found the top-right corner.

Although Stranraer awoke briefly from their slumbers, creating and missing a couple of half-decent chances, going down to ten men for the last 20 minutes put paid to any hope they had of turning the game around. Not for the first time Andy McDonald was beaten for pace, leading to the centre-back tugging an opponent's shirt right under the nose of referee Grant Irvine. Repeating the offence within ten minutes had a predictable outcome of a second yellow card and not so much as a murmur of dissent was raised in the stands as McDonald made his exit.

In the time that remained, Dom Thomas drilled a low shot past keeper Max Currie, arguably the only Stranraer player who emerged from the game with any credit. And the Sons' much-needed victory was wrapped up when Ross Perry got on the end of a corner from the right to score from close range. If anything, 3-0 was scant reward for the visitors' almost total domination.

With a couple of hours to kill before my train back to Glasgow, I thought I might spend some time in the Stranraer FC 'Fitba' Bar in the town, have a drink with the locals and maybe watch the first half of a televised match. I only got as far as looking in the window as the few punters inside clearly had been to the football. I got the very distinct impression that most Stranraer fans who had might have gone home in a sulk given how poorly their team had played.

In the end I went for a bite to eat in a place next to the museum called Bar Pazzerello. Quite whose benefit that happening dance tunes of Ibiza were being played for was something of a mystery as I was the only customer, vainly trying to listen to the results on Sky Sport News. If you're not a grumpy old sod I'd recommend a visit as would, no doubt, the regulars turning up as I headed back to Glasgow.

Bored with the telly, I gave Liverpool v Barcelona a miss and went to Montrose v Queen of the South instead.

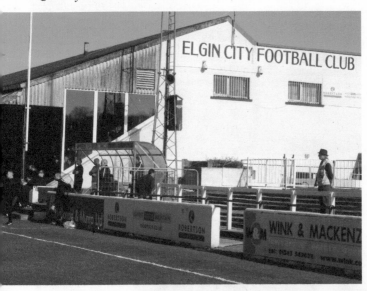

It's a long way from Elgin to Dover, particularly when you've lost your train tickets home.

I saw Ross Stewart play for three different clubs in three different seasons, winning promotion at the end of all of them. Now continuing the good work on Wearside.

Gayfield Park, Arbroath. Probably my favourite Scottish stadium.

I was promised 'one of the finest sights in Scottish football at Dumbarton'. I wasn't disappointed.

Ochilview, Stenhousemuir, where a drenched, bedraggled Englishman is guaranteed a warm welcome

A full house at Hampden. When I visited, 444 of us turned up to watch Queen's Park win 7-1.

Recreation Park, Alloa. The club's two play-off final games v Dumbarton were the best I saw in Scotland.

Rangers fans weren't having much fun when I last visited in 2015. I gather things have picked up a bit since.

Albion Rovers FC where romance is alive and well.

After four attempts and much time and expense, I finally overcame the Curse of Albion and saw Stirling play at the Forthbank Stadium. (You can see it from here.)

I travelled from Dover to Aberdeen to watch a Europa League tie, but someone switched the game to Tbilisi without telling me.

Known in Dover as 'the other DAFC', Dunfermline Athletic's East End Park.

The Global Energy Stadium, home of Ross County, a fine club constantly proving that size isn't everything.

He scores when he wants, especially when I'm watching. Nathan Austin (right) last seen at Kelty Hearts.

Journey's end at Queen of the South. You can do a day trip from Dover to Dumfries, but I'd recommend staying longer.

The Dover Sunday League was set up by a WWII veteran from Cowdenbeath. Not a lot of people know this.

Stair Park, Stranraer. If the football isn't up to much, I recommend bird watching in the harbour.

Rugby Park. Handy for some decent pubs and home of the celebrated Killie Pie.

Liam Henderson – a class act. Currently strutting his not inconsiderable stuff in Serie A for Empoli.

MOTHERWELL v
HEART OF MIDLOTHIAN

Scottish Premiership
Sunday, 17 February 2019

ON A Friday night in the first week of 2000 I lost a very dear friend; one of two best men on my wedding day. Walking home from the pub, Foxy keeled over and died. Nobody quite knows why to this day, but strong drink shouldn't be ruled out as a factor in his demise. He was 44 years old and our sense of loss is still felt in my home town today.

I mention this because Foxy frequently wore a silk Motherwell scarf. As a man who knew him better than most, I haven't a clue why. He'd certainly never seen them play or been to Lanarkshire, so I guess the secret went with him to his urn. I think I still have the scarf in the basement somewhere and could have worn it today had I first removed some interesting stains that I really shouldn't dwell upon.

As is always the case when I'm travelling from A to B in a pensive mood, nobody tapped me on the shoulder and said 'penny for them' as they often do in the films. If someone had – and frankly, I was hoping for Salma Hayek – I'd have told exactly the same story, given that this is a précis of the thoughts inside my pointy little head during the 25-minute journey from Glasgow Central.

Though 12.15pm on a Sunday is usually the worst time in the week to stage a football match, this particular piece of TV scheduling had worked out rather well for me. With opportunities of catching two games over a weekend in stadiums I'd yet to visit decreasing rapidly, I could watch this one and have plenty of time to catch the 4pm train back to London.

Leaving Motherwell station my heart sank within a couple of minutes, courtesy of a now happily defunct retailer that might as well have been called Gullible Paupers. Just the sight of the shop suggested a radio ad that might say, 'Tired of being a minimum-wage pleb? Well you too can have a £2,000 telly if you give us £2 a week for half a century.' On a straight walk along to Fir Park that screamed 'not much cash around here', I picked up the pace as I didn't have a great deal of time. Though these affairs tend to be solo expeditions, today I was meeting a mate who just happened to be 'popping up the road to Motherwell' – as you do when you live in nearby Chesterfield.

I met the chap in question, Chris Roberts, in a bar in Kraków where the last European U21 Championship was being staged and duly formed a friendship over a few pints of Tyskie. Though we only had time for a quick coffee and a sausage roll, it was nice to catch up with the old lad and his mate Dan before we shuffled off to our respective seats in different parts of the stadium. With no silk scarves of the type that David Niven might wear in the club shop, I just coughed up for the usual pin badge before finding my seat on the 18-yard line in the Phil O'Donnell Stand.

Fir Park looks bigger than its stated capacity of around 14,000, which I suspect is due to the South Stand, in which Hearts' supporters were housed behind one goal, being twice the height of the other three. The stadium lacked the symmetry and functionality of some of the grey, depressing new-builds I'd visited in recent times, which was just fine and dandy by me, and various other factors contributed to a good atmosphere just before kick-off.

With just over 5,000 fans present it might have been practical and cost-effective to close at least one stand. While I suspect that BT Sport may have had something to do with the decision, Motherwell opted to open all four stands. Thus, and while this might have had more to do with my disposition than the facts of the matter, Fir Park looked half full rather than half empty. With over 1,000 visiting fans in good voice and 'Well supporters buoyed by five wins on the spin, the place, if not rocking, was certainly humming a happy tune.

Given how the weekend had gone so far, I wasn't too surprised when the first bloke I spoke to inside the ground turned out to be an acquaintance from back home. Bill, a Maths teacher in a technology school ten miles from Dover, was staying in Sunderland visiting his mum. As another one who thinks of a 300-mile round trip in the same manner as normal folk might view a trip to the corner shop, he had picked Motherwell as his choice of 'local' live game. With good company sorted in mutual friends of Gerald – who I expect to keep popping up within these pages – we got comfortable as the game kicked off. With qualification for European competition at stake, it was the best live match I'd watched in a while.

Good games so often require a pantomime villain and in this respect Hearts' Steven Naismith filled the role rather admirably. Whenever I've watched Naismith down the years, I've often thought he was born 40 years too late and would have relished playing in an era when teeth were considered a fashion accessory favoured by ballet dancers. With Hearts on a long-term loan from Norwich City, Naismith seemed to be enjoying the fag end of his career, blundering into challenges that were robust but just about fell within the right side of legality. Referee Nick Walsh, refreshingly tolerant of a full-blooded tackle, seemed to be enjoying himself – albeit in irritating the life out of the fans of both clubs.

Later that week while watching the game's highlights on BT Sport, I noted that the football family's avuncular uncle Chris Sutton saw Hearts' first-half equaliser very differently from Bill and I, describing Naismith's finish as 'a work of genius'. Here's how we saw it.

Naismith's strike partner Uche Ikpeazu – six feet-plus of pure muscle and looking the part of a world-class sportsman if not necessarily a footballer – got behind Motherwell's right flank to drill the ball low across the face of the six-yard box. Although Naismith completely missed his kick, he was given a second opportunity when the ball came back to him off a 'Well defender. His second attempt had all the zip of a three-legged tortoise, looped up into the air and dropped in just below the crossbar.

Sublime finish? Well, possibly. For my part, as Naismith celebrated just in front of me, I thought I recognised the smile that screamed, 'Fluke? Nah, I meant to do that. No, really. I did,' having seen it honed and perfected in the Dover & District Sunday League over three decades. Either way, it was 1-1 half an hour into an absorbing game.

If Chris Sutton I differed on the authenticity of Naismith's Messi-esque moment, we were very much on the same page regarding the quality of a Jake Hastie goal that gave Motherwell the lead after 12 minutes. Primarily left-footed footballers with pace hugging the right-hand touchline are one of the game's mysteries, of course. Though you know that that they'll try and go past you on the inside and have a crack at goal as soon as they get the chance, doing something about it tends to be more problematic. If it wasn't, Leicester City and Riyad Mahrez would never have won the English Premier League.

After doing a very passable Mahrez impression in his approach, Hastie fired in a swerving shot from outside the penalty box that three keepers wouldn't have stopped.

If the pace and momentum of the game let up a little in the second half, the level of entertainment didn't. Hearts missed a couple of good chances to win it late on but it was Motherwell who picked up the three points on offer with an extraordinary goal from virtually the last kick of the game.

Following a challenge on Liam Grimshaw that was as dangerous as it was unnecessary, Hearts' Australian defender Ben Garuccio was deservedly red-carded with 'Well being awarded a free kick in a central position some 40 yards from goal. Taking the somewhat optimistic view that a shot was on, David Turnbull found accuracy but barely sufficient power to reach the goal. Keeper Colin Doyle, who'd had a good game up to this point, kneeled near his left-hand post to take a simple catch that he made an utter dog's bottom of. As the action briefly went into slow motion, the ball hit Doyle on the shoulder, moved forward an inch or two then spun back into the net at approximately 0.125mph.

As Motherwell fans around us flung their limbs about in a display of reckless abandon, Bill and I, despite our position as neutrals, felt it would be impolite not to join them.

I had, of course, planned to conclude this chapter with a paragraph crammed with well-worn derogatory cliches about Scottish goalkeepers, purely as a matter of duty. As Colin Doyle is an Irishman, I'll reserve this pleasure for another time.

ROSS COUNTY v DUNFERMLINE

Scottish Championship
Tuesday, 9 April 2019

ALTHOUGH I worked in both PR and journalism at the same time for two employers, I never really hit the heights professionally. To do so in either occupation a fellow needs to convince others that he believes his own bullshit. I had a bash at it but could never keep a straight face. That said, those who've never worked in either occupation would be amazed how many freebies you can acquire, even working for concerns that are strictly third division.

Football? By dint of doing a couple of modest favours for a businessman in Leicestershire, my trips to Leicester City games always came with a gratis three-course meal and a gallon of pop for about five years. For a similar period I owned a laminated press pass that would get me into any cricket ground in the country. The demands of a young family ensured I never used it once, but it saved a good friend a tidy sum. Golf? Horse racing? Formula 1? I've lost track of the number of offers I politely turned down due to a complete lack of interest.

The point I'm long-windedly trying to make here is that when I was flush and could easily afford my own tickets, the freebies came flooding in. Nowadays, when I wash pots at weekends to earn a few extra quid, I'd be chuffed with a free raffle ticket. Money goes to money is the adage I'm fumbling for, I guess.

I was thinking along these lines as I was queueing for my first trip on the Caledonian Sleeper up to Inverness. It's around 15 years since I legitimately sorted a few free cross-channel trips for this particular branch of Scotrail and was frequently offered a reciprocal deal should I ever need one. I was made redundant soon after and that was pretty much that. Or so I thought.

Initially I figured that, having made a 22-hour coach trip across the Andes from Buenos Aires to Santiago, I reckoned 11 hours in a similar seat would prove a doddle. The problem was that at the end of a run of 6am starts I was shattered, having second thoughts about a hastily arranged trip and in desperate need of my bed. I wasn't in the best of moods when I handed over my ticket for inspection, but soon perked up on hearing these words, delivered by a cheery lady with a broad Ulster accent, 'Ah, Mr Winter, it's your lucky day. Your reserved seat isn't available, I'm afraid, so we're upgrading you to a cabin at no extra charge.'

I didn't ask why my seat wasn't available. I simply thanked my new best friend profusely and followed her directions before she changed her mind. Moments later, I was struggling to recall when I'd been quite so happy or comfortable in such a small space. They don't come along often, so this was one of life's little victories I intended to savour. Ensconced like the proverbial bug in a rug, I read for a while then enjoyed the best night's sleep I'd had in a very long time indeed. Waking up for my 4am wee – it's obligatory post-50, I'm afraid – I peered out of the window to find we'd arrived in Perth. Three more hours of the dreamless later, I watched the sun rise over the Scottish Highlands; an experience that was everything I'd hoped it would be and more.

Previous experience had led me to believe that I'd be shattered at the end of my journey and would be needing caffeine and autopilot to get me through to early afternoon and a siesta in my B&B in Dingwall. In the event, feeling a spritely as a puppy with an extra willy, I dumped my bag in left luggage and sought a little educational tourism before dedicating the rest of my day to football, ale, and pies. Initially, I thought a visit to Glamis Castle might make for a lively conversation starter, the next time I find myself attempting to batter a few lines of *Macbeth* into a gaggle of unreceptive 14-year-olds. Then I remember the resounding 'Yeh, whatever!' my recollection of a trip to Hamlet's Castle in Helsingor had inspired in a GCSE literature group and I changed my mind. Instead I went to Culloden Moor, the site of the last battle to be fought on British soil in 1746 (if you're visiting yourself, the number two Culloden bus doesn't go there. You need the number five from outside Marks & Spencer).

I didn't pay to go into visitor centre – £11 was a bit steep, I thought – but contented myself with a walk around the moor. I felt I knew the salient points of the battle that finally put paid to the Jacobite uprising of 1745 anyway. I know, for example, that my lot, under the command of the Duke of Cumberland, didn't behave very well, particularly in the aftermath of an hour-long battle widely regarded as a slaughter. On a moor as flat as Lincolnshire there would have been no hiding place for close on 2,000 Jacobite troops who died that day. As I type these notes, Scottish National Heritage face a latter-day battle against some money-grubbing soulless bastards who are planning to put up a housing estate here.

With half an hour to kill before the next bus back to Inverness departed, I visited the gift shop and found myself unable to resist the obligatory fridge magnet and a model cannon that handily doubles up as a pencil sharpener. Later, after a carefree stroll along the banks of the River Ness, I jumped on the train to Dingwall.

Although it doesn't happen too often, there are times when all aspects of a football trip fall into place perfectly.

Today was one of those days. As I got off the train and stood outside an inviting looking bar called The Mallard, I could see my B&B across the road. Judging from the floodlights behind me, Ross County's Victoria Park (or the Global Energy Stadium if you want to be a pedant) was barely a five-minute walk away. A cheery Highland lass called Gillian – whose delightful Garfield Guesthouse sponsors her local club – promptly checked me in before I went for a wander.

Not for the first time, Scotland's geography got the better of me as I walked behind the stadium adjacent to a local caravan park. Although I thought I was as far inland as it was possible to be in Scotland, the sight of what proved to be the Cromarty Firth proved me wrong. I guessed that what appeared to be an oil rig platform on the distant horizon would have stopped functioning years ago. Although I'd read somewhere that the firth was to home to dolphins and minke whales, none had come out to play today, so I went to buy my match ticket from a young lady who was kind enough to chase after me when, in a frequently reoccurring act of elderly bewilderment, I left my debit and rail cards on the counter. Time for a silly old sod to have his afternoon nap, I reasoned.

Although I've developed an aversion to small, all-seater grounds that have more than a touch of Legoland about them, I rather liked Victoria Park. The far end of the stadium was closed and served only to keep the wind from howling in off the Cromarty Firth, but the other three stands were comfortably packed as I settled down in a seat parallel to the 18-yard-line some 20 minutes before kick-off.

In recent times I've found that just about every club in the country claims to be a community club, though many haven't looked beyond the buzzwords to think about what this actually means. Ross County fans, however, had that bounce and buoyancy about them that suggested a feeling of belonging. Of course, it could be argued that such displays of hail fellow well met might be expected of supporters whose team were running away with the Scottish Championship. That said, I found plenty of them in exactly the same frame of mind in Perth on the day they were relegated barely nine months ago, when they stoically accepted a little rough was long overdue following so many seasons of uninterrupted smooth.

Due no doubt to a widely admired academy, County's support had a very high percentage of youngsters. Refreshingly, on an evening when Champions League football was live on Sky TV, kids had come out of the house kitted out in their local club colours and watched the football rather than their mobile phones. Although the Staggies wouldn't quite guarantee promotion with a win over Dunfermline, it would give them an eight-point lead at the top that would be all but unassailable. For their part Dunfermline badly needed a win to have any hopes of nicking the division's final play-off spot.

As the game kicked off I started to recognise a few players; something that wouldn't have happened a year ago. For County, Ross Stewart, who I'd watched win promotion to the Championship with Alloa in last season's play-off final, started up front and looked to have grown to about 7ft 1in. A couple of feet lower, busy midfielder Michael Gardyne, who was voted man of the match tonight, impressed me as he had against St Johnstone. For Dunfermline, Myles Hippolyte, who I'd seen scoring a quite brilliant League Cup hat-trick for Falkirk, started up front.

The occasion was better than the game as both sides were a little tentative and nervy given the importance of the occasion. Dunfermline had the better of the first half with Matthew Todd hitting a post and bringing a good save out of County keeper Scott Fox. If they hadn't looked like league leaders and were fortunate to go in level at half-time, they bucked up considerably after the break and scored the single goal that always seemed likely to prove the difference between two well-matched sides.

It came as Josh Mullin's corner from the left was met by substitute Tom Grivosti who headed firmly home from eight yards out.

I applauded when the night's attendance of 3,222 was announced, reasoning that this was some effort in a town with a population of just 5,000 souls. I was the only one who did applaud, as everyone else seemed to take the view that supporting Ross County was the natural thing to do if you lived in or near Dingwall. They were promoted back to the Premiership two weeks later.

Although I was spoilt for choice as to how I might spend my second day in the Highlands I opted for a trip to Aviemore, which proved to be a bit disappointing given my expectations of bonny Morags, roaming in the gloaming, salmon, and rivers. There was an element of all that, I suppose, as a bridal path took me away from the tourist areas and along the banks of the fast-flowing River Spey and to the kind of tranquillity I was hoping for. However, when the track led into an expensive-looking new-build housing estate, rather than the splendid isolation I wanted, I headed back into town.

Milling around disinterestedly amid the overpriced tartan and shortbread, hindsight, as it invariably does, hinted that I'd have made better use of my time travelling through the Cairngorms on the Strathspey Railway. With a trip to watch Inverness Caley Thistle still to come, I reasoned this was an oversight I could still rectify as I headed back to catch the night sleeper to Euston.

With an hour to kill, I had a steak and a beer and watched the first half hour of Barcelona's Champions League win over Manchester United at Old Trafford before climbing aboard the Caledonian Express and immediately upgrading myself to a cabin. Reasonably expensive and indulgent, granted, but it was my 64th birthday and I figured that, what with Monday night's freebie, the return trip had still come in at 50 per cent off.

Ten hours later I awoke as we were passing through Hemel Hempstead. With a couple of hours to kill before I could catch my off-peak train back to Dover, I was rather hoping that we might be delayed in order that I might have a lie in. In the event we pulled into Euston bang on time.

ANNAN ATHLETIC v STIRLING ALBION

Scottish League Two
Saturday, 13 April 2019

MORE OFTEN than not, this ruinously expensive project of mine, great fun though it is, has been a solo project. It's not something I'd recommend to anyone not comfortable with their own company. Just as well I'm made that way, really, as there aren't too many people living in Dover who'd respond positively to an offer to join me on an 800-mile round trip to spend an hour and a half in a Scottish town they'd probably never heard of.

Having discovered I could visit Dumfries on a day trip in November without the slightest of mishaps, I felt that Annan, which is even closer to the English border, shouldn't present any significant problems, particularly in the middle of April.

I'd chosen well for once, it seemed, as today I would have the affable and familiar company of a few fellow Dover fans on the outward leg of the journey, at least as far as Lancaster, on their route to Barrow. All I'd really checked earlier in the season was that today's game at Annan wouldn't clash with a Dover Athletic home game, or an away match at a club I'd yet to visit. With all due respect to those who take civic pride in living there, Barrow was a place I was only likely to visit once. That said, if an outbreak of plague and foul pestilence should scupper my Scottish fixture, I'd at least have a backup plan in which I might make a second visit and hopefully watch the Mighty Whites secure their National League status for another season.

Rising at 4.30am on my day off in the middle of a run of early shifts, my sense of fun was almost instant. At the time I hadn't given so much as a nanosecond's thought to the idea that my previous attempts at any form of association or discourse with Stirling Albion FC could have gone better, but I'll get back to that.

For the time being, the period between our 5.49am departure from Dover Priory and our 9.41am arrival at Preston included moments of ale-assisted, high-speed conviviality during which even the usual row about Brexit had yet to materialise. A couple of minutes later we pulled out of Preston. Then we stopped. Then we didn't move again for well over an hour.

Looking back a few days later in a reasonable frame of mind, I reflected on how difficult it must be for a train manager to respond to such a pressurised situation when he or she is forced to wing it just like the rest of us. It all starts off reasonably well, of course, when the first five or ten minutes of any delay might simply be to allow another train to pass us in the opposite direction. At this point we're a good 20 minutes away from when the first passenger mutters a heartfelt, 'Oh, for fuck's sake!'

As the minutes dragged by and the punters became more agitated, the problem slowly but surely began to emerge. Apparently a train had stopped and was blocking the line at Lancaster due to a ruptured fuel tank (those of us who thought that trains just ran on electricity kept quiet for fear of showing our ignorance).

From here we moved into the realms of 'we've heard', which could just as easily have meant that somebody in a distant control centre had just lifted something from Facebook.

Among the most salient things that 'we've heard' was that the train in question was now on fire and the fire brigade 'with at least one engine' were in attendance. More curiously, 'we've heard' that animals, species unspecified, were also blocking the line, though there was no speculation as to whether they were there out of curiosity or warming themselves up on a chilly spring morning. When the driver walked past us through the train in a distinctly southerly direction we knew we were really in trouble. Moments later it was announced that we'd be returning to Preston because, 'Sometimes, these things take hours and hours to clear.'

At Preston, in scenes reminiscent of when the last American chopper left Saigon, chaos reigned supreme. All trains were delayed or cancelled, passengers wandered around gormlessly, and precious little information was forthcoming. What was certain was that, even if I was lucky enough to get as far north as Carlisle, getting a connection to Annan in time for a three o'clock kick-off was probably a non-starter. Even opting for Plan B and heading off to Barrow wasn't going to happen while we couldn't get as far as Lancaster. Furthermore, experience has taught me that whatever heads north late returns south even later. Defeated and demoralised, I boarded a train that was heading back to London at some point and sulked pathetically for a bit.

Having calmed down a tad, I wondered if my fellow Dover fans had caught the same train home. I'd lost them amid the chaos of Preston and, gearing myself for another relentless whine, I rang one of them, a certain Phil 'Packet' Smith, as we pulled into Warrington Bank Quays. Our conversation went like this.

Me, 'Hello, mate, where are you?'

Phil, 'We're about ten minutes away from Barrow.'

Further conversation was made impossible by a poor phone reception and what sounded suspiciously like noisy Herberts made incoherent by that heady mix of strong drink and (usually unfounded) pre-match optimism.

Although I'll doubtless find out what happened at some point, it will suit today's narrative to state that somebody sprinkled a bit of fairy dust about and problems on the network in the north-west of England miraculously disappeared from the very second I started moving in a southerly direction. It would be fair to say I became quite bitter and twisted on receipt of this nugget of information and immediately started my search for a scapegoat. I found one rather easily.

If you've been paying attention, you'll know this was my third attempt to either watch Stirling Albion or a game at their Forthbank Stadium. I have yet to see a ball kicked. Was this a curse reserved for me personally or one inflicted upon all Englishmen since 1297 and the Battle of Stirling Bridge? Evidence was mounting to point squarely in the direction of the former.

I briefly looked to salvage something by finding a game to watch on my way home but, having one of those King Midas in Reverse days, I felt it might be best if I just got home and put the day behind me as quickly as possible.

The day in summary, then! I spent £80-odd to undertake a 612-mile round trip to sit on a train, stationary or otherwise, for 11 hours. While they travelled further for similar outlay my fellow Dover fans had a much more enjoyable time. Trailing 2-0 at Barrow, Dover scored three times in the last 17 minutes to secure an unlikely three points that staved off any remaining threat of relegation. A little further north, two more late goals gave Annan a 2-2 draw with Stirling.

In the midst of all the action I arrived home around half-time. Very much in keeping with the rest of the day, I found myself locked out and duly sat on a wall for an hour until my daughter returned home from a visit to her in-laws.

Once indoors, I gave up and went to bed.

MONTROSE v
QUEEN OF THE SOUTH

Scottish Championship Play-off Semi-Final First Leg
Tuesday, 7 May 2019

IF YOU'VE never visited Dover, I think I can recommend it once you've escaped the nail bars, the charity shops and 12-year-old mothers texting while shoving their pushchairs in front of oncoming traffic. Within a ten-minute walk in any direction from the town's increasingly boarded-up and grubby centre is some breathtaking scenery that never fails to add wings to my soul. On a clear day you can gaze across the 22-mile stretch of the English Channel and get the time, albeit usually an hour ahead, from Calais's town hall clock. While this is something you're never going to see, in much the same way as you're not going to see a monster poking its pointy little head above the surface of Loch Ness, this is what we tell the more gullible tourists.

If you love a good walk, and you'll be spoilt for choice in my home town, the one I'd pick for you is the comfortable 12-mile stroll across our celebrated white cliffs from Dover to Deal. I should warn, however, that there comes a misleading point in the walk just after you've passed through the quaint yet snooty village of St Margaret's and reached the Dover Patrol War Memorial. It's around here, maybe an hour and a half into your walk, that you'll spot Deal Pier poking out from behind a chalk headland. It's here you'll say, 'Ah, nearly there then!' quite possibly to a dog who will wag its tail in a trusting manner and look at you with expressive doe eyes. The truth of the matter is that you're still about two hours and eight miles away, as close as your destination may seem.

I mention all this purely because it's suddenly dawned on me that this is the stage I've reached with this book. While the end is in sight the longest and hardest part of the journey still has to be undertaken.

Although I knew that the days of visiting four new grounds over the course of a weekend were a long way behind me, I'd hoped that I'd get three games in during the first week of the play-offs. However, with plenty still to play for on the final day of the regular season, planning a week ahead wasn't an option. All I knew for certain was that Montrose, already assured of fourth place in League Two, would be playing at home on the Tuesday night. Accordingly, I booked a single ticket to Edinburgh and a one-night stay in the capital on Monday. After Montrose, I looked at the possibility of moving on to either Forfar or Inverness on Wednesday then, after mooching around as a tourist for a couple of days, I could take my pick from three or four options on Saturday prior to heading home on a night sleeper.

Then, of course, the usual thing happened! Results didn't go my way and all five play-off games were scheduled to kick-off at the same time on Tuesday night. Disappointed yet slightly relieved – funds were low, particularly after the aborted trip to Annan – I opted for Montrose, a second night in Edinburgh and an early train home on Wednesday morning. Though I'd hoped to finish this book in July, that ambition now seemed wildly optimistic.

Whatever the problems with the Annan debacle, this trip to Edinburgh couldn't have gone better; I left Dover just before 10am and had dumped my bag at the B&B (the titchy yet ideal room three at the Sakura) by 5pm.

On what was one of those perfect spring evenings in which Scotland doesn't always specialise, I was out of the door sharpish and back to nature in Holyrood Park within a few minutes of arriving. Having recently celebrated, or more to the point ignored, my 64th birthday, I wondered if I was still up to the task of reaching the summit of Arthur's Seat having decided against a cottage on the Isle of Wight, given that it was far too pricey for a place that didn't have much in the way of football going on. I made it comfortably and in a time I felt was impressive for a codger soon expected to retire to the shed and await death. Feeling I'd earned a treat, I went to The Abbey, a cracking little pub within a minute's walk of my digs, where I enjoyed good company, fine ale and Leicester City's spirited if unsuccessful crack at soon-to-be English champions Manchester City. Having recently spent three months free of alcohol purely out of curiosity, I decided I could do without it if I chose to. Tonight I chose not to go without and inserted rather a lot of it into my face.

The following morning, feeling only slightly the worse for wear yet still in self-indulgent mood, I rose early, necked a full Scottish (a full English with different-shaped sausages) breakfast ahead of a visit to Edinburgh Castle I had decided not to put off any longer. Previously I'd got as far as the top of the Royal Mile on more than one occasion before deciding I'd visit another time when it wasn't quite so busy. Having finally realised that there would never be any such time, I strode to the entrance leaving kilts, shortbread, and tartan rugs behind me and coughed up the necessary.

Frankly, I was underwhelmed and possibly with good reason. The thing is, whatever you might say about Dover – and I dare say I'd agree with 90 per cent of it – the place does give extraordinarily good castle. Thus, I shall remain blinkered as to any evidence you might put before me with regard to their being a finer castle anywhere on God's clean earth. Dover Castle stands alone and I'm afraid that's all there is to it, so don't waste precious oxygen on the subject. Besides, until Edinburgh Castle places copious amounts of 'No twats allowed' signs at strategic points around its battlements and insists that selfie-obsessed tourists are fitted with indicators, it will never be possible for the discerning customer to enjoy the experience to the full.

Although the line up to Montrose might be familiar, it won't ever breed contempt in the soul of a punter who will never tire of the sights that the journey provides. In a quiet and virtually empty carriage I continued to marvel at the bridges over the Forth and the Tay, made a mental note to walk a stretch of the Fife Coastal Path before I popped my clogs, had another fleeting glimpse of Stark's Park in Kirkaldy and pondered over why such an aesthetically pleasing place as Carnoustie would wish to associate itself with such an immeasurably tedious game as golf. Although I had a fine Khaled Hosseini novel in my bag, I left it there in favour of the shimmering silver sheen of the North Sea on my right and the almost constant blaze of sunshine yellow gorse to my left, all set below an implausibly cornflower blue sky. Naturally, it was really bloody cold when I alighted at Montrose.

Not for the first time I'd been caught out by the Scottish weather, thinking that a T-shirt and a light waterproof training top would be just right for a bright spring evening. In the event I was perished within minutes of leaving the train; a problem duly rectified by the local Barnado's who, for the piddling sum of £3.50, sorted me out with a fetching grey cardigan of the type favoured by Pep Guardiola when it's a bit nippy (maybe it was one of his old ones that his wife had chucked out?).

I found Links Park in around 15 minutes, having followed some basic instructions to leave the town centre via John Street and walk in a straight line before hanging a sharp left at the local bowls club. Other than a brief chat with Queen of the South's kitman I've never known a place so quiet, with birdsong drowning out what passed as Montrose's rush-hour traffic.

Although I'd considered many permutations as to how the play-offs might pan out and reckoned on being in Montrose tonight, I hadn't considered that Queen of the South might be the visitors. I didn't even realise that it was a possibility, as I'd expected the opponents to be either Alloa or Partick Thistle. How Queens had managed to get themselves into such a pickle I really couldn't imagine.

When I visited Dumfries in November for the Doonhamers' game with Inverness, they were well placed for a crack at promotion. While they'd chucked away a 3-0 lead that day due to some rank bad defending, they looked great going forward. It seemed implausible that a team including Stephen Dobbie could get relegated. Dobbie, who was to finish up with 43 league and cup goals for the season, duly breaking the club's all-time scoring record, would be missing from tonight's line-up due to a niggling and persistent hamstring injury. In the final analysis, I guess a mid-table side in a ten-team division is never too far away from promotion or relegation; a dilemma I thought I might ponder over a few pints.

When I last visited Scotland during the play-offs, I hadn't contributed much to the economy given that a rather unpleasant bug dictated that I would mostly get through the week on Imodium and Lucozade. A year on and restored to rude good health, I was in a mood to make up for lost time and started off in a lively boozer called the Market Inn. I liked it there as the locals were friendly, the staff were a cheery and efficient bunch, and the beer was decent and very reasonably priced. The pub had, however, committed a crime I can forgive but can't tolerate for too long. Ergo, they had both

Sky Sports News and MTV showing at the same time on half a dozen screens, which is quite clearly an either/or situation waiting to be resolved. Although I can and often do watch Sky Sports News with the sound turned off, I can't cope with Jeff Stelling wittering on soundlessly as a soundtrack by chaps rapping about shooting police officers and smacking up their respective bitches offends my aural sensibilities. Disorientated, I wandered off in search of relative peace, quiet and a steak and found all three in what might reasonably be referred to as a family budget pub called the Picture House.

After I'd got a beer and ordered a meal, I spent some time with a couple of Aberdeen fans who, spotting the Leicester City crest on my jacket, asked me how James Maddison was doing. The answer, of course, was very well indeed, given that statistics – much as I despise English football's current obsession with them – had shown that Maddison had created more chances than any other player in the Premier League. What I hadn't realised was that Maddison, while still a Norwich City player, had spent time on loan at Aberdeen, earning cult status courtesy of a last-minute free-kick winner v Rangers.

Although the three of us were in for a meal and a couple of pints prior to watching some football, I was the only one of us who was certain which game he'd be watching. With the Champions League semi-final second leg between Liverpool and Barcelona due to be shown in the pub in an hour's time, I couldn't blame them if they stayed put.

Although Montrose are the lads' local team, they were very much their second team. I left them with the wish that I'd hope to see them later and left them pondering over what they claimed was a 50/50 course of action.

Very similar to Stranraer's Stair Park, I rather liked Links Park and had already decided that I'd watch the game from a cavernous main stand that ran along one touchline and could probably accommodate half of the stadium's stated capacity of just shy of 5,000. Although the attendance was given out as just 1,124 the place certainly had the feel of a full house about it, particularly given that there were still queues at the turnstile just a couple of minutes before kick-off. If the atmosphere wasn't exactly boisterous there was certainly a feel of anticipation about the place.

Even though I was 575 miles and a 12-hour drive from home, it seems to go without saying in these parts that I wasn't the only Dover Athletic fan in the house. Although I didn't recognise the face underneath it, the club woolly hat with its distinctive logo was unmistakable. He didn't recognise me either but we soon got chatting about mutual acquaintances and the fact that he was in the area visiting his daughter at St Andrews University, before we went back to our respective seats.

If the game didn't quite live up to the occasion, it was entertaining enough once the sides had got through a tentative 15 minutes. Queens had marginally the better of the first half and might have scored on a couple of occasions. Lyndon Dykes missed both opportunities, however, dragging one shot wide and striking a post with another. With the sides looking likely to go in level at the break, Montrose took the lead courtesy of the kind of defensive calamity that put the Doonhamers into this situation in the first place.

The goal was a shambles from a defensive perspective as a hopeful ball in from the right should have been cleared without too much trouble. In the event, an attempted clearance was sliced directly into the path of Ross Campbell who drilled it between keeper Alan Martin and his left-hand post to put Montrose 1-0 up.

With manager Gary Naismith having been sacked at the weekend his replacement, Allan Johnston, would at least have been delighted with the quality of the Doonhamers' equaliser which came midway through the second half. Without much in the way of options open to him, Connor Murray simply dropped a shoulder to wrong-foot a couple of Montrose defenders before firing in a 25-yarder that swerved away from the keeper and into the top-left corner.

The celebrations of the visiting fans behind the goal barely lasted a minute, however. Another ball in from the touchline should have been cleared, wasn't, and Campbell thumped in his and Montrose's second of the game. In the last knockings of a keenly contested match Montrose might have had a two-goal lead to take to Dumfries had Terry Masson's effort gone in, rather than rebound out off the angle of crossbar and post. In the event a 2-1 win, in the opinion of those around me at least, gave Montrose a fighting chance in the second leg.

With plenty of time to kill before the last train back to Edinburgh, I popped back into the Picture House for a nightcap and the last few minutes of Liverpool v Barcelona. I'd picked up a buzz going around Links Park that something was remarkable might be happening at Anfield. Few had given Liverpool much chance of overhauling a 3-0 deficit from the first leg, but they did just that by battering a shell-shocked Barca 4-0.

Closer to home, the two Aberdeen fans I met earlier weren't in the bar, leading me to think they may have gone to watch their local team and might consider doing so again.

With nothing much to see out of the window and few people to talk to on the two-hour journey back to Waverley, I immersed myself in my Khaled Hosseni novel (*The Mountains Echoed*), finished it, then fell back on the time-honoured pastime of filling my head with all sorts of rubbish after crossing the Tay Bridge. I even composed the start of a song based on my journey which fitted the tune of the Matchroom Mob's 'Snooker Loopy'. It goes, 'Cuper, Leuchars and Dundee, on the train from Aberdeen. These are places Marky goes, when he's on the way home from Montrose.'

Thinking I might avoid a lawsuit if I didn't try and sell this to The Proclaimers, I thought I might leave the 2018/19 season behind me and start again in July once I'd earned a few quid and refilled the coffers. I was back in Dover in time for *Pointless* the following evening.

It turned out that Queen of the South needn't have worried unduly. Although he only played 54 minutes of the second leg, Stephen Dobbie scored three of the five first-half goals that saw his side comfortably through to the final against Raith Rovers. They could only draw 0-0 in Dumfries but a 3-1 first-leg win in Kirkaldy saw them retain their Championship status.

THE SPARTANS v LIVERPOOL

Pre-season Friendly
Monday, 15 July 2019

THE OLDER I get, the easier it is to make me happy. While I wouldn't say I'm blissfully floating through what people tell me will be my 'golden years', it seldom ceases to amaze me how comfortable and content I can become if somebody puts a decent TV drama, a hot drink, and a packet of chocolate digestives in front of me. I sometimes think that is how I'd like to 'go' providing I get to watch the show through to the credits and finish off all the biscuits.

Given that I'm so easily pleased these days you can imagine my deep joy when the Scottish League Cup draw gave me two new grounds to visit on consecutive nights in Peterhead and Aberdeen, barely 30 miles apart. As fixture scheduling went, this was ideal and unlikely to happen when the season got under way in earnest and, with time off in lieu to take from school, I could save myself untold expense and sodding about later in the year. Although I already had plans to visit during the last week of July, this was the perfect opportunity to enjoy a short break, pop back home and earn a few quid from the summer job, then start again. It seemed that this book of mine would be finished in no time at all and I could already envisage the rejection letters piling up on the doormat.

Having not flown to Scotland for a while, I thought I might sort myself a return flight to Aberdeen given that prices quoted by the budget airlines seemed reasonable enough. Then again, as a bloke with a morbid fear of dying in a plane crash (not totally irrational, given that my uncle Alec passed away in these very circumstances) did I really want to fly into an airport called Dyce? It seemed like tempting fate somehow, so I opted to go by train and break my journey en route. It was at this point that the Gods of football fixtures, so often cruel, vindictive masters, decided to squirt another large portion of jam into my doughnut.

Quite how The Spartans managed to persuade Liverpool's under-23 side to visit Pilton for an evening I have no idea, and I didn't bother to check. That they had was enough for me to book both a return train ticket and a one-night stay at the Sakura – both reasonably priced before the school summer holidays sent the prices soaring – and set off just before 10am. At the end of another journey that went without a hitch, I dumped by bag at my favourite B&B around a couple of hours before the game's early kick-off time of 7pm.

Having made the trip to Ainslie Park before, I was almost on autopilot as I strolled down to The Mound, jumped on the number 27 bus to Silverknowes then alighted, without prompting, at the supermarket that the stadium is just behind. Arriving at 6.30pm it was to prove a very different experience to when I pitched up on a freezing February night in 2018, but no less enjoyable.

On that occasion, during what was to prove a Lowland League championship-winning season, around 100 fans pitched up to watch the club's derby with Edinburgh University. Tonight I queued for ten minutes to get into a sold-out game having received my ticket through the post a fortnight previously.

Having worked behind the scenes for a club at a similar level in England, I knew what a coup it was for The Spartans to get the reigning European champions to send a young side to visit. Although ticket prices remained more than reasonable – my concession cost a tenner – this was a classic case of a club making hay while the sun shone. Commemorative T-shirts and programmes, again reasonably priced, were shifting like the proverbial hot cakes and it seemed clear that today's receipts would dwarf the takings for the remainder of the season and, quite possibly, the one after that. At what was clearly a dyed-in-the-wool, bona fide club that existed purely for the benefit of the local community, it seemed clear that the windfall would be invested wisely.

I don't suppose I was the only one in a crowd of 1,975 to expect the game to be a bit one-sided. Yet while Liverpool's kids could and did keep possession for minutes at a time, The Spartans gave a good account of themselves and arguably created the better chances. Whether they deserved to win or not was up for question, but Liverpool took a keenly contested affair with the only goal of the game seven minutes from time.

Although the goal was supposedly down to a goalkeeping error, it would be fair to say that Lionel Messi would have struggled to have controlled a back-pass that wasn't so much rolled as hammered back to Spartans keeper Blair Carswell. Although Carswell made a decent fist of trying to atone for a defender's error, 17-year-old Jack Bearne fired home the loose ball, giving Liverpool both the win and the Ronnie Swan Trophy, which marked the tenth anniversary of the club's community arm.

It was around the time of the goal that I clocked an act of kindness and downright common decency that I felt summed up this wonderful little club rather well. While in the process of closing up the snack bar behind the goal for the evening, one of the young members of staff, who must have had a much busier evening than is usually the case, came out with a tray of leftover hot pies and bridies and dished them out gratis on a first come, first served basis. In essence, a little kindness that lives long in the memory and keeps the punters coming back for more.

With the next bus not due for another 45 minutes, I figured I'd have a crack at walking back. It was a trek, but the early kick-off gave me more of a glorious summer evening to enjoy as I checked at each bus stop that I was still on the route of the number 27. Far sooner than I expected, I found myself walking past Edinburgh Castle where Kylie Minogue was performing a live concert. While I'm not great fan of the diminutive antipodean songbird, I took her advice and by 'spinning around' away from the castle I found myself traipsing across The Meadows in full bloom beneath a pink and purple twilight.

I decided there and then that matters were pretty much all right with the world.

PETERHEAD v INVERNESS CALEDONIAN THISTLE

Scottish League Cup Group Stage
Tuesday, 16 July 2019

I WAS rather sternly ticked off by a couple of contributors to a Facebook group the other day. Although not a complete slouch when it comes to a little internet research, I'd got bogged down in seeking directions from the centre of Aberdeen to Cove Rangers' stadium and asked for advice that was instantly forthcoming. However, it came with a barbed additional comment that it had taken the guy who came up with the required information barely a few seconds to find it online and maybe I'd like to try a little harder in future. A cheeky young Scandinavian, who was probably handed a smartphone within seconds of leaving the womb, asked if I considered using Google Maps as some sort of magic trick? I replied that it is if your phone is a Nokia. I got a few likes and smiley faces for that one, which I felt justified my 21st-century existence for at least another day.

This afternoon, with my Nokia switched off in my travel bag, I found Peterhead's Balmoor Stadium in somewhat more traditional fashion, courtesy of a process that the elderly refer to as looking out of the window. As the number 63 bus rolled slowly downhill along the coast road into Scotland's most easterly settlement, I spied a set of floodlights away to my left and I made a mental note of the ground's location en route

223

to the bus station. When I was good and ready I backtracked from my hotel and found the place in about 25 minutes. Having discovered the feeling Bear Grylls must experience when he's found a long-lost Amazonian tribe, I wandered back into town and treated myself to a steak dinner.

Initially, I really hadn't fancied a 32-mile bus ride to Peterhead from Aberdeen, following a longish train trip from Edinburgh, but continuing the journey via my preferred method of transport had been scuppered by Doctor Beeching as long ago as 1965. In the event the trip was just fine and dandy, particularly given that the bus station in Aberdeen's Union Square is a two-minute walk away from the railway station via a shopping mall. I waited ten minutes for a bus that left hourly and was on my way. After a slow trudge through the busy city centre, the journey picked up once we'd crossed the Bridge of Don. Looking around at my fellow passengers, it was clear I'd left the tourists behind and was back in the world of the wifey where the headscarf is the fashion accessory to be seen in. As we left the A9 motorway we passed through villages that, though outlandishly twee, were a riot of summer of summer blooms that were quite beautiful. With the trip becoming a stop-start affair I was reminded of a lesson I'd heeded on the number seven bus from Kirkaldy to Methil; that the road to obesity isn't all about fish suppers and hidden sugar content, but often down to being the type of lazy sod who gets on a bus to travel 200 yards.

It would be fair to say that I took to Peterhead almost from the moment I stepped off the bus. If the main high street – which was just around the corner from the bus station – could have been in a British town almost anywhere, it was unusual in the manner in which people seemed to have the time to stop and talk to one another. If the place didn't exactly look prosperous, it seemed to have avoided the ravages inflicted on so many seaside towns in Kent.

I've so often found travel worthwhile when unearthing an unexpected gem and it seemed that the 'Blue Toun' wasn't going to let me down in this respect. I'd booked to stay at a place called the Waverley Hotel and having paid just £30 for one night's B&B, my expectations weren't high.

I'd expected to file the place in the memory bank marked 'one-star rat trap I'll never see again, so just suck it up'. In the event the Waverley was one of the nicest hotels I've ever stayed in. You'll have stayed in hotels yourself, of course, so now seems a reasonable juncture in which to skimp on adjectives I might use later.

Suffice to say that if I were to book comparable accommodation in London, even in one of the many manky parts, I wouldn't have expected much change from £150. Here, once I'd stumped up my £30, the smiley young lass on reception simply said, 'Thank you, Mr Winter. Here's your key. You're in room 105, which is first on the right just up the stairs there.' Call me old-fashioned, but I found this preferable to filling in the same form I'd completed online three months previously, then being told that, despite my being knackered after a long trip, my room wouldn't be ready for a couple of hours.

As I wandered around later I thought that Peterhead was just the type of place I could move to if family ties weren't destined to bind me to Dover until I slipped off the dish. Previously, what little I'd heard about Peterhead would have been much the same as everyone else, I'd imagine, in that I'd half expected to find a tatty old Jacobite town made impecunious by the terminal decline in a fishing industry upon which it was completely reliant. In truth, fishing still provides a livelihood for 700 of the town's 18,000 population, while plans are being hatched to open up the town as a gateway to the Scottish Highlands. Development of Peterhead Bay should soon provide berthing facilities for cruise ships and the piles of cash they bring with them. While I didn't fancy a trip to Peterhead Prison Museum myself, I was told that the town's main tourist attraction is bringing in punters from all around the world in increasing numbers.

The walk to the stadium was possibly the quietest I've ever undertaken. If the town is subject to a rush hour it had long since dispersed and, but for the low murmur of distant traffic, only the ever-present seagulls provided an audio backdrop to a leisurely stroll in the summer sunshine. Back at my hotel the owner had told me that, until very recently, Peterhead had been one of the five cheapest places to live in the whole of the UK. A glance into a couple of estate agent windows confirmed his point and as I got closer to the ground, it was difficult to dismiss the thought that I could sell my scruffy 'in need of extensive modernisation' three-bedroom terraced hovel in the south-east and buy two of the immaculate three-bedroom semi-detached houses of which the town has an abundance. Although this won't happen, I'd spend a lot less time moaning about litter if I did.

I went straight into the stadium some 45 minutes before kick-off and instantly liked what I saw. Although Balmoor has a capacity of just 3,150 – offering plenty of space to the 606 who'd turned up – it seemed larger somehow, with 1,000 seats housed in two covered stands on either side of the pitch. Behind each goal was uncovered hard standing, mostly favoured by young fans of whom Peterhead seemed to have a pleasing number.

Having grabbed a strong coffee to perk myself up, I did something I can't recall ever doing before by taking a seat in the stand and just listening to music. I suppose I've become largely immune to the relentless pap that constitutes 'pre-match entertainment' usually in the form of over-produced power ballads, cheesy Eurotrash and 'classics' from the 1980s, otherwise known as the decade that taste forgot. Tonight the lad on the decks – as I gather some youngsters say – had put a bit of thought and effort into his selections. Suffice to say he came up with an eclectic mix of great songs I hadn't heard for decades and great songs I've never heard before but would like to hear again. All this was concluded as the teams came out to Peterhead's club anthem, 'The Blue Toon Tune', which rather nicely expressed the sentiment, 'So if you're Russian or you're Polish or you're from another land, you can come and join our crew.'

As a chap from another land, I took this as a personal invitation to have a good time and settled down in a seat by the 18-yard line to watch the game.

I'd looked forward to watching ICT play again having seen them score eight times in just two away games. Today, however, we weren't too far into the game when I realised that the current side might not be quite so gung-ho and good to watch. Exceptionally big lads – you could tell they were the professionals, as their names were printed on the backs of their rather natty black shirts – Inverness had a lot of the ball without looking likely to do much with it. As Peterhead didn't create a great deal either, 'intriguing but needing a goal' would sum up the first half.

If Peterhead manager Jim McInally had picked up his share of medals in a distinguished career with Dundee United, it seemed he was making an equally good fist of management having just led Peterhead to the League Two title. Having decided that ICT weren't a side they needed to fear who could be got at with pace, it was admirable the way in which they changed tactics at the beginning of the second half. Using the full width of the pitch, Peterhead looked to get in behind either flank. They did so frequently and with ever-increasing ease. Although ICT did have one good chance to win the game, the second half was largely a tale of keeper Mark Ridgers keeping Peterhead out with a string of fine saves. As the game got better the longer it went on, nobody seemed to notice that the floodlights hadn't been switched on until five minutes before the end. Responding to a tremendous din provided by the local kids hammering on the advertising hoardings, Peterhead deserved to win comfortably, but had to be content with a 0-0 draw which dictated that a penalty shoot-out would decide who took a bonus point from the fixture.

Initially, it seemed like we might be here all night as both sides seemed to think this taking penalties malarkey was a bit like shelling peas. Each and every outfield player scored, most with a textbook penalty, and it was 10-10 when both goalkeepers stepped up to have a bash. Having been mainly responsible for ICT claiming one point, Ridgers put his effort wide to scupper his side's chances of claiming another one. Opposite number Greg Fleming scored comfortably from the night's 22nd penalty to give Peterhead the two points that were the very least they deserved.

In the event, the result didn't matter too much. Dundee won the group while Peterhead and ICT, despite having decent enough campaigns, couldn't scrape together enough points to qualify as one of the four best runners-up.

Strolling back into town later, where builders were still working on a derelict church at around 10pm, I couldn't help but think that this was the sort of place I could happily retire to given different circumstances. I could settle down in my smart and spacious semi, shove £100,000 in the bank (assuming the kids haven't taken it off me) and volunteer myself to do something useful in my spare time. I could write a paragraph or two for the Peterhead programme, maybe work an afternoon or two in the club shop, or knock on a few doors in the hope of signing up a few folk to the weekly tote. A friendly bunch, I reckoned they'd welcome a spare pair of hands, albeit in my next life.

The following morning, following a damn fine hotel breakfast, I was stopped by an earnest young man, possibly 19 but going on 55, with thick glasses and perfect teeth, looking for all the world like Buddy Holly on his way to a job interview. My guess that he was a patron of the Kingdom Hall of Jehovah's Witnesses, a landmark I'd spotted en route to Balmoor the previous evening, proved correct. With an unusual opening gambit, he asked, 'Sir, do you mind if I ask what makes you happy?'

'Football!' I instantly replied.

I'd have chatted longer, but the bus back to Aberdeen really was just leaving.

COVE RANGERS v DUNDEE

Scottish League Cup Group Stage
Wednesday, 17 July 2019

I THOUGHT Cove Bay might be a rather swish, exotic type of place you wouldn't necessarily associate with Aberdeen. And while Cove Rangers are currently the newest addition to the SPFL I've known I'd be coming here sooner or later, but somehow imagined my trip to the stadium would be altogether different. In my mind's eye I'd strolled along a tree-lined promenade where Tom Selleck lookalikes prepare cocktails on the decks of schooners the size of aircraft carriers. In either direction, legions of Farrah Fawcett clones with implausible white teeth and trousers would be pulled along on their skateboards by identical golden retrievers. They'd all halloo me with a 'hi, handsome' as they celebrated the arrival of their menstrual cycle in a manner they'd never have thought possible prior to the invention of the dry weave top sheet.

Reality was a little different. Following instructions to the letter, I got off the number three bus at the roundabout with a Burger King on the third exit. In drizzle so thick you could float a lump hammer on it, I found Balmoral Stadium behind a Royal Mail depot. With recce duly completed I went back to the centre of Aberdeen on the same bus that had brought me here. 'Folk never stop long,' said the driver.

Although Cove Rangers were always going to leave the Highland League behind them – they missed out on promotion in controversial circumstances in 2018 – the team they replaced came as something of a surprise. Although Berwick Rangers were awful when I saw them lose 7-1 to Queen's Park in February, they were 13 points clear of League Two's bottom club Albion Rovers at the time. Yet while the Wee Rovers bucked up considerably from this point, the Borderers continued to sink like a stone. In a classic case of the English being sent homeward to think again, Cove won both legs of their promotion-relegation play-off against Berwick to win 7-0 on aggregate.

For once, an almost ideal scenario cropped up in that I'd hoped to stay in the north-west for three consecutive nights. After games at Peterhead and Cove, however, Aberdeen didn't play at home in the Europa League but travelled to Finland instead. Taking the view that two out of three was reasonable, I opted to travel home on Thursday, work the weekend and come back the following Tuesday. If they got past their Finnish opponents Aberdeen would be at home in Europe a couple of nights later, but I'll get back to that.

You can never legislate for Scottish weather, of course, and I'm become quite stoical about that now. I simply pat myself on the back nowadays for packing for all eventualities. Knowing that I'll have already seen Aberdeen seafront look much better than it will today, I thought I might save myself the bother of staring at the slate-grey North Sea for a couple of hours and just relax until it was time to go back to the ground. I'd spent a lot of money on hotels in recent weeks without spending a great deal of time in any of them, so I thought I might buck that particular trend for an hour or three. I had a nice hot bath, watched smug people buying holiday homes on TV, read another 20 pages of the wonderful Kate Atkinson's latest tome, then had a couple of swift liveners in the bar. Although the Station Hotel was undergoing extensive renovation while I was there, I rather liked the place.

The short walk from the number three bus stop was much busier second time around, given that this was a big game for Cove Rangers; their first at home as a fully fledged SPFL club. The fixture against Dundee was both segregated and all-ticket and mine had been booked, delivered, and paid for a couple of weeks back.

Although it had more to do with the miserable weather than the place itself, I was underwhelmed by Balmoral. Cove had been compelled to move to a new stadium in 2015 if they wished to progress, given that their former home at Allan Park didn't meet SFA licensing criteria. I feel unkind saying so but looking around Balmoral did make me wonder what the minimum criterion for membership actually is. While the stadium boasted 306 seats as part of its 2,322 capacity, I'd be hard pressed to think of any ground I'd been to that had less cover against the elements. With 45 minutes remaining until kick-off, all seats and the limited amount of covered standing had long since been filled. There was nothing for it but to fret miserably in the kind of drizzle that takes its time to get into your clothing but stays there once it has.

Still on the high that promotion invariably brings, Rangers were out to prove they could mix it with Scotland's relatively big boys. Dundee, relegated from the Premiership at the end of what was a pretty rotten 2018/19 season, had seen plenty of comings and goings during the summer and were fielding what was very much a new look side tonight in front of travelling supporters who'd turned up in good numbers. Dundee had already signed nine new players and more seemed to be in the offing.

Although Dundee saw a lot more of the ball, it was difficult to escape the feeling that one or two were trying a little too hard to impress. If there were 30 places between the sides at the start of play it didn't show, as Cove held off their more illustrious visitors with a degree of comfort. Indeed, in a game of few chances it was the home side who came closest to winning it when Daniel Park's long-range effort went over via the top of the crossbar.

It finished 0-0.

I've often thought that if we really can't cope with a drawn game (though not being an American myself, I'm usually fine with one) we might look at reducing the teams to eight-a-side and playing an extra 15 minutes to find a winner. For now, an extra point would go to the winner of the usual penalty shoot-out.

If last night's events at Peterhead had resembled a training video as to how these things are done properly, matters at the Balmoral had a touch of the circus about them. Only five out of ten went in, with Paul McGowan slotting in the last of them to make it 3-2 in Dundee's favour. Although I'm sure Cove manager Paul Hartley wouldn't have allowed the fact to detract from a very good night's work, three of his side's penalties missed the target completely.

It was a long walk back to the city centre but I figured I'd give it a go. The weather had improved, the bus wouldn't be along for another 20 minutes, not all of us would get on it and at least the journey was all downhill. I was joined by Matt, a Nottingham Forest season ticket holder and young dad around half my age. Matt had an interesting take on why so many English groundhoppers – there were several at tonight's game in a crowd of 1,410 – tended to be wary of one another, 'I think we come in two kinds. Some can't bear a silence and a gap in conversation and always feel the need to fill it with whatever comes into their heads. The rest of us are sociable under our own terms but are happy with our own company, so we have to be careful who we talk to, particularly on a long train journey.'

Twenty-four hours later the final piece of the jigsaw of my next trip fell nicely into place when Aberdeen won in Finland to qualify for the next round of the Europa League, and they would be at home the following Thursday. Within a few minutes of the result I'd booked the same hotel, a train ticket up from Edinburgh and an onward one to Elgin where I'd watch another game on Friday night. I made non-refundable bookings and paid up front to ensure I got the best prices.

The following morning I found out that while I'd probably still see the game against Georgia's Chikhura Sachkhere I wouldn't need to shell out for a match ticket given that the clubs had agreed to switch the first leg of the tie to Tbilisi.

I was not best pleased!

ANNAN ATHLETIC v
GREENOCK MORTON

Scottish League Cup Group Stage
Tuesday, 23 July 2019

IF YOU'VE been paying attention you'll know that my last trip to Annan was spectacularly aborted. This time I thought I might try travelling by another route, sneak up on the place and take it by surprise.

For whatever reason the midday train from Euston to Glasgow had proved unusually and ridiculously expensive enough to almost rule out the trip altogether, before a rare moment of clarity resulted in my finding another option. The price of a single to Newcastle proved much more reasonable and, as I'd never travelled the line before, I figured I'd cut across to Carlisle from there.

Although I normally prefer to travel quietly and alone, I had pleasant company on the train from King's Cross in the diminutive form of a retired Indian doctor, returning home after spending a week with her daughter in the Smoke. It was a glance at the book I was reading that triggered off a two-hour conversation. She too was an Ian Rankin fan working her way through the *Inspector Rebus* series but didn't wish to know too much about this most recent novel, given that she was half a dozen books away from bringing herself up to date. Although I usually find myself doing all the talking, I was happy to sit back and listen to a lady who came to England as a young girl and became a doctor 'mostly because a teacher told me I didn't have what it took when I was 18. She was the first person I showed my diploma to after I'd qualified'.

I would think I'm not alone in thinking of myself as reasonably multicultural, yet seldom spend any length of time talking to people about the culture they come from. Anjum was a Hindu who described herself as 'practising, but not to the extent that I've become particularly good at it' and had an interesting take on the topic that was neatly dividing our nation in half. She told me, 'I'm just about a Remainer, but I have seen the damage that can be done to a community that has a surplus of cheap labour and a shortage of housing and the way these problems lead to people being treated shabbily.' She added, 'Population growth across the world is something that the generation following you and I are really going to have to take seriously, as the planet can only produce so much.'

It was only after she'd toddled off to the taxi rank that I noticed how tiny Anjum was. Barely 4ft 6in in her socks, I'd wager, but not the type of girl you'd want to take on in a fair fight. While I tend not to seek out conversation and company on a long train journey, I'd enjoyed hers enormously.

I'd looked forward to travelling on the Tyne Valley Line. Friends from the north-east had told me it was probably the most scenic railway in the country and that the 60-mile journey to Carlisle would pass in no time at all. Although what I saw of it was spectacularly cinematic, I found myself overwhelmed by a terrible sadness and in something of a world of my own after we'd stopped at Prudhoe.

One of my best friends was from Prudhoe, a lad called Davie Bell, who loved his football and added a certain *je ne sais quoi* to every away trip with the mighty Dover Athletic. A fun guy to be around, Davie had an unknown side that few knew about and he decided to resolve his problems by taking his own life in 2013. I was just one of many who was devastated by the news and continue to think of him fondly on an almost daily basis. Contradiction though it may be, I came to terms with a dreadful sense of loss by realising I wouldn't come to terms with it and tried to move on.

I'd got to the stage where I thought I might have a little blub, proving Davie's point that I was just a soft, shandy-drinking, southern nancy boy, when a memory popped into my head. It was of Davie, after a UEFA under-21 game in Helsingborg, drunkenly explaining to an equally drunk and bewildered Belorussian that you could tell the difference between an elk and a moose by asking it trick questions. You had to be there, I guess, but I laughed out loud, startling an old boy dozing in an adjacent seat, and started to cheer up from that point. Within an hour I'd arrived in Annan feeling just fine and dandy.

By dint of asking a youngster familiar with Google Maps, I found my hotel within about five minutes, it being a straight walk from the station. The Old Rectory, rather cleverly named due to the fact that the building was once an old rectory, was a nicely appointed guest house run by an English couple called David and Tara.

I don't know if this is just my experience, but an English couple wandering around Scotland, deciding they like the place and opening a guest house seems to be a more commonplace course of action than you might think. In my circle of friends alone three couples have done so and haven't looked back, with all six claiming it was the best thing they ever did. I haven't got around to visiting to any of them yet – mostly due to their establishments' distance from a football ground – but intend to rectify this oversight as soon as I can. As for now, the room was fine and very reasonably priced and, after a shower and a coffee, I set out to find the stadium.

I walked to the ground with George, a local lad a year or seven junior to myself, who was 'loving every minute' of a retirement based on a substantial pension following 40-years in the same well-paid job. George didn't tell me what that job was, but I assumed it was something to do with successfully forecasting events. I surmised this due to the fact that, while I'd not uttered a word in requesting directions, he somehow made the spot-on assumption that I was a gormless elderly football fan on his way to a game despite heading in the wrong direction. 'Follow me, old son. I'm going that way myself,' he said cheerily. Ten minutes of enjoyable chat later he deposited me underneath a big yellow sign marked 'Galabank Stadium' and trusted me not to lose my way from here.

Although Galabank had the stamp of new-build non-league about it, I don't mean that in any derogatory sense. Breezily decorated in the same bright yellow as the club shirt, the stadium is a three-sided affair with uncovered standing at one end, covered standing at the other and 500 seats in the main stand that ran from one 18-yard line to the other. As another of Scotland's smaller clubs who saw the commercial benefit of having one to rent to the local community, Annan's playing surface was a plastic one.

While you'd have needed a shoehorn to fill the ground to its 2,500 capacity there was plenty of room for tonight's crowd of 478, a fair percentage of whom had made the trip from Greenock. Some 0.6276 per cent of the crowd came from Dover, however, and it rather goes without saying these days that I can't spend a few days in Scotland without bumping into somebody I know.

As they 'just happened to be passing' when I bumped into them at Arbroath v Ross County almost a year ago to the day, my fellow Dover ultra Mick Palmer and his good lady wife do not need further introduction. As their Scottish holiday location was a short drive from Annan, I was able to enjoy their company again as the game got under way.

George had earlier expressed the opinion that Annan might find the going a bit tough at the start of this season. He reasoned that most clubs suffered a hangover of sorts following a play-off defeat – Clyde were promoted from League Two after beating Annan in the final – and figured his team might look a bit jaded for a while. George's views were spot on tonight.

The previous Friday, I'd spent half an hour watching Morton getting battered by group favourites Motherwell on BT Sport and figured tonight's game might be a tight one. In the event it was the most one-sided game I'd seen since watching Dundee beat Forfar 7-0 a while back. It took Morton just seven minutes to take the lead. A long throw was flicked on and Aiden Nesbit, looking to kick-start his career after being released by Dundee United, took one touch to control and another to smack in a sweetly struck half volley.

By the end of a first half they completely controlled, Morton added a couple more. First, Reece Lyon ran half the length of the field before rolling the ball across the 18-yard line for Nicky Cadden to fire home. A couple of minutes before the break, Cadden banged another sweetly struck effort into the far corner.

If Annan mounted a revival of sorts, in which they created and spurned a couple of half chances, this proved merely a five-minute break from being completely under the cosh against a team who knew that a comprehensive win would put them right back in the frame for a place in the last 16. Though some poor finishing, desperate defending, the woodwork, and a couple of smart saves from Annan keeper Lyle Avci kept the score down, Morton added two more goals in the last ten minutes.

First, Nesbit cut in from the left unhindered by a challenge and nonchalantly rolled in his second of the game. In the final minute of the 90 substitute Robbie Muirhead, light on his toes for a big lad, carried the ball from inside his own half prior to netting from 20 yards. Annan, lucky to get nought as the saying goes, were mightily relieved to hear the final whistle a few seconds later.

With all day to get to Edinburgh for my next game, I figured I'd just leave my bag at the B&B and, with no particular agenda, have a wander around Annan prior to getting a midday train back to Carlisle and my onward connection. On a bright morning, albeit with one or two flecks of rain in the air, I followed the route towards the town's high street and took a turning on to a stone road bridge and over the River Annan. In the water meadows below I found just what I was looking for before the carnage of Edinburgh gearing itself up for the festival; a little peace, tranquillity, and colour in a Scottish countryside I'd spent nowhere near enough time walking around in.

As a means to avoiding a herd of cattle, most notably a couple of hefty bulls walking slowly towards me with a 'do you want some, pal?' look in their dull, dead eyes, I took a detour around a clump of gorse bushes close to the river's edge, duly disturbing a heron the size of a Lancaster bomber. Although he raised his wings briefly and thought about flying off, he gave me a cursory glance in the manner of a matchday steward deciding whether it was worth the time and effort to search the bag of a harmless old man. Knowing he had the insurance of a beak as long and sharp as a Samurai sword, he gave me the benefit of the doubt and let me pass within a couple of yards of him.

After bounding over a couple of stiles with no little athleticism, I found myself on a riverside path and in the company of a lass who was the spitting image of USA World

Cup winning footballer Megan Rapinoe, and her two lunatic canines. The dogs, a black Labrador and Springer Spaniel, jumped in and out of the river in a manner that suggested that, if the activity gave one more iota of pleasure, they might both spontaneously combust. A mile or two away from the nearest other human at this point, 'Megan' possibly dismissed the idea I might be an axe murderer as we walked and chatted for 20 minutes in the manner dog lovers do. Reaching a bridge that would take me somewhat reluctantly back towards the town, I wished Megan a happy life and headed back to the B&B.

Annan was waking itself up by this time but seemed in no rush to do so. After exchanging pleasantries with a few more dog walkers, I had a coffee outside a high street cafe and watched folk sedately going about their business.

Within an hour I was on the boneshaker back to Carlisle and would be heading further and further north over the next three days.

HEART OF MIDLOTHIAN v STENHOUSEMUIR

Scottish League Cup Group Stage
Wednesday, 24 July 2019

IN JUNE, I went to Italy for the UEFA Under-21 Championship. I had a fabulous time with old friends and made some new ones while I was there. It didn't go well for England, however, who started the competition as favourites.

In their first game against France in Cesena, they led with a sublime Phil Foden goal. They rode their luck as France missed two penalties – the second of which was awarded for a foul that saw Hamza Choudhury sent off – and were still ahead as the game entered the final minute of normal time. Somehow England contrived to lose as Manchester United's £50m signing Aaron Wan-Bissaka scored a comedy own goal with the last kick of the game.

The following morning, I was at Cesena railway station en route to Bologna when my attention was attracted by a couple of Hearts shirts containing a couple of fans with similar miles on the clock to myself. Naturally, I engaged them in conversation.

'That must have been a cracking game last night for a neutral,' I said.

'Whatever makes you think we were neutrals, pal?' replied the shorter or the two.

I mention all this for a couple of reasons. Firstly, having travelled the length and breadth of Scotland, I had to travel all the way to Emilia Romagna to hear a Scotsman make a derogatory remark about the English. Secondly, if these lads had told me they wanted England to win, I wouldn't have trusted them any further than I could have thrown them and certainly wouldn't have enjoyed their company all the way to Bologna.

Although I didn't really think about it at the time, I guess I was hoping I might bump into them tonight as I was breaking my journey up to Aberdeen and beyond. In the meantime I fancied a beer or two and a game.

I started off in the Oxford Bar, a place of modern legend thanks to the *Rebus* novels of Ian Rankin, just a short walk from the bustle of Princes Street. Rankin is a customer himself but didn't pop in during the half an hour I was there. A little nearer to Tynecastle, Ryries, a listed building said to be largely unchanged since Edwardian times, was equally sociable and cosmopolitan, where an old boy sang and played old American blues standards in the corner, seemingly in exchange for having his pewter tankard constantly refilled.

I hadn't expected much from tonight's game other than a one-sided affair that Hearts would win comfortably in front of a crowd of diehards who lacked the wherewithal to stay away. In the event cheap tickets attracted a crowd of over 7,000, most of whom were housed in a packed main stand.

As the game got under way I soon got the impression from those around me that the natives hadn't been happy with the football Hearts were playing under manager and club legend Craig Levein, with many holding the view that he does his best work behind the scenes and upstairs. I saw their point as Hearts turned in a rotten performance against part-time League Two opponents in a first half that finished goalless.

Essentially, Stenhousemuir were comfortably holding Hearts by virtue of defending deep, rolling their sleeves up and keeping their shape. Although they seldom ventured beyond the halfway line, they took the lead with ten minutes remaining much to the joyous disbelief of their 100 or so fans in the upper stand behind the goal they were attacking. A good goal it was too as Alan Cook found some space on the left before supplying a perfect cross for Mark McGuigan to get in front of two defenders and prod the ball over the line.

This was the point when I saw Scottish fans at their most volatile and abuse got a wee bit ugly for a while, as 'find some other daft fucker to pay your wages' was a widely expressed opinion. Irrespective of how poorly Hearts were playing, I didn't see the need for desperation just yet. With ten minutes plus stoppages still to play Stenhousemuir's players looked dead on their feet, having put so much into the game.

While Hearts' goals came from an unlikely source, they turned the game around in the closing stages. Centre-back Craig Halkett, a summer signing from Livingston, scored twice in seven minutes to give his club a win they barely deserved. At the end it was Stenhousemuir who were applauded by the home support – even former Hibs youngster Graeme Smith who'd had a quite brilliant game in goal.

More than satisfied with my evening's entertainment, I began the long walk to the cold comfort of a bleak room in a hostel I'd no intention of staying in again, given that the tight buggers didn't even give me a towel.

Hearts got better in the competition and made it as far as the semi-finals. Four days after sacking Craig Levein, they went down 3-0 to Rangers at Hampden. See if you can guess who won the other semi-final.

CHIKHURA SACHKHERE
v ABERDEEN

Europa League Second Qualifying Round First Leg
Thursday, 25 July 2019

GIVEN THAT you've read thus far, you won't need telling that I'm no stranger to pointless journeys and the amounts of time, energy, and cash they invariably chuck away. Abortive trips to Annan and Stirling you know about. I simply don't have the time or space to go over similar experiences in Santiago, Montevideo, Rijeka, Split, Newport and Swansea to name just a few abortive outings I'd just as soon forget about. In some cases problems were of my own making and might have been avoided with a little more research. However, booking to go to Aberdeen for a game that actually took place over 3,000 miles away was largely unavoidable.

Having thoroughly enjoyed my previous visit to Pittodrie for a European occasion, it made sense to stop off and pay another on my way to a Friday night fixture in Elgin. I'd been sensibly cautious for once, deciding not to book a train ticket or a hotel until I knew for certain that Aberdeen had made it through to the second qualifying round. Having beaten Rovaniemen Palloseura 2-1 in the first leg I knew they still had plenty to do in the return. After winning by the same score in Finland I knew that Aberdeen had secured another winnable looking tie against Georgian opposition. Within ten minutes of the results confirmation I made non-refundable arrangements then went to bed.

It was only while chatting on a Facebook page the following day that I suspected something might have gone horribly wrong when a Dons fan expressed admiration for my speed of thought and actions in booking such an intrepid adventure at such short notice. When the fellow asked how much my flight to Tbilisi cost, I found out what had actually occurred. Long story short, two Georgian clubs who share the same stadium had both qualified for the next round, causing the necessity for one of them to switch the home leg of their tie. Thus, the story of my life continues to dictate that given a choice from two, I'll pick the wrong one.

For once my feelings of exasperation didn't last too long, safe in the knowledge that a night out in Aberdeen would break my journey north rather nicely. Having spotted the place from a coach window on the way back from Peterhead, I decided where I'd watch match on TV: the Pittodrie Arms in King Street, not far from the stadium.

You know how watching a game in a pub works, I'll wager. I strolled in, got a pint, and told everyone about my predicament, a tale that invoked amusement and sympathy in just about equal measure. Suffice to say that the locals were good people, and I enjoyed their company a lot more than a game that was actually pretty rotten. Both sides were awarded a dodgy penalty and scored from the spot, then played out an uninspiring 1-1 draw in a huge stadium that seemed to contain about 25 people. Typically enough, the home leg I should have watched finished 5-0 in Aberdeen's favour. They missed out on the group stages again, however, losing both legs to the aforementioned Rijeka.

Meanwhile, back at the Station Hotel, I was in a relaxed frame of mind – as relaxed as a newt, in fact – and chose not to reflect on the fact that I'd lost 90-odd quid's worth of train tickets that would get me to Elgin and home again via Larbert, Edinburgh and London.

Some things are just best left until the morning.

ELGIN CITY v HIBERNIAN

Scottish League Cup Group Stage
Friday 26 July 2019

ENGINEERING WORKS, not to mention a thick head from the previous night's excesses in the Pittodrie Bar, dictated that today might be a long one. Shelling out another £90 at Aberdeen travel centre for tickets to get myself home did little to improve my mood. A train to Dyce, a bus to Huntley and another train to Elgin with lengthy gaps in between meant that I wouldn't have much time in Elgin and wouldn't arrive until mid-afternoon. No matter, as a good book and a gawp at parts of Scotland I've yet to see made light of the most arduous of journeys. Getting out of Aberdeen and the area around the airport proved the most time-consuming, but an hour in a cafe at Dyce and catching up with last night's results from Europe soon passed and the bus and the trip up to Huntley departed packed and bang on schedule.

After leaving Huntley's tiny yet immaculate railway station, we fairly zipped through a part of the world that would make an ideal location should the Highland League, if they haven't already, ever decide to hold a groundhoppers' weekend, given that just about every stop boasted a team that played in it. I was pondering how many of the Forres Mechanics team are actually mechanics when we pulled into Elgin and I spotted my digs, the Laichmoray Hotel, from the station exit.

Although I liked the Laichmoray – and I should stress that the staff were efficient, polite, and overwhelmingly friendly – I think I might make a point of avoiding hotels that cater for wedding parties in future, given that everyone who turns up to them seems to be dressed up to the nines. Naturally, when I pitched up in scuffed trainers, shorts and one of my interesting collection of every-stain-tells-a-story T-shirts, I tend to turn a few heads and just as many stomachs. Also, when anyone sells anything that comprises the word 'wedding' it seems to be accepted custom and practice to jack the price up by a few quid. Comfortable and accommodating as it was, what the Laichmoray had to offer was wasted on a scruff like me so I dumped my bag and used what was left of the afternoon to see what Elgin is about.

I've long since given up judging a place on what I get to see in a couple of hours but didn't see a great deal to make me think I'd slipped up by just booking a one-night stay. I toyed with the idea of taking a look at Elgin Cathedral but, given that the place was just a shell that nobody had considered doing up over the course of the last few centuries, I figured I'd just content myself with a stroll into the city centre on what was becoming a blisteringly hot afternoon. If I'm honest, I wish I hadn't bothered. An absolutely average scampi and chips in a greasy spoon later, there was nothing for it but to get showered, get naked and enjoy a snooze in the tiny but air-conditioned room I'd shelled out a tidy few quid for.

On what was surely the hottest day of the year so far, I didn't move a great deal before showering again and setting off for the ground as soon as the early evening heat had become a little less brutal and headache inducing. Following some fairly straightforward instructions, I ambled along a gentle slope uphill from the railway station and immediately saw a different side to Elgin, with its neat and substantial semi-detached housing and array of corporate conference facilities that suggested that the city was a renowned centre for something or other. Conferences, probably.

Coming over the brow of the hill I put the instructions in a bin, safe in the knowledge that I wouldn't need them, but could enjoy the rare treat of following fans en route to a stadium.

Entering with a ticket I'd bought a couple of weeks previously, I was instantly impressed with a fine stadium that the purist would struggle not to love. Although Borough Briggs had just grass banks and some hard standing behind either goal, a splendid, if antiquated and a bit of a rusty covered terrace ran the full length of one touchline, while seating could be found on the smaller main stand on the other side of the pitch. As I fell into conversation with a couple of old boys who'd been fans here for years, one of them told me, 'They used to play the Highland League Cup finals here and the place would be absolutely rammed. Even though those days are long gone, nights like these are probably as near as we'll get to them again.'

Although Elgin are one of the better supported clubs in Scottish League Two – usually attracting crowds around the 600 mark – tonight's game against one of the country's leading lights had been made all-ticket. While the attendance fell some way short of the ground's 3,927 capacity it was over three times the average, it seemed as near to a full house as made no difference.

Hibernian, well supported by those who'd made the long trip up from Edinburgh, put out a strong side, fielding a number of players I'd watched before, mixed with one or two summer signings. In what ultimately proved to be a routine win for Hibs, it was one of the latter, a lad from Tamworth called Joe Newell, who put them ahead inside the first ten minutes. The goal resulted in equal measure from some downright shoddy defending and some first-class officiating from referee Willie Collum. Expecting a fairly clear-cut foul to be awarded against them, Elgin's back line pulled up briefly while Collum waited a split second to see if an advantage might develop. As Hibs played to the whistle, Daryl Horgan got behind Elgin's left flank to square the ball across the six-yard box for Newell to slide in and convert.

If Elgin were outplayed from start to finish, there was still just a single goal separating the sides after an hour's play. It was around this point, however, that Elgin handed Hibs the tie with a big green bow wrapped around it.

With a back-pass that was both lazy and careless, Elgin winger Rabin Omar simply provided Hibs with a perfect ball that sent Swiss striker Florian Kamberi clear through on goal. Though Kamberi can often look like a player who fits snugly into the class-act-who-can't-be-arsed category, he made light work of beating keeper Thomas McHale. That was that in terms of a contest that Elgin emerged with a great deal of credit from.

As the crowd trundled out expressing the view that they'd had their money's worth, nobody seemed to mind that the heavens had opened, soaking everyone but clearing the muggy and oppressive Highland air. It didn't dampen the spirits of the wedding guests at the hotel, however, who kept me awake until about one o'clock in the morning. Tolerant and romantically inclined to the last, I took the view that you only get married two or three times in a lifetime and found an old film to watch until they went to bed.

STENHOUSEMUIR v COWDENBEATH

Scottish League Cup Group Stage
Saturday, 27 July 2019

TODAY DID not begin well, as I opened a text I hadn't noticed last night. It came from my daughter who told me that my tickets from Larbert back to Dover had turned up where I knew I'd left them on the living room table. Only this morning did it suddenly dawn on me that I'd known about the problem for a full three days. Had I alerted my daughter to the problem, no doubt she could have posted them to my hotel in Larbert. Morosely, I did a mental calculation as to how many hours I'd need to work washing pots in the summer job to recover the cost.

After rising at six o'clock and necking a fulsome breakfast, I caught a train from Elgin that zipped me pretty efficiently through the Highland League towns of Nairn and Forres into Inverness in good time for my 7.55am connection to the south of the country. I'd expected to be travelling on a quiet and virtually empty train, which is exactly how things panned out for around five minutes.

What I'd completely forgotten was that today was the first day of the school summer holidays and the train was absolutely rammed. As we left I applauded Scotrail's policy of prohibiting the sale of alcohol at a time of day when the more docile among us wish to slip gently into the day with a newspaper and a hot beverage. The flaw in this plan was that a good proportion of today's customers didn't need more alcohol, given that they'd come directly from clubs that kicked out a couple of hours ago.

Initially I took the view that this was something I could put up with for a while. I couldn't be too po-faced, given that my tendency towards acute oafishness was quite advanced through my teens to mid-20s. I lost a little patience when a gang of Ibiza-bound hairdressers decided that what the world and I needed to make it a brighter and better place was to listen to Whigfield's 'Saturday Night' on continuous loop and 'have a wee dance'. Not for the first time, I had cause to reflect on the indisputable fact that people with a taste for the world's worst music are always keen to share it. Knowing that this particular song could penetrate even the thickest of earplugs and stay inside my pointy little head all day, I opted to move. In fact I played musical chairs throughout most of the journey until I changed trains at Stirling.

Having needed to stay out of the heat in Elgin yesterday I'd come south into what must have been the foulest weather I'd encountered in Scotland since I started this project, with rain now coming down in proverbial stair rods. At Larbert, just a single stop away from Stirling, it's maybe 200 paces from the station to the Station Hotel, but I still got soaked to the skin by the time I made it to reception bang on midday.

With an hour to kill and time to luxuriate in a hot bath, the thought occurred that today's game could well be postponed. There was no escaping the fact that I was feeling thoroughly miserable and wishing I was somewhere, anywhere, else. Although the thoughts soon passed, I began to see the attraction of watching football in a pub all afternoon, calling myself a 'passionate fan' and regurgitating the opinions I'd just heard on Sky TV while passing them off as my own.

Other than that Ochilview is a straight 20-minute walk away from the station, I couldn't tell you much about Larbert given that I strolled briskly and with my head down as protection against the elements, while reflecting that my rainproof jacket was nothing of the bloody sort. Spotting some floodlights behind a rather appealing cake and coffee shop, I hung a sharp left and found a stadium and a couple of gentlemen clad in orange vests, from whom I expected to hear that the game had been called off and that I might try my luck again in January when the weather had bucked up a bit. Instead one confirmed that, due to the installation of a 3G pitch, postponements were a thing of the past. He suggested, 'You might like to get yourself out of the rain, son,' as he pointed out a door leading into a football Nirvana.

After the club's receptionist confirmed that not only was I allowed into Stenhousemuir's social club but would viewed as a very welcome guest, I squelched into what is the smallest clubhouse I'd ever set foot in. What it lacked in size it made up for by giving off the feel of a much-loved relative's living room in which family would gather. If Stenny's social club was a bit like your nan's living room, you certainly knew you were in a football stadium. Indeed, I felt a slight pang of guilt in that I seemed to be the only visiting fan who'd turned up without a gift to hang up, given that just about every square inch of wall space was covered with flags and pennants from all over Britain and Europe. Once again, the old don't-let-them-hear-your-accent advice proved outdated and utter tosh as the home fans couldn't have been more welcoming once I'd told them where I was from and what I was doing, particularly after I mentioned how I'd witnessed their club's moral victory at Tynecastle a few nights previously. 'In these parts, that makes you pretty much a regular,' said one old lad prior to giving me an impromptu tour of the main stand from which we'd all be watching the game.

The main thing that struck me about Stenny fans, even following a relegation season, was their boundless enthusiasm and optimism, not necessarily for a successful campaign, but one that would provide plenty of days out and anecdotes that go with them. Although Stenhousemuir and Cowdenbeath would meet again four times in League Two this season, today's game was about who would finish bottom of a cup qualifying group that also contained Hearts, Dundee, and East Fife. In truth it had the look of a wooden spoon scrap since the day the draw was made. Under the circumstances, full credit goes to both clubs for putting on a show rather than going through the motions of the pre-season kickabout the game effectively was.

Any preconceived ideas I might have had about this not being a competitive fixture were dispelled inside the first five minutes, after Stenny keeper Graeme Smith and Cowdenbeath captain David Cox were booked for asking one another if they fancied what is known in these parts as 'a square go'. Three minutes earlier, the visitors had been unfortunate not to take the lead after Jordan Allan's long-range shot came back off the crossbar.

If Cowdenbeath were the better side in the first half an hour then Stenhousemuir perked up a bit to take the lead as Mark McGuigan joined that select band of Scottish footballers I'd watching scoring in different games, finishing confidently with his left foot after Alan Cook had set him up.

While the second half was largely a tale of niggly fouls and a few more yellow cards, the game was still entertaining enough and Stenny made sure of winning it with a second goal five minutes from the end. It came as Cook won back possession, went clear down the left flank, and knocked a perfect ball low across the face of the six-yard box. McGuigan would surely have tapped in his third of the week if Jamie

Todd hadn't got in front of him to turn the cross into his own net.

With no plans for the evening beyond a reasonably early night, I returned to the clubhouse for a final pint and a chat with fans now even more confident of a swift return to League One. Stenhousemuir would need more supporters from somewhere though as the majority in a crowd of just 262 were my age or thereabouts and would need to be replaced once they'd slipped off the perch. That might be a problem given that I was told, 'We just provide affordable housing for people who work in Glasgow nowadays and most of them haven't got a clue that we're here.' Although there aren't too many to spread the word, I can only hope Stenhousemuir FC can persuade a few punters that they're a club with so much to offer.

I rounded off the evening sitting on a concrete bench outside Farmfoods, eating a fish supper with just a few seagulls and a couple of Aberdeen Angus (I think!) bronze statues for company. Scenic Scotland it wasn't, but it suited my mood. Thanks to a decent game, some good old-fashioned hospitality, and a change in the weather it was a good mood.

INVERNESS CALEDONIAN THISTLE v GREENOCK MORTON

Scottish Championship
Friday, 30 August 2019

I DIDN'T quite have the same good fortune on the Caledonian Sleeper out of Euston this time. For whatever reason I could only book a seat rather than a cabin online, even though I'd have been happy to push the boat out and treat myself before I went back to work on Monday. I found my seat on the 9.15pm service in a carriage in which the aircon didn't seem to be working on an uncomfortably warm night. After five minutes of sweating profusely, I tracked down the train manager and tried to upgrade myself to a cabin. I come from a town in which just about anything can be accomplished for a drink, so I'm sure Scotrail will be thrilled to bits to hear that their onboard staff are immune to the type of innuendo that is about a millimetre away from being attempted bribery. Although I'd happily have paid £100 in cash to repeat the great experience of my last trip to the Highlands, the going rate, during the legalised robbery period known as the school summer holidays, was £220. Thus, five blue notes stayed in my wallet and a cabin stayed empty and went to waste.

Matters improved to the extent that the aircon bucked its ideas up just north of Watford and the seat next to me remained vacant all the way to Inverness. So while I was aware of every station we stopped at en route, I'd guess that

I managed six or seven hours of sleep during an 11-hour journey. Whichever way you looked at it, I got damn good value for just shy of £40 and arrived, bang on time at 8.40am.

After re-mortgaging the house as a means to buying a coffee and bun in the Costa on the station concourse, I made plans for the day and fell back on the time-honoured excursion of finding my hotel and ICT's ground before drink was taken. Having had the foresight to bring an umbrella, I got underneath it and through the pouring rain to find the hotel in double-quick time (it transpired that its proximity, within five minutes' walk of the station, was the only good thing about it, but I'll get you back to that). While the walk to the stadium took a lot longer it proved a pretty straightforward if uninspiring trip, and at least the rain had let up.

As I strolled along the main drag out of town, most likely in the direction of Aberdeen, the first thing that struck me was that Inverness must be a city in which at least some of the population aren't short of a few bob. Although my hopes of owing a half-decent car have been postponed until the next life, BMWs and the like seemed readily available to drive off a variety of forecourts if you had about 40 grand in your back pocket.

In about half an hour I came within sight of a set of floodlights and a busy roundabout with various options to pick the wrong exit. After a magical mystery tour involving a lane made impenetrable by blackberry bushes, a recycling plant, a travellers' camp, and a council office, I found myself taking the correct route via the Kessock Bridge.

Having watched Inverness on TV once or twice, I knew that the Caledonian Stadium backed on to a body of water or another so I found myself strolling along the banks of the Beauly Firth, an inlet of the Moray Firth.

Although my perambulations had taken a more scenic turn, the waters in these parts are disappointingly short of monsters so I took myself to the club's reception where I was greeted by a charming lady of some 40-ish summers who I would certainly have taken a shine to when I was alive. With a match ticket and a lapel badge in my pocket, I returned from whence I came wondering how to spend my time before kick-off.

The fact that I couldn't enter my hotel until four o'clock made life a little more difficult, as did the downpours that were periodic but constant and heavy. After putting my case into left luggage, an early dinner passed a little time before a cunning plan suggested itself as to how I might entertain myself before the day brightened up as I was assured it would. I'd already made plans to see the new Tarantino film when I got home, so simply brought that forward when I discovered it would be screened shortly at the Eden Court Theatre, a short walk away on the banks of the River Ness.

Although it seemed like a few people had the same idea, I was confused as to why so many had turned up in kilts and full national costume. I found out when my request for an old git ticket was refused on the grounds that 'this afternoon's screenings have all been cancelled because of the pipers'. I didn't seek further clarification, safe in the knowledge that these were words I'd never hear in a cinema again. However, given that a good number of the kilt-clad pipers were women, I did briefly wonder if the same underwear rules applied *vis-à-vis* traditional Highland costume, but I thought it best not to ask.

Although viable options were disappearing at a rate of knots, the weather had brightened up even though this state of affairs seemed likely to be temporary. Taking one of my better decisions, I opted to stroll along the riverbank and see where it took me if I just kept going for an hour. Instantly I found myself in my natural habitat, drinking in the scenery and birdsong and exchanging pleasantries with dogs and their owners. Not for the first time, I thought I'd treat my Scottish adventure very differently if I could start again from scratch and walk about in the open a lot more. I turned myself around via the Ness Islands, linked by a couple of ornate 19th-century suspension bridges, and walked along the opposite bank in the direction of the castle which was barely 200 yards from my lodgings for the night.

The less said about my hotel the better, as it was one of those ghastly places that's effectively a hostel charging hotel prices. I had a cold shower in the only bathroom that was available on two floors, made a coffee with the two nasty little plastic milk pots I'd generously been given for my £55 and reflected on the fact that I'd have been better off sharing a dormitory for £15 in one of the numerous hostels down the road. Rather than spend more time in such a cheerless place, I uttered a heartfelt 'bugger this' and set off for a match that would be kicking off early at 7.05pm for the benefit of BBC Scotland and its viewers.

Arriving about 15 minutes before kick-off I got comfortable in the main stand, close to the touchline and almost within touching distance of the dugouts. Although I'd expected the stadium to be larger, an all-seater three-sided ground with a capacity just shy of 8,000 seemed more than adequate for the club's needs. With both sets of supporters housed in the main stand and a few more behind one goal, the crowd seemed larger than the declared gate of 2,136.

I hadn't expected any Morton fans at all to make what must have been the most awkward away trip of the season; travelling through Friday night rush-hour traffic as part of a near 400-mile round trip that would have involved at least an afternoon off work for most. A good 40-odd had made the effort, however, rather than save themselves a few quid and watch from their armchairs. I thought I recognised one or two from their recent trip to Annan and chatting to them proved me right. Essentially, though they had cause to question the sanity of their actions on occasion, this was a kudos trip to talk about at the next home game while scoffing at the commitment of perceived part-timers as they did so.

When the game kicked off I had the good fortune to find myself sitting next to Joe. Dressed for an Arctic expedition rather than a summer evening in the Highlands, Joe could add ten years to my 64 but he looked bloody well on it. Originally an Inverness Thistle fan, Joe had opposed a merger with local rivals Caledonian that had resulted in a newly formed club being admitted to the Scottish Third Division in 1994. After agonising as to how he would spend his Saturdays, Joe eventually settled on a compromise that struck me as a good one. Rather than pine for Highland League fixtures he'd watched since before he started primary school, Joe opted to watch Clachnacuddin and to bite the bullet and see how things went at the new club. He ended up with a season ticket at both and if ICT's history is a short one, it remains fairly illustrious, with the highlight being the Scottish Cup Final win over Falkirk in 2015. 'The best day of my life, but best not tell the family that, eh son,' said Joe. Essentially, if blokes in the next seat were put up for retail sale, Joe is the one Harrods would sell you.

If ICT had been a bit sluggish and leaden-footed when I saw them at Peterhead a few weeks back, they had a lot more zip about them today. Morton, with manager David Hopkin appointed to bring the same success he had at Livingston, were just as keen to show what they had to offer as the game developed into an entertaining end-to-end affair. If it was anyone's game as half-time approached, the pattern of the match changed dramatically after ICT took the lead. Morton keeper Daniel Rogers might have done better than to parry a well-struck shot from Aaron Doran. Yet while the stopper might argue that half a dozen defenders were on hand to help him out, none reacted as quickly as James Keatings who knocked the ball over the line.

Although I gathered that Keatings had endured his share of problems in recent times, his smile was as wide as the Moray Firth after he scored his second goal a minute after the break. It came as Jamie McCart's long ball found Tom Walsh, with his back to goal on the 18-yard line. Walsh cleverly rolled a defender and left the ball for Keatings to control with his left foot and drive firmly into the corner with his right.

Hopkin blew a gasket in front of us, said something rude that the pitchside microphone probably picked up and his team were soundly battered from this point.

ICT's third goal came courtesy of one of those lovely, languid footballers who make the game look so effortless and easy. Englishman James Vincent, who'd impressed me before in a Dundee shirt, played a perfect angled ball that caught Morton's back line square, leaving Jordan White to go clear and roll his shot under Rogers.

If Morton hadn't already got the idea that it wasn't going to be their night, it was confirmed a few minutes later when they were awarded a penalty for a handling offence against David Carson that looked harsh in the extreme. It didn't matter in the general scheme of things, as Nicky Cadden's penalty was more pancake than Panenka, allowing Rogers to make a comfortable one-handed save.

Moments later it was 4-0 when Coll Donaldson headed in a Keatings corner before Bulgarian Nikolay Todorov, played onside by a defender who appeared to have nodded off, completed the scoring within a minute of coming on as substitute.

If the sunset resembled a furious Hopkin's complexion in glorious shades of pinks and purples, the black clouds soon returned as Joe and I wished each other well and said our goodbyes.

In a subsequent downpour, I got completely drenched before getting as comfortable as possible in the lower bunk of my wonky bunk bed, grateful that I'd only booked for one night and would be leaving in the morning.

FORFAR ATHLETIC v CLYDE

Scottish League One
Saturday, 31 August 2019

I'D ALWAYS planned to visit Perth again, but this really wasn't what I had in mind. I had just enough time to take a ten-minute walk away from the station concourse, grab a coffee, then catch my onward connection to Dundee. When I got there, I barely recognised the modernised station with its highly polished plate glass and stainless steel. Down by the Tay at least, the city had changed so much since my first visit not so very long ago. On a travel show recently I'd heard the place described as 'up and coming', which essentially means that poor folk won't be able to afford to live here anymore. With four hours to kill until kick-off at Forfar, I strolled along familiar streets with the air of somebody who knew where he was going.

Rather than sod about with 'cheap and cheerful' and running the risks that entails, I'd booked myself into a hotel priced well beyond my usual budget and found it within 15 minutes. Although the Best Western Queen's Hotel afforded a relative opulence that was wasted on me, it did at least offer a 24-hour reception at which to dump my bag and bugger off to the football. While I'd allowed myself a ridiculous amount of time to travel the 16 miles to Forfar, I managed to find Seagate bus station and the appropriate bus soon after.

Back on a Scottish bus and in the land of headscarves, impenetrable accents, and Saturday morning purchases – one of which was a house plant the size of a small giraffe – I settled into the warm fug and detachment that only a trip to the uncharted terrain of a new stadium can bring, as another Scottish town contrived once again to welcome me with all four seasons in the space of a few hours.

I found Station Park easily enough after getting off the bus at Barclays, prior to hanging a sharp left and walking in a straight line for 20 minutes. It would have been ten minutes had it not been for a short, sharp downpour of horizontal rain and gale force winds rendering my umbrella fit for nothing other than the nearest bin. It was a cheap one, but even so. With my destination found with a maximum of fuss and effort I found myself sitting on a bench just ten minutes later, eating chips and if not exactly basking, then certainly drying out in the late-summer sunshine. In essence, the perfect day to find a decent pub and stay there until a few minutes before kick-off.

On the corner of the road leading up to Station Park, I found just what I was looking for: decent beer, a live game on BT Sport and 30 to 40 Clyde fans enjoying themselves while always staying on the right side of boisterous. All in all, a regular home from home.

I found the Clyde fans in the best frame of mind that you might expect at the start of a new season. Still pumped up and optimistic following promotion via the play-offs just a few weeks previously, most seemed reasonably confident that, in another ten-team division, another crack at promotion might not prove beyond a club currently on something of a roll. Confidence grew with every pint of Bellhaven Best and certainly wasn't harmed by the disclosure that I'd watched Forfar on three occasions and had seen them take a fearful battering each time.

Although none of the Bully Wee's travelling support could hark back to the club's glory days of the 1950s, I did have one tenuous link in this respect having once known a Dover resident who'd won the Scottish Cup in 1955, the year of my birth, when Clyde beat Celtic 1-0 in a replayed final. Suffice to say I'll get back to this, but it was a tale that held everyone's attention at the time.

Although a few TVs around the pub were showing a live game between Southampton and Manchester United, few gave the match more than a passing glance as anecdotes were swapped, relived and doubtless embellished. As a gobby yet friendly barmaid hurled a few 'Weedgie' jibes their way, Clyde fans responded in kind, and everything was taken on the chin in the spirit it was meant. I enjoyed a fine session in equally fine company and wisely allowed myself an extra ten minutes to wobble back to the stadium named after a station that didn't actually exist.

I've often found that the worst part of a good day out occurs between 3pm and 5pm. Today was one of those days.

This is not to say I didn't enjoy myself. Under normal circumstances I'd find a seat with a decent view and watch the game and the world going on around it. Today, made more garrulous and sociable by some three pints in excess of a sensible lunchtime intake, I had a chat with a few locals and visitors alike. My Leicester City training top is always a useful conversation starter, more so since 2016 and particularly during a game that's no great shakes. Given that Station Park has cover on two sides and none at either end I wandered about, took in bits of the game from all four sides of the ground, never straying too far from a toilet.

While those of us who watched the game through beer goggles – and there were certainly a few of us – seemed to enjoy the game more than others, it always seemed destined to finish goalless. The BBC website told me a few days later that Forfar hadn't managed a single shot on target. Reverting to memory, Forfar keeper Marc McCallum had a good game and was probably the man of the match, duly aided by some desperate last-ditch defending, earning a point and staving off the dicking that previous experience of watching the Loons had led me to expect. Clyde, despite being the better side throughout, chucked away a couple of points by dint of poor finishing and wanting too much time in front of goal.

Getting away a bit lively, I managed to make the bus back to Dundee that left just after five o'clock. It took 33 minutes to reach Seagate bus station. Had it taken 34 minutes I would almost certainly have wet myself.

Knackered and in need of a good night's kip ahead of a long trip home, I opted for a nightcap – if such a thing exists at 6pm – in a popular pub close to my hotel, frequented by Dundee's young and glamorous. As I settled into a quiet corner to watch some football, I noticed a gorgeous young thing, who bore an uncanny resemblance to the Irish actress and comedian Aisling Bea. Stylishly dressed and with legs that went on forever, she was difficult to ignore. When she looked at me and made a come-hither motion with her index finger, I did what any red-blooded 64-year-old would do and looked behind me to see who she actually wanted to speak to. Raised eyebrows and a smile that could charm a duck off the water indicated it was me. Gathering I was a bit slow on the uptake, she came and sat next to me. This is a verbatim report of the exchange that followed:

'Sorry to interrupt your game, but could I ask a big favour?'

'You can indeed, young lady.'

'Would you mind if I sat with you until my mates get here. They're only about ten minutes away, but I keep being bothered by creeps. You look like the only bloke here who isn't on the pull.'

'Oh, gotcha. A chaperone type of thing and act like I'm your dad?'

'You've done this sort of thing before, haven't you! I knew I'd got the right man!'

She had indeed and I like to think that Lynn (a 26-year-old nurse from Cuper) and I were good company for one another for a while. If I bored her by prattling on about my little grandson, she hid it brilliantly. Right on cue her mates, three other attractive young nurses, pitched up for a night out that was beyond me by about 40 years.

'This is Mark from Dover,' said Lynn. 'He's a lovely daddy I borrowed for a while.'

With this endorsement of my latter-day talents ringing in my ears, we said our goodbyes and I toddled off, squiffy and gormless, to my plush hotel to pack in readiness for the journey home.

With 39 grounds visited and just three to go, I reckoned I'd have the book done and dusted by Christmas. Mind you, they said that in 1914 about the First World War.

HEART OF MIDLOTHIAN v CELTIC

Scottish Premiership
Wednesday, 18 December 2019

AS I finished packing for a long weekend away, the contents of my case told tales of previous trips to Scotland. As backup trousers, the cream-coloured chinos – purchased in a Stirling charity shop after it became clear that shorts alone wouldn't get me through a Scottish summer – had been neatly folded. In the unlikely event that smart-casual might be required, my Pep Guardiola cardigan, purchased from Barnado's to stave off hypothermia on a May evening in Montrose, completed my suave second-hand ensemble. To be on the safe side I chucked in the cheapest woollen scarf Edinburgh's Royal Mile had to offer from my daughter's extensive dad's crap present collection, and packed a hot water bottle. Naturally, when I got to Edinburgh the weather was so mild, in the daytime at least I wandered around the city with my coat under my arm.

With just three grounds to visit to finish my project, I hadn't envisaged a third trip to Tynecastle. Indeed, my match ticket had been bought for an excellent fellow called Simon Harris. Simon – who I've effectively used as a free, one-man Viagogo for the last three decades – had sorted match tickets for me all over Europe. It was nice to return the compliment when he, knowing I had a purchasing history at Hearts, asked if I could get him a ticket for a game against Celtic which coincided with his visit to Edinburgh.

My call to the Hearts ticket office was answered promptly by a lady with a south-east Asian accent for whom politeness was a watchword. In the finest new-found traditions of globalisation, she spoke perfect BBC 'American English' while working for a Scottish club, talking to a chap whose constant use of colloquial English made conversation stilted and difficult at times. Thus, the oft-asked question as to what could possibly go wrong didn't take long to emerge. Having encountered a computer glitch, she asked if I would mind her using a shortcut to produce my ticket. I replied that I'd be happy with any procedure that got the job done; an acceptance that led directly to the following conversation:

'I'm sorry, Mr Winter, but I'm afraid I can't issue you with a ticket for the Celtic game!'

'Why not?'

'You don't have a purchasing history with us!'

'Yes, I do, we discussed this earlier. I was at the Stenhousemuir game in July.'

'Well, you did have a purchasing history with us, but I'm afraid I've erased it.'

'How on earth did you manage that?'

'Uhmmmm … is there anything else I can help you with today?'

In the interests of brevity I shall simply state that, after I'd hurled my phone at the sofa in a fit of pique, my call was returned, my application processed, and the ticket plopped on my doormat the following day.

With favour duly returned, I presented Simon with said ticket at the next Dover home game. It was at this point that Hearts cocked everything up by reaching the League Cup semi-finals; the Celtic fixture was postponed, rearranged, and Simon made other plans.

When he gave me the ticket back with the instruction to give it to whoever might want it, I had a rethink. I'd had a testing few weeks at work and a few nights away in Edinburgh might be just what the doctor ordered. With Hibernian playing at home to Rangers a couple of evenings later, I could escape the madness that is Dover during the week leading up to Christmas, take in a couple of Edinburgh v Glasgow derbies, head off to Clyde v Airdrieonians on Saturday, then get an early train back to King's Cross on the Sunday morning. Deciding that matters had panned out rather well, I gave Simon his money back in a spirit of seasonal bonhomie.

I really hadn't looked at my ticket until I arrived outside the Tynecastle Arms as I'd just taken what I was given in what I expected to be a sold-out stadium. It turned out that my seat was in the Gorgie Stand, where home fans congregated behind the goal and, judging from the photos taken during my first visit I was in much the same place as when I saw Hearts lose to Dundee seven years ago.

Although tonight's crowd of 17,297 was the largest I'd been a part of in Scotland for years, there were plenty of empty seats around me. It didn't take me too long to work out why so many Hearts fans had decided to stay at home and watch this one on the box.

At the other end of the ground, where there wasn't a spare seat to be had, a giant yellow flag proclaimed that we would be watching 'the Pope's team' tonight. This set me to wondering if His Holiness had popped down the road to watch Celtic when they beat Lazio 2-1 in Rome's Olympic Stadium a few weeks back. The number 32 bus leaves from right outside the Vatican City and is just a straight ten-minute run to the ground. I didn't dwell on this unlikeliest of possibilities for too long, safe in the knowledge that Big Frank, a Buenos Aires lad, is actually a big San Lorenzo fan and is probably busy on Thursday nights anyway.

It had been a while since I'd been in a crowd where the atmosphere had been quite so hostile and tense, a factor not helped by the fact that Hearts were enduring a rotten season that might reasonably end with them returning to the Scottish Championship. Thus, a quick song in praise of the Irish Republican Army and Scott Brown's early booking for a typically robust tackle allowed three sides of the ground to forget all this seasonal bonhomie nonsense, give the veins in their necks a decent workout and let loose a little anti-Glaswegian invective.

I've never quite been able to make my mind up about Brown, son of the same Fife village as the late, great Jim Baxter, trying to take the view that you don't play top-level football for 18 years just by running around and lamping people. Although 'club legend' would doubtless be the view of anyone connected with the green and white hoops, the overwhelming consensus of those around me was that Celtic's skipper was nothing but a shaven-headed thug of dubious parentage. Under the circumstances I thought I might leave neutral, reasoned debate for another time and just sit quietly.

The following day, I read both the free *Metro* paper and the BBC website and learned that Hearts had played rather well tonight and had the lion's share of possession on a 52-48 (sound familiar?) ratio.

This seemed to prove the rather salient point that possession statistics seldom make allowance for a team that takes 25 passes to cross the halfway line. Whatever our views on our national game's obsession with statistics, it remains an indisputable fact that there's very little point in having 95 per cent of the ball if your opponents end up with 100 per cent of the goals.

Hearts started brightly enough without really creating a great deal, but it was always going to be Celtic's night as soon as they inevitably scored the game's first goal. It came after 28 minutes as Odsonne Édouard held the ball up with three Hearts defenders in close attendance. Although I suspect he intended to lay it off to James Forrest, it fell perfectly for Ryan Christie to effortlessly roll into the bottom-left corner from 20 yards out.

Just before half-time Celtic added a second goal after Brown had won possession and sent Forrest haring down the left before getting behind Christophe Berra and crossing to the far post. Although Édouard completely missed his kick, Olivier Ntcham scored with a cleverly cushioned volley. It finished 2-0 but Celtic could have won by half a dozen as the game petered out as a contest long before the end.

For Hearts' new boss Daniel Stendel, the club's third managerial appointment of the season, it looked like he might have his work cut out to keep the club in the top flight. I simply thought this heading towards the exit, while the locals expressed the opinion just a little more strongly.

HIBERNIAN v RANGERS

Scottish Premiership
Friday 20 December 2019

ALTHOUGH I hope to never be one again, I often look back to my days as a shift worker with fondness, particularly my time as a customer service agent on the trains at Eurotunnel. A standard night shift would start when our crew of eight – half of whom were extraordinarily lovely women in their 20s – would take an empty train across to France and leave it somewhere. For the next six hours we'd sit in a crew room, drink coffee, eat macaroons (which were free if you knew the exact spot to thump the vending machine) and just chat and laugh. We'd then take another empty train back to the UK, dump that somewhere where there was a better than even chance of someone finding it, then bugger off home. Occasionally a customer or two might show up, but they tended not to inconvenience us too often. It was under these circumstances that I met a Scotsman called Frankie Bell.

Frank, a train driver, was a lovely, lyrical guy who was exactly how he seemed. If memory serves, he was working on the Orient Express when he met the love of his life in Deal and settled there. His broad accent softened not a jot in all his time living on England's south-east coast. A dedicated family man, Frank didn't always say a great deal and you could sometimes forget he was there. When he did speak, he'd usually come up with something profound or something that would make you laugh, with the latter often being an anecdote from his youth in Scotland. As so often happens to guys with the lovely bloke gene, Frankie Bell passed away a good three decades before his time.

Having received the rotten news that he wasn't long for this world, Frankie was at least granted a little time in which to revisit some of the places he often spoke about. One was Celtic Park, and another was Loch Lomond. Having watched Celtic the previous evening, I felt I might continue following in his footsteps the following day.

Although Scotland wasn't offering me much in the way of daylight – it was still dark on Nicholson Street after I left the B&B at 9am – I was glad I made the effort, taking the train to Glasgow Queen Street then getting straight on to another out to Balloch and the southern end of the loch. As the second train crawled through a bleak post-industrial landscape towards the middle of a grey, damp day, I'd started to consider the possibility that I'd taken the wrong option out of two. Encouraged by an episode of the BBC's excellent four-part series, *A History of Scotland*, I'd considered a visit to Linlithgow Palace rather than an outing spending hours on a train looking out of the window at parts of Scotland I'd seen before.

I bucked up, however, when I spotted Dumbarton Castle and the vast volcanic rock it stood upon and was reminded of the time Dumbarton's groundsman invited me to take photos of 'one of the finest sights in Scottish football' from the centre of the pitch he was preparing for their play-off game against Alloa Athletic.

Arriving in Balloch, I realised how I'd unwittingly missed a trick by not staying here for a night or two to coincide with the Dumbarton v Alloa game.

Finding myself in what I felt looked like a film set for a gentle drama in which the village doctor was constantly kept on his toes by an octogenarian housekeeper called Morag,

I instantly got the feel of the place and wandered around without a care in the world. Initially I was tempted to visit a tandoori restaurant by a huge mural advertising Bombay Jock's. Jock himself was kitted out in full national dress incorporating both kilt and sporran, topped off with the beard and turban of his Sikh religion. Somehow it perfectly illustrated the tolerance and humour of a nation that had much to teach its southern neighbour. With just a little pang of regret I passed on the spicy delights that Jock had to offer, turned tail, and sought out Balloch Castle Country Park and found it within a couple of minutes.

At a different time of year I'd doubtless have taken a boat trip on the River Leven and into Loch Lomond. All the boats were tied up out of season, so I contented myself with a walk along the footpath that ran by the side of the river and loch and into the country park to enjoy a little tranquillity and, once away from the main road, to listen to sounds that came purely from nature. Foremost among them were from dogs having a whale of a time, bounding in and out of the loch and never losing energy or enthusiasm in constant pursuit of a rubber ball. Lost in thought and only speaking to exchange pleasantries with the occasional dog owner, I mooched around the loch and through woodland, strolled around the perimeter of the castle and visited a beautifully kept ornamental garden until a lack of daylight sent me back to the station to begin my long trip back to Edinburgh.

The following day I opted for the familiar, spending my daylight hours by the Water of Leith and marvelling at the peace and quiet that could be found five minutes away from the centre of a bustling capital city.

Feeling I'd earned an hour propped up by my fat backside, I found myself in boozer on the quayside of Leith that hadn't been subjected to the relentless march of gentrification. After I'd asked for a coffee – drinking at lunchtime tends to extract a heavy toll these days – the landlord looked me up and down in a manner that suggested I'd asked him to hand over his youngest daughter for sacrifice. Seldom has the word 'no' been uttered in a less contemptuous manner. When I asked for a large glass of Merlot his features softened a little, as he weighed up whether or not he still wanted to kill me and dump me in the basement. Once he'd served me, I had a very happy hour or so in my kind of pub – one in which punters popped in for a drink and a chat and a quick glance at the daily papers. The boozer is called the Malt and Hops and I recommend it very highly.

If I'd failed to find Irvine Welsh's dark heart of Leith again, I got a little closer to it later that evening at Easter Road. Time for a little context. A week previously, the British Isles woke up to learn that Boris Johnson's Conservative Party had won a comfortable majority in the UK's third general election in four years. At the same time the Scottish Nationalists had a great night, pretty much sweeping the board north of the border, duly suggesting that Scotland wanted a Tory government and Brexit as much as it wanted an STD. So when Rangers fans belted out a heartfelt rendition of 'Rule Britannia' the locals weren't overly impressed, didn't join in, but did express their own views quite clearly. I just kept quiet.

Having obtained my ticket from a guy on a Facebook page, I found myself in a section of the main stand which had earned a reputation for the occasional display of volatile behaviour. From where I was sitting, that reputation seemed well deserved. The bloke behind me seldom said anything that wasn't tinged with anger, outrage, or sectarianism.

Every sentence began with 'for f***s sake' and ended with 'ya c**t'. As often as not, he failed to put any meat in the middle of his linguistic sandwiches and left more than a spot of spittle on the back of my neck. You may imagine my surprise when I turned around at half-time to listen to a rather dapper septuagenarian intelligently discussing the key points of the game thus far.

In the seat in front of me, a spotty, callow youth in his late teens had a lot of points to raise and – surprisingly for a bloke who weighed about four stone wringing wet – threats to make. Unfortunately he felt the need to stand up to make each and every one of them, much to the annoyance of those just trying to watch the game. Luckily, a bloke the size of Arthur's Seat in a North Face jacket said, 'Will ya sit the f**k down, ya doss wee c**t!' in a tone that suggested ignoring his request might result in violence and no little pain. Despite muttering something about it still be being 'a free country, despite the f***in' Tories' the lad – a ringer for Plug from the Bash Street Kids – had the sense to do as he was told. A few seats along, two quite beautiful young women – one blonde and tall, the other petite and dark – occasionally stopped taking selfies of themselves for long enough to flash a masturbatory gesture (copyright the Metropolitan Police) in the general direction of those of the red, white, and blue persuasion.

If the Hibs fans around me hadn't been in the happiest frame of mind at kick-off, they were apoplectic when their team went 2-0 down inside the first eight minutes.

Rangers' opener was a real horror show from Hibs' perspective as keeper Ofir Marciano should have made light work of clearing a straightforward backpass upfield. As he dithered, Joe Aribo closed him down and forced a grade A howler as the Israeli international sliced his clearance straight to Ryan Kent. Looking straight down the throat of the gift horse, Kent drilled the ball into an unguarded net from the 18-yard line.

Howls of derision from three sides of the ground had barely died down when Rangers doubled their lead four minutes later with a goal that had more than a touch of genuine class about it. After swapping passes and getting behind Hibs' left flank with consummate ease, Kent set up Aribo to net with the coolest of side-footed finishes into the far corner.

Having watch this same fixture in Glasgow in the Championship, I reflected on how rapidly fortunes can change. On that occasion the visitors outclassed a side going through a difficult time, while the travelling supporters took the opportunity to indulge in some heartless gloating. Tonight the boot was very much on the other foot. Previously, I'd seen the 'bouncy, bouncy, la, la, la, la, la, la' chant and accompanying choreography performed by 30 to 40 fans at an English non-league game. Watching a thousand Rangers fans doing the same thing proved a far more memorable experience.

At half-time, a two-goal lead was scant reflection of Rangers' total domination.

If his most recent sending off and suspension denied me the pleasure of watching Rangers' Colombian striker Alfredo Morelos, his absence did allow me to renew an old acquaintance in the form of Jermain Defoe. Now 37 and seemingly having a great time at the fag end of his career, I'd first seen Defoe as a 16-year-old playing for Bournemouth where he'd just scored in ten consecutive games. Although he didn't find the net in an LDV Vans Trophy game v Dover that Bournemouth eventually won on penalties, Defoe was on target against Hibernian.

A fine goal it was too, as Defoe's sublime first touch killed a hopeful ball into the box that dropped out of the sky. After dumping his marker on his backside and cutting inside, Defoe drilled the ball into the gap between Marciano and his right-hand post. Expecting even more of a rout in the half an hour that remained, a couple of thousand Hibs fans left as soon as the ball hit the net.

Although Rangers somehow failed to boost their goal difference in the last 30 minutes, the early leavers did miss a remarkable few minutes that ended with referee Nick Walsh dishing out three red cards after the dust, blood and feathers had settled.

This rather unfortunate sequence of events began with one of those challenges we so often see when one side is taking the piss out of well-beaten opponents. Although such tackles are intended to indicate that the perpetrator has pride in his shirt and hasn't given up on a game that's lost, he just ends up looking a bit of a tit. Such was the case when Ryan Porteous hurled himself into a tackle he really didn't need to make, duly leaving Rangers' Borna Barišić in a heap on the touchline, just a few yards from where Hibs' more vociferous supporters were gathered.

As a few missiles – an empty vodka bottle included – were hurled in the prone Croatian's general direction, rules governing acceptable behaviour were set to one side for a time. I thought about leaving at this point but watched by the exit as Hibs' assistant manager John Potter and Rangers' coach Tom Culshaw were shown red cards along with Porteous.

Lothian and Borders Police decided I couldn't leave via the way I came in for 'safety reasons'. While a roadblock was aimed at keeping home fans away from Glaswegian visitors, it had the somewhat predictable effect of leading me straight into the middle of the latter.

As a coward of negotiable loyalties on such occasions, I joined in with joyous renditions of 'Rule Britannia' and 'Follow, Follow' before slipping unnoticed down the first available side street that eventually led me over the North Bridge and back to the B&B.

CLYDE v AIRDRIEONIANS

Scottish League One
Saturday, 21 December 2019

IT WAS probably longer ago than I imagine when I was working in a Year 8 English class discussing future options and careers. At one point we got on to the topic of what I'd done in life before becoming a teaching assistant, the implication being that as I was so crap at my current job I couldn't have just winged it since leaving school and must have done something else better. After mentioning that I spent a few years working as a sports writer for the *Dover Express*, our local newspaper, a quiet, barely audible voice piped up from the front row, 'My grandad used to work for them.'

Investigations revealed that the young lady who uttered these words – I'm embarrassed to say I've forgotten her name – is the granddaughter of a Scottish gentleman called Davie Laing. Though I never had the pleasure of meeting Davie – he'd retired before I started working for the local rag in my mid-40s – I was a fan. In an era when you needed to know your patch and the people in it rather than how to cut and paste from a variety of websites, reading Davie's work was a non-negotiable part of my day when the paper came out every Thursday. Perhaps the only thing Davie and I had in common was that we both turned to a career in journalism after another working life had ended. I was a redundant shipping clerk, while Davie was a professional footballer from Fife.

After an eight-year spell with Hearts, Laing opted to move on when his wing-half spot was given to a young whippersnapper called Dave Mackay. This was to prove a blessing in disguise, however, as in 1955, the year of my birth, Laing won the Scottish Cup with Clyde. After the first game against Celtic had finished 1-1, Clyde won the replay 1-0. Davie was reported to have been the man of the match in both games, which attracted a total of 175,065 paying punters to Hampden Park. To my amazement his granddaughter was unaware of any of this, only knowing, 'He played a bit of football when he was younger.' At the time I couldn't help but think that if I ever won the FA Cup – admittedly, at 64, I appreciate I might have left it a bit late – a conversation with any of my grandchildren might have gone something like this:

'Do you want a cup of tea, Granddad?'

'Cup? Did you say cup? Did I ever tell you about the time I won the FA Cup with Dover?'

'Only five times this morning, Granddad, but carry on if it makes you happy.'

'Well, we were 0-0 with Manchester United going into the last few minutes ...'

Clyde won the cup again three years later, but by that time Davie was in my neck of the woods playing for Gillingham. He appeared for a few Kent clubs but once again we missed one another. He was playing for Margate when he retired in 1965, the year before I started watching Dover on a regular basis. I saw him play just once one memorable afternoon at our local leisure centre.

Although I can't be sure of the year or even the decade, I was playing in a five-a-side tournament that was particularly well supported given that it was held in aid of several local charities. Although I was in sparkling goalscoring form, despite my team going out in the group stages, it was an elderly Scotsman who made the greatest impression on the tournament, if not necessarily for the right reasons to begin with.

Never the tallest of men, our hero's diminutive stature was topped off by one of those ice-cream cone, snow white hairstyles made popular by the former home secretary and foreign secretary Douglas Hurd. Having presumably not put on his kit for a while, his shorts, of the style favoured by the British Army when engaged in jungle warfare, were knee-length, while his socks looked as though they'd been filled with concrete. He almost certainly wasn't wearing carpet slippers, but nobody could be too sure what he did have on his feet. He was 65 if he was a day and the butt of a few snide asides from a few young crackerjacks who fancied themselves as footballers. I knew better and felt that I knew what was coming. In essence, why run when you can pass the ball with metronomic regularity to those who can, while making an opponent 45 years your junior look a complete and utter tit. I didn't pay to watch this ten-minute gala exhibition, but it was worth £20 of anyone's money.

What I'm saying, I guess, is that if you'd spotted me gazing gormlessly out of a window of a Glasgow-bound train calling at Croy, and offered me a penny for them, the above is a reasonable summary of what you'd have got for your money.

Having somehow got the idea that Croy was lively and happening kind of place, I reckoned on arriving around midday and finding a pub. Hopefully it might contain a few of the Clyde fans I'd bumped into at Forfar and provide me with a pint or four and a decent meal. Although Edinburgh has any number of decent restaurants, getting into one for a quiet solo dinner hadn't proven possible, hence I'd spent the last four days either grabbing takeaways or snacking in my room at the B&B.

After taking around 20 minutes to find my way out of a vast car park and to the main road, I found precisely nobody wandering around from whom to ask directions. Eventually a dog-walking couple attached to a little yappy thing caked in mud pitched up, enabling me to pose the question, 'Which is the easiest way into town?' I hadn't bargained on a reply of 'Which town?' and stood around open-mouthed and flummoxed for a while until they elucidated further and emphasised, not for the first time, that I hadn't done my homework. If I had, I would know that, 'Croy is a village in North Lanarkshire, Scotland. A former mining community, it is situated some 13 miles from Glasgow and 37 miles from Edinburgh. It has a population of about 1,390.' Or, in non-Wikipedia speak, it's in the arse end of nowhere where no sod lives, at least until they've finished building what's going to be another commuter town.

It turned out that Cumbernauld is the nearest town from which Clyde FC draws the bulk of its support. If I was to find what I was looking for, I faced a three-mile walk there and back or I could try my luck with an infrequent Saturday bus service. With the better part of three hours until kick-off, I figured that circumstances dictated that I should just find the ground and hope the bar was open.

Thus, I set off on an uninspiring trek through a vast building site that would probably be rather nice when it's finished, once little afterthoughts like shops, pubs and schools had been thrown up. Though the odd light and net curtain suggested that some of the houses were populated, I bumped into two pedestrians in the 40 minutes it took me to find Broadwood Stadium.

Although I've heard Broadwood described as 'an uninspiring new-build' by some fans who've been there, 'new' seems to be employed in the loosest possible sense of the word. Clyde have been playing here for 26 years. The fact that Clyde moved here in 1994 following a nomadic existence – caused by being kicked out of their former Shawfield home in Rutherglen – speaks volumes. I guess it was around this time that somebody, somewhere, decided that what we all wanted was more and more centralisation and everything in one place. This was simply the kind of muddled thinking that gave Milton Keynes Dons FC to an ungrateful public.

How wonderful it would be, it was argued, if the nuclear family could do the weekly shop following a ten-minute drive, then spend an hour or two looking at wildly overpriced Swedish furniture. After taking in the delights of a 'soccer' match they could enjoy a dinner courtesy of a multinational chain before rounding off the perfect day at a multiplex cinema, watching the latest hilarious animated offering from the good old US of A. All this within a 50-yard radius of where the Range Rover was parked.

Each to their own, of course, but I would sooner spend a Saturday inserting live wasps into my anus. Unless it is completely unavoidable I like walking to grounds, spending time in good company before and after the game, in one or two decent pubs. Today this simply wasn't an option.

At the stadium itself, there was no room at the inn. Although the guy on reception was perfectly affable about it – and added that he hoped I'd stay for a drink after the game – the club's bar was closed due to a Christmas function. He suggested I try Broadwood Farm, a pub/restaurant I'd find at the top of the slope leading away from the ground. I did, walked in, and heard Wham's 'Last Christmas' playing at Motörhead-esque volume to the seeming delight of assorted family gatherings. 'Bugger this,' I muttered before I left in search of other options of which there was just one. I could get a takeaway coffee from an adjacent garage, make it last for two hours and stand next to a dual carriageway in the drizzle. I bit the bullet and returned to Broadwood Farm.

Having found a quiet corner where the Christmas number ones could easily be partially ignored, I decided it really wasn't such a bad place. It just wasn't my sort of place. Families seemed happy enough and given it was they who the place was set up for, I opted to stop being a grumpy old bastard and get a bite to eat and opted for the carvery. In order to save myself the bother of a first Tripadvisor review, I'll just add that the meat and gravy were stone cold while an impressive selection of vegetables, admittedly hot, had the consistency of porridge and all tasted exactly the same. Three large glasses of Argentine Merlot hit the spot though and my *joie de vivre*, such as it was, had been restored when I left half an hour later.

If my previous day watching Clyde had been spoiled by a dull couple of hours in mid-afternoon, today, my last in Scotland for a while, was rescued by a cracking game of football.

While I hadn't thought of it as such, this was a derby that was about as local as they get. Although I realised that both clubs were based just outside of Glasgow, what I didn't know was that they're separated by a 20-minute drive of less than ten miles. On the last Saturday before Christmas when crowds usually go down by around 20 per cent, Airdrie were well supported, both numerically and vocally, in a crowd of 1,094.

Seven minutes in Clyde won a free kick in a promising position, and it didn't take a tactical genius to work out that if the dead-ball delivery was right, they could put it on to the head of their centre-half who seemed to be about a foot taller than anyone else in the penalty area. So it proved, as Mark Lamont curled in a free kick that Aleks Petkov, here on a month-long loan from Hearts, headed in without bothering to raise his 6ft 3in frame off the deck.

If Clyde had forgotten to bring their shooting boots when I saw them at Forfar, they looked like they might run away with this game as they put Airdrie under pressure for a sustained period. They made it 2-0 not even midway through the first half courtesy of one of a handful of players I'd seen play on either side of the border.

It's widely known that David Goodwillie's career had largely been one of great promise that failed to materialise as had been predicted. It's also well known that Clyde's decision to sign the former Blackburn Rovers and Scotland striker had drawn widespread and vociferous criticism for reasons I really shouldn't go into, hence I will speak solely of what he did during today's game.

Although Goodwillie took a fearful buffeting all afternoon, he took it without much in the way of complaint, gave as good as he got, and scored the first of two fine goals after 21 minutes. After a corner was only partially cleared, the sides engaged in a game of head tennis before the ball came his way in what we old folks refer to as the inside-right position. Tightly marked, Goodwillie watched the ball drop over his shoulder before firing a peach of a volley over and beyond the keeper from the tightest of angles.

Airdrie seemed on course for the mother of all batterings but they stuck with it, albeit more by luck than judgement at times, and slowly but surely started getting back into the game. As possibly the only neutral in the ground, I reckoned an Airdrie goal would make a good match even better in the second half. So it proved as they pulled one back just before half-time.

I'd yet to see Clyde concede a goal in two and a half games but they showed they weren't immune to defensive frailty, passing up three opportunities to clear a corner. When the ball was headed back into the mix, Dale Carrick turned sharply and scored with an emphatic finish that put Airdrie back in the game.

A point for Airdrie would have taken them top in a division that was fabulously competitive and open. And although the second half was much more evenly contested and just as absorbing, it was Clyde who wrapped up the three points on offer when they scored with the last kick of the game.

Although he riled the fans of both clubs at times, I rather enjoyed referee John McKendrick's tendency not to award free kicks if he could avoid it, preferring to allow a second or two to see if an advantage developed. Pleasingly, for the man in charge as well as me, this was a contributory factor in Goodwillie's second goal.

It came as keeper David Mitchell launched a huge clearance downfield, aiming, I suspect, to merely eat up the few seconds of the game that remained. Although Goodwillie, not for the first time, was being pulled all over the place, he brought the ball down with his first touch then scored with a sublime volley with his second from some 30 yards out. Once wild and lengthy celebrations died down, the final whistle concluded the best game I'd seen in months.

Rather than hang about, I decided to give up on Croy until someone finished building it and headed back to Edinburgh on the first available train. On arrival, I spent some time in one of the capital's swisher pubs watching Kevin De Bruyne and Riyad Mahrez in electric form as Manchester City beat Leicester City 3-1; the second time I'd watched this fixture in an Edinburgh pub. Reflecting on the view that the game was almost as good as the one I'd seen earlier, I headed back to the B&B and packed in readiness for the long trip home.

PS: Davie Laing passed away in July 2017 at the ripe old age of 92. He had been inducted into the Clyde Hall of Fame in 2011.

KELTY HEARTS v EAST FIFE

Scottish League Cup Group Stage
Saturday, 17 July 2021

I HADN'T expected to cross the Firth of Forth again and venture into the kingdom. The lure and magic of Cowdenbeath is irresistible to some, I guess. Today, when the Blue Brazil were at home to Brechin City, it just seemed a bit weird to be walking away from Central Park rather than towards it, in order to visit a club I hadn't even heard of as recently as a couple of years ago.

If Kelty Hearts haven't exactly come from nowhere, their history is a short one having been formed as recently as 1975. After 40-odd years as a successful junior side Kelty, in December 2017, became full members of the SFA, making themselves eligible not only to enter the Scottish Cup but also have the opportunity to move onwards and upwards in the Scottish league pyramid system. Moving up to the East of Scotland League, they opted not to hang about for too long and won the competition at the first attempt.

If the casual observer might have expected Kelty to find the going a lot tougher in the Lowland League, that wasn't how things panned out. When the 2019/20 season was subject to a Covid cancellation they won the title at the first attempt, albeit on the baffling average points per game system. Although there was no promotion and relegation between Scotland's fourth and fifth tier at the end of the season – duly preserving Brechin's place in League Two – Kelty were to have better fortune a year later. Although they held a seven-point lead at the top of the Lowland League, they'd only completed 13 of their scheduled 32 games when the season was abandoned. Once again they were declared champions and, after making light work of overcoming Highland League champions Brora Rangers in the promotion play-off semi-final, they met Brechin in the final. After losing both legs narrowly, Brechin couldn't earn a second successive reprieve as Kelty, following three remarkable seasons, earned a place in the SPFL.

Whichever way you looked at it, they'd had a bloody sight better time during the pandemic than I did!

I'd done my research for once to discover that the village of Kelty, without a train station, was about three miles from the centre of Cowdenbeath. There was a bus service, apparently, but I figured that a six-mile round trip, even on increasingly ancient legs, wouldn't prove too difficult on a glorious summer day. Naturally I received the usual advice along the lines that this wasn't a task to be taken lightly and that a taxi would be my best bet. While this is advice I'd normally take with a pinch of salt, I took it a little more seriously when given by a lycra-clad runner in her 20s out training for her first marathon. Regardless, I set off. It wasn't the nicest of walks.

Living in an era when neither is socially acceptable, it's been a very long time indeed since I saw anyone drop litter in the street or fail to clear up after their dog. That said, the walk from Cowdenbeath to Kelty really drove home the problem of single-use plastic and the need to come up with biodegradable packaging alternatives given the number of people who don't take recycling seriously.

Indeed, in this part of Fife it seemed that chucking litter out of a car window was the area's most popular participation sport. It wouldn't be an exaggeration to say that the roadside and hedgerows en route to Kelty were marked with either a drinks can or a plastic bottle every five yards along the way. It was a depressing spectacle, as I reckoned that if I'd have picked everything up I could have filled a skip quite comfortably. On the plus side, Kelty isn't on a main route to a port, so no clear bottles of urine decorated the road into the village. Luckily the residents of Kelty took much more pride in the appearance of their village and my spirits were raised as soon as I got there.

Suffice to say that Kelty isn't a big place. With a population of around 6,000 it came as no great surprise to hear that Kelty is a former mining village, with a pit that provided work for 3,000 before it shut down in the 1980s. Though I didn't spot any evidence of the place's mining heritage I did find the club's stadium, New Central Park, in double-quick time in a neat and tidy housing estate on the outskirts of the village. If Central Park wasn't exactly new, it looked like it had been given a fresh coat of paint ahead of its newfound status in the big boys' league.

As per usual custom and habit, I'd arrived three hours before kick-off as a means to getting my bearings before drink was taken.

The problem was, with Covid still rampant all over the island, a busy pub really wasn't the best place for a 65-year-old fat lad with asthma, tempting though the prospect was. Under the circumstances, it seemed reasonable to grab a meal deal from the local Co-op then park my backside on a bench outside the local community centre and watch the world go by while absorbing a few rays.

Back at the stadium, where I produced one of those fashionable yet ghastly print-at-home match tickets and received a hearty welcome, the first thing I noticed about Hearts' tiny, yet tidy stadium was the grass banks behind each goal.

Grass banks in England are invariably the first thing that has to go when ambitious clubs seek to move up the pyramid and need a stamp of approval from the dreaded ground-graders.

I speak from painful experience when I say that these guys have a penchant for the ugly and pragmatic, with a love of concrete and a dread of anyone slipping over in our increasingly litigious society. The once-omnipresent grass banks have all but disappeared in English stadiums and I'm sure I'm not alone in mourning their passing. The Scottish authorities seem to take a different view, I'm pleased to say, clearly feeling that a ground is fine if it can safely accommodate as many fans as it's likely to welcome, rather than dictate that so-and-so must have 1,000 covered seats even though their average home gate is 327. Although Scottish football briefly mucked about with this kind of nonsense – making Inverness play Premiership home games at Aberdeen – an ambitious club with a small stadium can progress and win things as Ross County have proven.

With an hour to kill before kick-off, I figured a death-defying trip to the bar might be worth the risk. As a few punters had the same idea, social distancing was being strictly observed, so I took my pint to a seat that allowed me both space and proximity of conversation. While the locals were friendly enough, many were engrossed in Sky's coverage of some golf tournament that was taking place ten miles from my front door.

Never a fan of garish knitwear and a tedious sport I gather the Scots gave us, I wandered off for some outdoor entertainment in the form of a Fife derby.

I'd wondered how Kelty, having come so far in such a short time, would fare against an established League One side. Somehow I'd expected them to show up well in a narrow defeat and hadn't imagined that a one-sided affair would develop from the first whistle. Unfortunately, from East Fife's perspective at least, it was they who were on the wrong end of a battering.

In Kelty's starting line-up were a couple of familiar faces in Nathan Austin and Kallum Higginbotham; players I've watched so frequently now that we can't be far from being on one another's Christmas card list. As a 4-5-1 formation gave the home side width and pace that East Fife struggled to cope with, the game was effectively done and dusted once Austin had scored twice against his former club to put the 'Maroon Machine' 2-0 up inside the first 20 minutes.

The first came as centre-back Dougie Hill gave him something to chase with a long ball down the left-hand touchline that caught the visitors' defence hopelessly square. Austin duly took advantage of the acre of space in front of him and effortlessly rolled the ball into the opposite corner.

With Higginbotham and another Englishman, Joe Cardle, hugging either touchline and firing over crosses at will, it didn't take a genius to predict that Kelty's second goal was coming soon and from what source. So it proved as Cardle's cross from the left should have been headed clear, wasn't, leaving Austin to volley home at the far post.

If Kelty's domination was almost total, the second half petered out a little in an encounter that didn't have much of a derby feel to it. I've often felt that pre-season is just an opportunity to stand around and chat and a couple of local lads kept me entertained with the match all over as a contest. Possibly the game's only benefit of the last last two years is that a growing number of fans, on either side of the border, have learned to appreciate that there's much more to football than top clubs and spending 'Super Sunday' in the pub. Denied the possibility of being part of a large crowd, these two had opted for the socially distanced benefits of lower-league football – much as I had with my club's neighbours across the cliffs at

Deal – and setting off to whichever game took their fancy. Released from the shackles of loyalty they were finding, as I had, how enjoyable a game can be when you watch from a neutral perspective. They invited me to join them in midweek at a Linlithgow Rose match and I'd have certainly accepted had I not booked a train home earlier that week.

Although Kelty effectively declared with the withdrawal of Austin, his replacement, a Ghanaian lad raised in Italy, proved as much of a handful for a well-beaten side looking forward to the final whistle. Alfredo Agyeman made it 3-0 with a few minutes remaining after going clear through the middle to get on the end of Jamie Barjonas's sublime pass. He duly rounded the keeper and rolled the ball into the net to give the final score a margin of defeat that flattered an East Fife side that barely mounted a noteworthy attack all afternoon.

I took the more direct route back to Cowdenbeath, did my best to ignore all the litter, and was feeling a tad footsore by the time I arrived back at the railway station. It still seemed odd having come all the way to Cowdenbeath without going to watch a club I'd developed a soft spot for, so was pleased to hear, courtesy of a Blue Brazil fan waiting for her train back to Kirkaldy, that they'd managed a rare victory by beating Brechin City 3-2.

With just a long-awaited visit to Stirling Albion left to finish my project, it seemed oddly deflating to think that I was almost there. Given that the pandemic had stopped me from finishing as long ago as April 2020, this was a topic I chose not to dwell on as I crossed the Forth for possibly the final time.

EDINBURGH CITY v ELGIN CITY

Scottish League Division Two
Friday, 7 January 2022

IT SEEMS strange to think that my first visits to Edinburgh were just for an afternoon before I flew home. Having first caught the slow train across from Glasgow to watch Hearts play at Tynecastle as long ago as 2012, I knew I'd have to return soon to watch Hibs play at Easter Road. That way, though my chances of living in Edinburgh might be unlikely in the extreme, I'd know where I'd be buying my season ticket if I did. Almost ten years on I've learned the valuable lesson that life's a bit more complicated than that.

For one thing, though I get an inkling that Hibs' brand of football might have just a little more swagger to it, I'd felt comfortable at both clubs and warmed to them equally. Yet while a season ticket at both presumably wouldn't contravene any local bylaws, such a course of action might limit my visits to a little spiritual home I'd not so much discovered as stumbled across in the allegedly rough district of Pilton.

Although this trip had been geared towards rounding off the 42 by finally getting a game in at Stirling Albion on Saturday – the promise of a ticket came through a couple of days previously – another game at Ainslie Park (home of The Spartans and current lodgers Edinburgh City) had been a major factor in booking a trip on a weekend when Covid and the weather might reasonably be expected to play havoc with the fixture list.

After a good night's sleep following a fairly chaotic trip up from King's Cross, I'd had a good day catching up on some of the tourist stuff I'd planned to do before football, as it invariably does, got in the way. It was closed for the winter and undergoing extensive repairs but Linlithgow Palace had provided an absorbing diversion, as did a walk around an adjacent loch teeming with wildlife and dogs with the happy knack of knowing if humans like them or not. In Mary Queen of Scots' shoes I think I might have been a tad miffed at being shunted out of my birthplace and shipped out to France at an early age, but I gather that 16th-century Stuart folk viewed such matters differently. In the afternoon, still in a back-to-nature frame of mind, a stroll around Edinburgh's botanical gardens proved just the ticket until it dawned on me that I'd been walking virtually non-stop for the last six hours and that a curmudgeon of my advancing years should probably sit down in the warm for a bit.

Despite being a guy who likes his walks to be a little wild and unpredictable and a good few miles from a town or city I rather enjoyed the lovingly manicured gardens and pathways, not to mention the fact that entry was free. I'd planned to visit before but could never quite find the place. This was careless of me given that I'd walked within 200 yards of the entrance a few times while walking the pathway that follows the Water of Leith.

Later, warmed by a lie down and a good meal, I set off on what was now a familiar journey, taking a stroll across the Meadows, through the Grassmarket and following the road round to The Mound and jumping on the number 27 bus to Silverknowes.

I needn't have worried about being turned away due to a Covid-inspired restriction of 500 on tonight's gate, but I still pitched up an hour before kick-off to be on the safe side. While waiting for the turnstiles to open, I chatted with a university student with similar groundless concerns and was reminded what the attraction of football at a lower level in general and Ainslie Park in particular have for a chap like me. I'm a garrulous old lad when the mood suits me, but there are times when I can wander around hopelessly lost in thought for three or four days before it dawns on me that I haven't spoken to anyone for a while. At the 'Pilton Paradise' the atmosphere dictates that the more personable side of my nature will emerge, making me oblivious to the possibility that I might be boring someone to death.

In England, I've long since held the view that, in the 1980s, somebody, somewhere, decreed that anyone who is even remotely working class would not be allowed to have fun at work anymore, particularly if involved in selling stuff. The staff at Ainslie Park don't seem to have got this particular memo and a friendlier bunch I've yet to come across. Whether you're handing over your money at the turnstile, buying a bridie and a tea at the snack bar or looking for the obligatory memento at the club shop, the staff always make time for pleasantries in the manner of folk being friendly because that's who they are, rather than who they're told to be. That they want you to have a nice time rather goes without saying, in a stadium in which an English accent is met with a 'thanks for coming' safe in the knowledge that a January night in Pilton doesn't make the front cover of too many Edinburgh tourist flyers.

As the game got under way, my new found friend and I indulged in a little groundhopper chat that outlined how much had changed since I was his age (I reckoned about 22). I'd just about introduced myself to the wide world of European culture circa 1977 with my first day trip to Calais, having chosen not to accept my mother's firmly held belief that 'abroad' simply 'wasn't for the likes of us'. Dan (at least I think his name was Dan; he looked like a Dan, so let's stick with it) by contrast was already a widely travelled, fully fledged European, who viewed boarding a Wizz Air flight to Vilnius with much the same nonchalance as I'd have hopped on the 102 bus to Folkestone Harbour. His Rangers-supporting father had evidently introduced him to the joys of European travel as a toddler while I, at the same age, spent a week at Butlin's in Clacton while waiting for Freddie Laker to make Europe a bit smaller.

When we discussed Dan's forthcoming entry into the world of work, it soon became very clear that this was an area in which my generation had had things so much easier. After graduation, Dan had a couple of options of going into well-paid employment with a logistics company. Though far too thick for university myself I'd followed a similar career path in my first 20-odd years of working life, buying my first house when I was 27. Dan had similar plans regarding owning his own place but feared he'd probably have to leave the country to bring them to fruition.

Despite turning into a backdrop to a good natter, a half-decent game between two well-matched sides was developing in front of us. Although Kelty Hearts were miles clear at the top of League Two and Forfar and Annan were already looking nailed on for the play-offs, Edinburgh, in fourth place, looked as good a bet as any to take the final spot on offer.

While Elgin were second from bottom, Cowdenbeath, already looking hopelessly adrift at the foot of the table, seemed unlikely to give them any serious relegation concerns. Accordingly both sides knocked the ball around in a manner that suggested that neither had too much to worry about and looked like they were enjoying themselves.

As a little gang of like-minded souls gathered by the corner flag – all of us ineffectively stamping our feet as a means to combating a freezing January night – conversation turned to the last time an Edinburgh club had been crowned champions of Scotland. Well, almost. Even at the other end of the British Isles we'd had huge sympathy for a Heart of Midlothian side who, on the final day of the season, needed just a draw to win the title at Dundee. After going unbeaten in their previous 27 games, Hearts went down 2-0 at Dens Park. Celtic, who else, snatched the title on goal difference by beating St Mirren 5-0 at Paisley. Worryingly, I haven't needed to look up any of this, given that I still remember the salient points of the day back in 1986.

Dan and I had only just started to recall these events when a guy in front of us visibly shuddered and it wasn't from the cold. Derek, a Hearts-supporting cab driver who'd turned up for an affordable night out with his teenage son and daughter, recalled 'one of the worst days of my life' having attended the game as a 15-year-old boy, 'I often look back to that day and think about how we were already celebrating on the coach up to Dundee. Not one of us had even considered the possibility that it wasn't going to happen. I cried all the way home and only stopped after I got back from school on Monday.'

He added, 'At 2-0 down we were hoping that St Mirren could do us a favour and apparently they were in the game for a while. Then someone with a radio told us they'd chucked in the towel, and we knew the title had gone. I'm a pretty mild-mannered bloke, but I still want to spit when anyone mentions St Mirren.'

Back in 2022, the game finished as a 2-2 draw after an on-trial defender called Michael Travis scored a late equaliser for Edinburgh. Within ten minutes I was back on the number 27 back to the city centre. I jumped off just beyond The Mound, took a stroll through the university grounds and the Meadows and was in bed by 10.30pm. As something of a Scotland veteran I'd put a hot water bottle in it before I left.

I hadn't taken much notice of either club since this game, after going back to Dover and watching a season that was the football equivalent of a death by a thousand cuts as my local team were relegated having amassed the princely total of one point. Edinburgh City (now FC Edinburgh) did rather better as things turned out. After finishing in the final play-off spot, aggregate wins over Dumbarton (5-2) and Annan Athletic (3-2) saw them promoted to League One for the first time in the club's short history as they return to their refurbished home ground.

Elgin, while never really bothered by the prospect of a return to the Highland League, finished second from bottom.

STIRLING ALBION v KELTY HEARTS

Scottish League Two
Saturday, 8 January 2022

GIVEN THAT it's taken me nearly six years to get to this point, I should probably recap how my attempts to visit the Forthbank Stadium and/or watch Stirling Albion really haven't gone too well. Here goes.

Friday, 28 July 2016
I pay a visit to watch a Lowland League fixture between Stirling University and The Spartans; initially perceived as a bonus game that wasn't initially on my radar. Once the office staff at the Forthbank work out that I'm harmless and not dangerously insane, they help me out by ascertaining where this match is actually taking place. It transpired that while the University of Stirling has around 2,000 staff and students, nobody was available to update the website to advise that the uni's football team had moved to Falkirk.

Thursday, 27 July 2017
One year later, I return to watch a pre-season friendly between Stirling Albion and Notts County. This time the office staff, who seem to recognise me as the bewildered oddball who bothered them 364 days previously, tell me that no such fixture is taking place or has ever been scheduled. When we

get to the point where the receptionist is clearly thinking of asking if I have any children who might come and pick me up, I resign myself to the situation and depart with a mixture of good grace and exasperation.

Having seen a guy in a Notts County shirt wandering around Stirling earlier, I dismiss the thought that this might be pure coincidence but make a call home as a means to confirming that I haven't gone completely squirrel nutkins. My good friend Simon confirms that the fixture is still listed on the SFA website as it has been for several weeks.

Saturday, 13 April 2019
Having successfully negotiated a day trip from Dover to Dumfries, I thought I might try my luck again with a visit to a Scottish town that's even closer to the English border, to watch Annan v Stirling. I duly book a train and plan to travel most of the way with Dover-supporting friends en route to Barrow and a National League fixture that will serve as a backup option should the bosoms head in a northerly direction at any point.

All is going swimmingly until the train stops dead a mile out of Preston for reasons that vary and depend on what you're prepared to believe on social media. An hour or so later we returned to Preston to scenes reminiscent of the last American chopper leaving Saigon. Nothing was moving north, so I opted to jump on the first southbound train.

Naturally, within 20 minutes of the train leaving, a text tells me that obstructions north of Preston have miraculously cleared. My friends made it to Barrow with an hour to spare to watch Dover come back from 2-0 down to win 3-2. I made it home at four o'clock to find myself locked out of the house.

I should further stress that Stirling Albion were blameless for this unfortunate sequence of events, with staff and volunteers being polite and as helpful as they could possibly be.

I had hoped to visit in July when stadiums were tentatively opening up the turnstiles again, albeit in hosting minuscule attendances and monitoring how things went. I figured that the possibility of getting into a League Cup group game against Hearts was non-existent, but I thought I'd give it a go, emailing a summary of my previous SAFC misfortunes in the hope of getting some sympathy and being flogged a ticket. It was thus I became involved in a series of email exchanges with the club's director of supporter and media liaison; a decidedly poncey name for a straightforward and genuine bloke called John Daly. Although blokes with fancy jobs titles seem to have developed a united front when it comes to ignoring me, John sent me a prompt reply that was refreshingly short of psychobabble. In short he said that while he'd look forward to welcoming me to the Forthbank in happier times, the club would only be admitting their small but dedicated band of season ticket holders for the Hearts game. At a time when folk were wandering all over the island passing on a potentially fatal illness, I had to admit that this was a policy that made sense. However, after spending some time perusing the club's website, I noticed that the club were calling for a small number of volunteers to act as stewards before and during the Hearts game. I duly sent John another email and offered my services. Another prompt reply soon followed in which John told me he 'liked a chancer' and would look forward to meeting me at a later date. The game duly went ahead without me, and Hearts won 2-0 in front of 211 locals.

Naturally, John was my first point of contact at the turn of the year. Even though restrictions were still in place and tickets weren't offered to opposition fans, I figured I'd be OK if I got in early and became one of the 500 fans the Scottish government would allow the club to let in. Another prompt reply confirmed my views but came with the proviso that there *should* be a few tickets left over once the club's loyal fans had been offered first dibs. Either way, John promised me he would contact me within a couple of days. He was as good as his word and told me a ticket was waiting for me in an envelope with my name on it that I could pay for when I picked it up.

Looking after your own fans first and foremost is a policy I rather approve of though I can't imagine it catching on in 2022.

A week later, following my time-honoured habit of arriving ridiculously early, I took what was a well-trodden path to the Forthbank for a game that would kick off at 1pm due to problems Albion had experienced recently with their floodlights. I crossed the railway bridge, followed the road past the Vue cinema and followed the more scenic path by the Forth river for as long as I could. What was originally described to me as 'a bit of a trek' wasn't much more than a 20-minute stroll that ended when I passed the local – and surprisingly neutral smelling – sewage works and hung a sharp left at the leisure centre adjacent to the ground. Although I'd convinced myself that nothing could possibly go wrong today, I still felt a slight pang of trepidation as I approached the club's reception for the third time for fear of a sudden earthquake or the possibility that the playing surface was covered by a plague of locusts.

Although he was casually dressed and adorned with the obligatory orange tabard rather than the sharp suit of his website profile picture, I recognised John Daly immediately, going about a regular matchday routine that would be familiar to thousands of volunteers around the country and beyond. I introduced myself, shook his hand and thanked him profusely for his help at a time when he had so many other things to be getting on with.

I joined a short queue in a spot that offered a great view of the William Wallace memorial and was duly handed my ticket. Although it wasn't embossed with gold leaf and attached to a huge bar of chocolate, it somehow felt as though it was. I handed over a few coins and thanked the couple manning the distribution point in a manner they must have found a bit gushing and unnecessary. While opinions will always vary as to what constitutes the hottest tickets in town, I was implausibly happy to have mine tucked into my wallet and I wandered off to see what the area had to offer in the way of fine dining.

The short answer was not much, but I was happy enough with a pot of coffee and a plate of calorific pastry-based comestibles in the cafe of the local Sainsbury's. If the place wasn't exactly a model of American style 'y'all come back now, y'hear' customer service, it certainly offered plenty in the way of cabaret.

Following a brief yet fearsome row behind the counter, a young lass taking payments at the till gave an exaggerated sigh, threw up her arms in exasperation and wandered off, while her colleagues just carried on with what they were doing as though this was a regular event and nothing to take too seriously. Once a queue – doubtless longer than anything seen over the road in a while – had built up, she returned after ten minutes as though nothing had happened and carried on in a manner that suggested she was doing everyone a favour. Not one customer so much as tutted, leading me to think that entertainment was taking on some weird and wonderful forms as we all started to cautiously emerge from lockdown.

Back at the Forthbank, a stadium that looked like it could accommodate more than its 3,800 capacity, various factors dictated that filling the ground wouldn't be an option for a while. With terracing behind either goal closed, an attendance of 483 paying punters weren't exactly crammed into the main stand and breathing over one another. On the other side of the pitch, the staff, and substitutes of either club spread out and basked in the weak January sunshine like they were holidaying in Ibiza.

If Stirling has a reputation for overcoming odds and an unsurpassed record for giving the English a good kicking, the football club weren't enjoying the best of fortunes at the time even though the previous weekend's derby victory at Stenhousemuir had at least put an end to a run of league defeats. Hope springs eternal in a ten-team division, however, and they went into today's game just a point off a play-off spot. The club also had a big day out to look forward as the Scottish Cup draw had paired them with Rangers at Ibrox later in the month when restrictions on attendances would be removed.

Kelty, who had barely put a foot wrong since I watched them in July, went into today's game much more in expectation than hope. With games in hand over second-placed Forfar, they led the League Two table by seven points and seemed certain to secure yet another promotion sooner rather than later. They too had a big Scottish Cup tie to look forward to with the visit of holders St Johnstone.

I'd been told I might expect a close game today, but that really wasn't the way things panned out once Kelty took the lead after three minutes. From this point Stirling didn't look remotely likely to get anything out of the game.

The opening goal came as Jamie Barjonas shrugged off a challenge to dink a delicious ball into the box to pick out Nathan Austin's diagonal run. After getting goal side of his marker, Austin made light work of delicately clipping the ball beyond keeper Blair Currie. In terms of my attendance alone this was his fifth goal in two and a bit games.

Ponderous at the back, outplayed in midfield and non-existent up front, Stirling were nothing if not industrious. Outclassed from the first whistle, their endeavour was admirable as they stayed in the game more through luck than judgement.

Kelty's long-overdue second goal was a route-one affair that was out of keeping with their measured and stylish passing game. As keeper Darren Jamieson kicked long out of his hands, both Austin and Kallum Higginbotham nodded the ball on in a game of head tennis from the halfway line. Joe Cardle duly went clear through the middle and, with the assurance of a dad nutmegging two toddlers on Blackpool beach, avoided a couple of ineffective challenges to roll the ball in for 2-0.

Around the hour, Stirling made a triple substitution that made not a jot of difference to Kelty's total domination. A couple of minutes later Austin came off in a change that had an air of declaration about it.

Although Kelty's small band of smartly besuited officials made their presence felt, Cardle's goal had the effect of sucking all the atmosphere out of the main stand. As Albion's diehard support chatted among themselves and checked their phones, Kelty rounded off the scoring with a third goal that was the least their dominance deserved. If Cardle had impressed me in a wide role in his side's win over East Fife he proved equally effective playing five yards behind a target man. Cardle made another late run to get on the end of Thomas O'Ware's fine ball across the 18-yard line. Given the choice of a first-time finish or skipping past a couple of defenders and walking the ball in, Cardle went for option B to round off an excellent afternoon's work for him and his team.

Kelty Hearts went on to win promotion with five games to spare and won the League Two title by a massive 21 points.

Filing out of the Forthbank with a resigned and passive crowd who seemed to have witnessed exactly what they were expecting, I found it difficult to shake off feelings of deflation now that my long-term project had reached the stage of 42 down, none to go. Having retired over a year ago to become a fully fledged, bona fide old person in receipt of a state pension, it was hard to escape the feeling that a void was opening up in front of me would need to be filled. While I couldn't imagine that life would settle down into a carousel of tea dances and bowls tournaments, I had no idea what was likely to happen next, other than slow physical and mental decline and the growth of a persona that was starting to disapprove of just about everything. Scotland had given me so much pleasure over the course of the last few years, not least in the planning and anticipation of travel, and it was difficult to take in that it had all come to an end.

I didn't think that Scotland and its football clubs were finished with me, however. Looking ahead to the start of the 2022/23 season, it seemed likely that the SPFL would have a new member and that would be a box I'd need to tick to retain membership of my own little club. I'd yet to stand atop Arthur's Seat in 2022 and had started doing so annually as a kind of yardstick to measuring my fitness in a manner more pleasurable than other options. A spot of mountaineering in the morning and a Bonnyrigg Rose home game in the afternoon had an appeal I'd find hard to resist.

Sadly Brechin City, who'd had much to do with my taking on the SPFL task in the first place, were now in the Highland League, having rather carelessly got themselves relegated before I got the chance to visit them. A fifth-tier club they may now be yet the appeal of a 1,200-mile round trip to take in a game and marvel at British football's most impressive hedge remained strong. A little closer to home, I'd rather liked Linlithgow and felt that the pull of visiting a club nicknamed the Rosey Posey might prove impossible to ignore.

For now, the tentative escape from the many tentacled beast of Covid-19 continued in Auld Reekie. Although I felt the completion of a task I'd set myself eight years ago was worthy of more vigorous celebration, I found myself a space in the centre of a two-metre radius and had a pizza. It would have to do until next time.

CELTIC B v CALEDONIAN BRAVES

Lowland League
Sunday, 9 January 2022

THE SLOW train to Glasgow Queen Street trundled though the gloom of a grim January morning, stopping at all the stations that had become so familiar. Pulling into one, I'd guess the next and only once came up with the wrong answer. As BBC News told me before I set off, the west of Scotland had seen the worst of the weather and the first snow I'd seen in a while duly materialised shortly after Falkirk Grahamstown. Apart from a light dusting on the distant hills it wasn't of the picture postcard kind, merely the stuff that hangs around for 36 hours before turning grey and slushy before disappearing to reveal litter and dog deposits it had briefly covered up. It was the perfect train journey for hunkering down in a quiet corner and reading the Sunday paper.

I still hadn't convinced myself that I really wanted to spend my last day in Scotland attending a game that, as far as I could tell, was the only one taking place that day. I'd been tempted to spend another day in Stirling, having a bit of a history day that yesterday's early kick-off had ruled out. I figured I'd have time to visit Bannockburn, Stirling Bridge, the William Wallace memorial, and Stirling Castle in the daylight hours if I arrived early enough. What changed my mind was that when I'd previously visited Airdrie and the Excelsior Stadium for two or three hours, I really hadn't given either a fair crack of the whip. In short, an evening kick-off after a lengthy session in Coatbridge and a game at Albion Rovers had taken its toll. With the beer wearing off, I simply wasn't in the mood for a plastic pitch, three empty stands, pristine toilets, and something clearly recognisable as meat in the pies. If I was a little tired and emotional that evening back in the winter of 2015, today I was refreshed, well-rested and in a mood to absorb all the culture, entertainment, ale, and tuck that the town could chuck at me.

If the decision to allow Celtic and Rangers B teams to compete in the Lowland League had been a controversial one, it had certainly given Scottish football's fifth tier a higher profile and brought in some gate money that the part-time clubs could put to good use. I'd seen an impressive young Rangers side win 2-0 away to The Spartans at the start of the season and thought then that the title race might prove to be an all-too-familiar scrap between the Old Firm, albeit one that wouldn't bring promotion to either. However, going into the new year it was Bonnyrigg Rose who looked like nailed on favourites to win the league and take on the winners of the Highland League in a promotion play-off. Even so, I'd enjoyed watching Rangers and was keen to see what Celtic's kids had to offer in the stadium they'd made home.

Before that particular delight, I'd had to wrestle with the thorny problem of what to do on a grey January morning in Airdrie at a time when it was too late for breakfast, too early for lunch and, while I hadn't exactly signed up to Dry January, Covid restrictions certainly seemed to be giving a hefty shove in that direction. As luck would have it, a signpost adjacent to the railway station directed me towards a countryside park a mile away. If the going was a tad icy underfoot, the air was certainly fresh and a good walk looked by far my best option for killing an hour or two if the rain held off.

By following a sign through a smart residential area and past a primary school, I found myself in what was effectively a brownfield site in a valley that ran parallel to a busy road. If the park wasn't exactly teeming with fauna and flora and could best be filmed in sepia, it was a nice enough place to stretch my legs and make the brief acquaintance of a few cheery locals and the occasional mental hound.

'Have you lost your dog?' asked a burly old lad in a flat cap and wax jacket, sporting what I'm reliably informed is a Clydeside suntan: a skin tone that could best be described as navy blue. When I replied in the negative, stating that my smelly old Lab was back in England, he replied in a surprised tone, 'Oh, I just thought you looked like a man who ought to have one.'

Crunching my way across ice and gravel back to the centre of the town around midday, I figured I might as well find my way to the ground, buy a ticket, then hopefully find a decent pub to stay warm in prior to kick-off. I had a vague recollection that when I last visited, Airdrie railway station was a short-to-middling cab ride from the stadium, even though Coatbridge Sunnyside was probably closer. There were three of us to share the fare on that occasion, however, so I decided to walk. Even though the majority view of Airdrieonian gentlefolk was that I'd never make it on foot, the Sunday bus service seemed non-existent so I set off.

Admittedly it was a bit of a trek, along a main drag that seemed to go on for miles. Apart from one old boy having his few strands of hair trimmed at a barbers that was surprisingly open for business, just about everyone else seemed to be out food shopping or queueing at the McDonald's drive-through. If it wasn't the Scottish central belt's most aesthetically pleasing hike, it was straightforward enough and, after staying lost in thought for half an hour, I arrived at the roundabout at which I'd been told to turn right and amble downhill to the stadium.

When I got there, it all seemed very familiar and nothing seemed to have changed much since John, Gez and I pitched up for an evening game seven years ago. One thing that was striking, however, was the variety of cars parked up ahead of the game. Simplistic and predictable perhaps, but I took the view that the aged Fords and Fiats had been driven there by the players and staff of the Caledonian Braves, while the 4x4s and low-slung two-seaters were owned by those expecting to be dining at Scottish football's top table in the not-too-distant future. At 1.25pm it seemed equally likely that I was the first fan to turn up for the game.

Given that it was far too early for any turnstiles to be open, I presented myself at a rather swish entrance that looked like the lobby of a hotel I couldn't afford to stay at. Though a couple of fat lads in orange bibs lurked about the place, at least giving a faint idea that we were there for a game of non-league football rather than a spa weekend, my query about ticketing was addressed to a Celtic club official. I instantly became concerned before the fellow had even opened his mouth.

Although the man in question didn't seem to be sporting a name badge, if he had it would have announced him to be something fairly poncey, like official matchday concierge. In England such fellows are invariably called Ted, I've found. Ramrod straight due to a strategically inserted broom handle, Tam (I'm guessing) was a man who'd clearly spent time in the military.

He sported an immaculate club blazer and tie, a lovingly laundered white shirt and grey flannels with creases so sharp you could have used them to slice bacon. I didn't see his boots but reckoned I would have seen my face in their mirror shine if I had. As he didn't look like a hail fellow well met kinda guy prone to exchanging excessive pleasantries, I got straight down to business and asked how I might procure a ticket to the game. He replied, 'You have to book online!' and left me in no doubt that, as far as he was concerned, our business for the day was concluded.

Although I was reluctant to appeal to a better nature Tam didn't seem to have, I gave it my best shot. I apologised for not booking online, believing that cash at the turnstile would be the norm for a Lowland League fixture. I'd do it now, I added, if only my phone weren't a Nokia. Putting on my best Hollywood smile I went through my gormless tourist routine, explaining that I'd come an awfully long way with this game in mind, without which I'd have returned home a day earlier. I offered my eternal gratitude in return for an exception being made for a silly yet harmless and grovelling Englishman.

In the time that's passed since Tam and I went head-to-head I've often thought how I might have handled the situation in his brightly polished footwear, assuming that online sales had actually hit the 500-capacity restriction. I like to think I'd have lent a sympathetic ear and asked the bloke in front of me to put a mask on, prior to sending him to sit quietly in one of three empty stands that had been closed for the foreseeable future. Further, I'd have asked him to donate the price of the ticket to his favourite charity.

Tam, clearly a man who preferred black and white to troubling grey areas simply said, 'Sorry, pal!' and walked off.

Although I should have been disappointed to be turned away, I simply wasn't overly concerned as I began the trudge back to the railway station and onward to a warm and welcoming Edinburgh pub and an early dinner. Regret was mostly centred around the fact that I could and should have spent my last day in Scotland wandering around Stirling but had squandered that opportunity.

I'd achieved my objective of visiting all of the SPFL's 42 clubs – making myself a few grand poorer in the process – but I couldn't help but wonder what I'd missed by concentrating my efforts almost exclusively on football.

Between Glasgow and Fort William there was a huge area in the west of the country I'd not so much as seen from a train window. I'd failed to spend a couple of nights in Oban as I'd planned to since I first saw *Local Hero*, never caught a ferry to an island, driven across the Great Glen up to Glencoe or seen Ben Nevis. The Jacobite steam locomotive trip to Mallaig was somehow overlooked, irrespective of the hours I'd spent planning a trip, prior to shelving it to a clash with a League Cup dead rubber in Kirkaldy.

By the same token I'd barely set foot north of Inverness and about a third of the country that lay beyond it. Could I really claim to have seen Scotland in anything other than a whistlestop tour of its football grounds and adjacent pubs? Observing the aesthetic splendour of the Airdrie branch of Tesco from the vantage point of a roundabout, I made a deal with myself that I'd come back for a month, forget I'm a football fan and try and discover some of what I'd missed.

Speaking of things I'd missed, Celtic B beat Caledonian Braves 2-0. How many turned up to watch the game without me was something I simply couldn't be arsed to find out.

POSTSCRIPT

I THOUGHT I might go somewhere else in the autumn of 2022 but family commitments dictated that, for the time being at least, I couldn't really go anywhere I couldn't guarantee being able to get home from in a few hours. Valencia will still be there in a year or two and hopefully I will be too.

In the meantime, Bonnyrigg Rose's elevation to Scottish League Two and Cowdenbeath's relegation to the Lowland League now means that I've only visited 41 of the SPFL's 42 clubs making me, in terms of this book at least, something of a fraud. While certain that this is a fact that not a single soul would be interested in or care about, I knew only too well that this would nag away at me until I renewed membership of my private and pathetic little club.

After picking out a Bonnyrigg fixture v Stenhousemuir, the news that Fiorentina would be visiting Hearts in the Europa Conference League a few days later sealed the deal. Everything was booked and paid for in a matter of minutes.

I booked a few other things while I was at it and thought I might have a look at another part of Scotland. After talking about it for 30 years, I'll be spending some time in Oban between games and catching a ferry to the Isle of Mull. I've no idea if any live football will be played while I'm in the area. If there is, I dare say I'll be watching it.

ACKNOWLEDGEMENTS

ALTHOUGH I seldom gave it much thought when I was doing it, travelling to 42 Scottish football clubs would have been a tough enough task if I lived in Edinburgh and owned a smartphone. When my starting point was Dover and the nearest club was 394 miles away, it was always going to be a time-consuming and expensive undertaking for an old man still holding down two jobs. That I got there in the end still sane and solvent was an achievement, I think, and due in no small part to the railways, most notably South Eastern Trains and Scotrail. Both got me to where I was heading in good time to the extent that I didn't miss a single minute of any game, even when services were disrupted by industrial action. That I didn't once claim on 'delay – repay' speaks volumes for the standard of service I received, once I'd given up flying to Scotland on the basis that it didn't seem to get me there any quicker.

While I type these notes before we've met in person, I should thank Jane Camillin at Pitch Publishing for taking me on. However sales pan out – and I hope they're significant enough to reward their faith in me – Paul and Jane have saved me the endless drudgery of listening to a stream of vanity publishers telling me that my tome is the best football book ever written and they'd be honoured to publish it if I give them several thousand pounds. On a similar theme, I offer hearty thanks to Duncan Olner of Olner Design for designing my book's cover. I hadn't the first clue what I was looking for, yet he still managed to come up with it with no help whatsoever from the author.

If most academics were recharging their batteries throughout the summer break, one worked tirelessly throughout this period to knock this book into shape. As an old friend of mine who went to a far more exclusive school, my editor Mike Harrison put his lifelong classical education to good use by pointing out the difference between a throwaway remark and one that could earn me a stretch at King Charles III's pleasure. I hope to reward him handsomely for his efforts over the coming months but currently owe him £10 for postage.

Growing up in the south-east with several Scottish exiles, I'd always been told that if I ever decided to visit Scotland in general and Glasgow in particular I should speak in hushed tones and only when spoken to, while making eye contact wasn't advisable under any circumstances. If that is or ever was the case, I can only say that the kindness and hospitality I've been shown in the years I've wandered gormlessly around the country asking daft questions has simply been without equal, guaranteeing that I will return.

Finally, my warmest congratulations go to fellow Dovorian James Brown. As fans of St Johnstone will know, James was an integral part of the Saints squad that won both the Scottish League Cup and Scottish Cup in 2021. I missed both games due to a global pandemic but hope to stay in Perth and watch him win something else in the not-too-distant future.